The Tumbleweeds

THE
TUMBLEWEEDS

*Somersaulting Up and Out
of the City Streets*

Frederick Johnson

HARPER & ROW, PUBLISHERS

New York, Hagerstown, San Francisco, London

FIRST EDITION

Designed by C. Linda Dingler

Library of Congress Cataloging in Publication Data

Johnson, Frederick, 1932–
    The tumbleweeds, somersaulting up and out of
    the city streets.
    1. Puerto Ricans in New York (City)
    2. Acrobats and acrobatism.   3.   Johnson,
    Frederick, 1932–   4.   Social workers—New York
    (City)—Biography.   5.   Social work with youth—
    New York (City)   6.   New York (City)—Biography.
I. Title
F128.9.P85J6   1977   301.45'16'8729507471   76-26236
ISBN 0-06-012216-1

77 78 79 80 10 9 8 7 6 5 4 3 2 1

To all the Puerto Ricans who have come to this rude and fascinating New York City. I hope they find opportunities. They certainly have given me plenty.

1

I was just twenty-one years old when I retired from my first career as an acrobat and became a youth worker in the ghettos of New York City.

I liked being an acrobat and doing shows, but the business part of show business—contracts, agents, selling oneself and that sort of thing—cooled my ardor for the profession. And right about that time I got married and decided to go to college. Since there were no athletic scholarships for acrobats, I had to earn a living and pay my tuition at New York University.

So I went to work as an assistant recreation leader for the Police Athletic League. The PAL is really a private agency, loosely connected to the Police Department. It's a poor agency, paying low salaries and operating out of renovated firehouses, warehouses, supermarkets, churches and the like, in the highest-delinquency areas in the most deteriorated, worst-of-everything neighborhoods in the city.

And what did the PAL get for their three-thousand-dollar-a-year salary in the year 1953? I was a white, well-coordinated, six-foot-tall, one-hundred-seventy-five-pounder with some skills in most sports, some half-baked ideas about kids, and a monumental ignorance of delinquents, drug addiction, school failures, the underprivileged and minorities. . . . And I had the ability to thread a needle while balanced on one hand, catch the outstretched hands of a one-hundred-forty-pound man hurtling through the air and hold him in a hand-to-hand stand, support several top-mounters with the steadiness of a statue, and duplicate at least two stunts in *Ripley's Believe It or Not!*

I was assigned to the Boylan PAL Youth Center on Seventy-ninth Street between Columbus and Amsterdam avenues—the mid-West Side of Manhattan. The center was a four-story converted town house. A judge had willed it to the PAL. The Seventy-ninth Street block was mostly large apartment buildings occupied by older, affluent whites, with many ground-floor professional offices. Few kids were visible. Except for occasional complaints about the youth center and its members, we had little to do with the residents of the block.

Most of our constituents were the many-hued Latin-tanned Puerto Rican kids from Eightieth Street, which is a Puerto Rican neighborhood in itself, directly in back of Boylan Center. Eightieth Street is a long block, overcrowded with maybe three thousand people in tenements, subdivided apartments, high-stooped brownstones with converted furnished rooms—sometimes housing eight to ten people in a space designed for a family of four; sometimes having four or five furnished apartments on a floor where initially there were two.

The humanity of Eightieth Street spilled out onto the window sills, the sooted stoops and the dirty, gum-blotched sidewalks. Restless, screaming, black-haired, wiry children darted between the parked cars, in and out of the beer-can-littered streets. In fair weather or foul, these same kids poured into the Boylan Center.

On the corners of Eightieth Street and on up Columbus and Amsterdam avenues are small, cluttered bodegas (groceries), sweaty laundromats, unappetizing luncheonettes, used-furniture stores, joyous storefront "hallelujah" churches, and bars, cool and dark inside.

Although Puerto Rican kids came to the center from other side streets, the numbers diminishing with distance, none of the white kids who lived two blocks away in the large, elegant Central Park West apartments or the sedate, substantial West

2

End Avenue buildings ever came. Sprinkled in with the Puerto Ricans were a few leftover Irish kids and still fewer newly arrived blacks. It was a normal New York City ghetto.

Upon entering the town house at 125 West 79th Street, one is struck by the plain green-and-white sign—BOYLAN PAL YOUTH CENTER—over the ornate iron-frame door, because it clashes with the conservative dignity of the town house. In the lobby, neighborhood kids are confronted by a husky registrar in a green satin jacket with felt PAL letters on the back. He sells membership buttons to the seven-to-twelve-year-old boys and girls for ten cents a year. The thirteen-to-seventeen-year-olds pay twenty-five cents for a yearly membership card, which entitles them to use the center from 7 to 10 P.M.

Miss Victor, the director, a severe-looking German lady, greets most new enrollees—and sets them straight. On first impression she appears a bit intolerant, unable to distinguish between high spirits and premeditated rowdiness. But the more important impression most of the children pick up is: "We work hard to give you a program, and we are glad you are here. But we don't stand for any fooling around!"

At three o'clock, over a hundred of the younger boys and girls stream into the center and let loose energies and emotions that have been building up in school all day. They disperse themselves throughout the four floors into refurbished, fluorescent-lighted rooms with walnut paneling and lavish moldings, but now empty of chandeliers and tapestries, where they play ping-pong and checkers, mold clay, braid plastic lace, perform skits, sing, dance, listen to rock music, develop photographs and hammer on drums, nails and junk jewelry. The whole building resounds with the hubbub of shrill voices, stamping, scurrying feet, the knocking and slamming of benches and chairs, and the whining, laughing and arguing of kids entertaining themselves by poking, punching, taunting, "sounding on" and annoying each other.

The fourth and top floor must have been an attic or servants' quarters, or both. The ceiling is lower than in the lower-floor rooms. The small back room has exercise equipment, wall pulleys and a rowing machine, and a heavy punching bag just about fits in the corner. Another room, in the center of the fourth floor, has two stall showers and eight lockers.

In the larger front room, with four windows facing the street, is a fifteen-by-fifteen-foot boxing ring with springy, green-corduroy-covered ring ropes and a dreary gray canvas-covered mat floor. The ring barely fits into the room. There's about two feet of clearance on three sides; the fourth side is the hallway, extended into the room.

In the evenings Joe DeFoe trains his boxers here for the Golden Gloves, which the PAL has dominated for years. DeFoe is a short, stocky, quiet-spoken ex-lightweight who, in his heyday, fought such greats as Kid Chocolate and Henry Armstrong.

In the afternoons this is my area. It's the nearest thing to a gymnasium we have. Each weekday, supercharged, restless boys, as multicolored as autumn leaves, bump and thump up the wooden stairs and throw themselves at the boxing ring and matted floor.

The boxing ring itself was a novelty, and the kids, all of whom had watched professional wrestlers on TV, emulated what they saw. Running and bouncing off the ropes was their favorite. Some would stand on the bottom strand, hold onto the top strand, and just bounce up and down. Others would run full steam into the ropes and catapult themselves like a slingshot into a flying block, slamming into another kid, who, if he wasn't looking, took a whiplash jolt. Sometimes two kids would run, bounce off the ropes, and go head on at each other, crashing shoulders in the middle of the ring, to see who would give way. Pretty soon there were a dozen kids bouncing and flying around simultaneously. I winced and cringed a lot.

"The ropes are losing tension," complained DeFoe when he came to the center in the evening. "And that's a safety factor for my fighters."

The ring ropes were more than a "safety factor" for me, for

even with all the hazards they created, they also kept my *niños* from crashing into the walls or flying through the windows. But my group was growing and soon there was a regular daily attendance of thirty kids. To avoid chaos and cracked heads, I began regimenting them.

I devised or adapted games for the small space within the ring. I divided the group into two teams of fifteen and fastened a string from the top ring ropes down the middle. This became the volleyball net and a two-cent balloon became the volleyball. The kids had to play on their knees, which made the net height just right and eliminated the need for a lot of running room.

One of the most popular games involved blindfolding two or three kids, arming them with rolled-up newspaper bats, and letting them whale the hell out of the non-blindfolded kids, who tried to evade the blows and if hit had to get out of the ring. The last one in was the winner. When I wanted a fast exit, I would tell them to put their shoes or sneakers in the middle of the ring and then have them stand with their backs touching the ring ropes. After mixing up the shoes and sneakers, I would say, "Go!" and thirty kids would dig frantically into the pile of footwear to find their own, put them on and lace them up before anyone else, so that I might hold up their hand and declare them the winner. Needless to say, even the slowest kids were laced up and ready to go much quicker than usual.

But tumbling and acrobatics was my specialty. Of course, I had to teach simple tricks and modified tumbling to these young beginners. Before long, most of the preteens who came to my program had learned to do the basic front roll. Hundreds must have heard me repeating over and over again: "Squat down, put your hands on the mat. . . . Duck your head. . . . Keep bending forward until you can look up between your legs and see the ceiling. . . . Roll on the back of your shoulders—not your head or neck. . . . Grab your knees as you roll forward. . . . Stand up! . . . Good! . . . Now shut up! Pay attention! . . . Off the ropes! . . . Watch me! *Mira!* And listen! . . ."

It was the same with an endless variety of rolls: backward,

5

sideways and combinations. Headstands, cartwheels, shoulder stands and flips. While I lay on my back in the center of the ring, the kids would run, put their hands on my knees, jump and duck their heads. As I caught their shoulders and gave them a push, they would arch their backs and land on their feet—or their behinds, depending upon their skill or how much practice they'd had. When most of them learned this trick, they would accelerate and run at me without stopping, going around again and again. They never tired. Sometimes I would have them do "leapfrog" vaults over my bent body. As I raised my back higher and higher, the kids who didn't get over were eliminated. When I was almost erect, one or two of the bigger kids would vault over as the others cheered. Other times I would sit on the mat as the kids, one at a time, sat on my feet, with their backs toward me. Holding on to their upper arms, I would roll backward and flip them over with my legs. When my stomach muscles ached from this, I would take down the heavy punching bag and lay it in the middle of the ring. The kids ran, put their heads and hands on the cushioned bag and snapped their bodies over, landing on their feet as I sat on the end of the bag and "spotted" them by using my hands to make sure they didn't land on their backs. Sometimes I would have fifteen kids up in headstands and one kid would falter and knock over another headstand and like dominoes a whole line would go down, followed by angry whining and recriminations as to whose fault it was.

Whenever there were "show and tell" affairs at the center, we would drag a few mats down to the game room area—which served as our auditorium—and my kids would give an exhibition. Seeing fifteen to twenty consecutive front rolls, cartwheels, head snaps, candle flips and a few simple tableau pyramids—five kids standing on the knees of five others—was pretty tedious for me to watch, but the children in the audience cheered every move.

My program grew in popularity and pretty soon I had to break up my afternoon sessions so I wouldn't exceed the thirty-kid maximum I had established as a "safety factor." The seven-to-nine-year-olds were to come to my gym area from 3 to 4:15 P.M., and then they would go downstairs to other programs while the ten-to-twelve-year-olds would come up till five-thirty, closing time.

As soon as this schedule was instituted there was an immediate and constant stream of kids up and down the stairs. I began to feel like a border guard policing these mini-"wetbacks." "How old are you? You belong in the next group! . . . You're ten? What grade are you in? . . . I don't care if you are nine—you're too big to be in this group! . . . I don't believe you. Bring your birth certificate. . . . Time's up! Get your shoes on and *out!* before the next group gets here. . . . Weren't you here the last session? . . ."

The sheer volume of kids was wearing out the canvas mat cover. I dreaded those little rips and tears which in minutes became gaping holes. And in the evening it was: "I know, Mr. DeFoe—'safety factor!' "

I tried having the kids take off their sneakers so we would be less rough on the mat cover. Although I got used to the rotten-cheese smell of sweaty feet and socks, Miss Victor would come into the room, her face soured up disapprovingly, and say, "Children! We want you to come here and enjoy yourselves, but you have to *wash your feet!*"

Actually, this was a minor problem. I was concerned about the kids who were embarrassed by the holes in their socks and didn't want to take off their sneakers. I made a rule: "Socks or bare feet—whichever you prefer."

Because the windows in the room always had to be open for air and fumigation, we froze in winter and steamed in summer and even got splattered on windy, rainy days. And as the late-afternoon sun streaked in through the windows, glistening the countless specks of dust beat up from the mats, I was unpleasantly reminded that this was the air we were breathing.

Not only was the total Boylan Center attendance growing, but there was a turnover. New kids were coming all the time as families moved into the neighborhood and others moved out.

Some classes in the local elementary schools had as much as a 75 percent turnover each year. Almost every day I had to orient some new kids, which made it difficult to develop continuity, stability and programs.

Although I knew some kids by name, and even had a relationship of sorts with others, most who came up to my canvased square play area appeared to me as an endless stream of dark-eyed street gamins, garbed in odds and ends of clothing and dirty sneakers. The tight program added to the depersonalization.

Yet the movements of certain kids in this mob kept grabbing my attention. Some raggedy kid would flip over with fluid grace, time a nip-up just right, instinctively arch and point his toes in a balance. Another would ignore my commands to "Bend! . . . Straighten! . . . Tuck! . . . Turn!" and let his natural coordination, tempo and timing carry him through a spinning somersault. A thin, shapeless eleven-year-old would throw himself, loose and relaxed, into twists, turns and gyrations with nothing more to guide him than the split-second photo image in his head, learned from my demonstration or explanation. The same kid who frowned dumbly at my instructions let his limbs and torso roll and dance, feet to hands, over and over, guided by some neuromuscular intelligence, his body flowing inexorably into paths of minimum effort and compatible rhythms, the laws of gravity and momentum harmoniously integrated.

For me this was sensuous physical beauty. But it was rough and raw. It cried out for shaping, training, discipline and definition so that such potential and talent would not be wasted.

Amid the daily turmoil I tried to squeeze in a little more attention and instruction for these few "naturals." In a sense, I couldn't keep my hands off them. And I found that I could take this raw talent and by words, demonstrations, gestures, threats, cajoling and sheer will power lead them to replicate sophisticated patterns of movement—not modified, watered-down basics, but real stunts, tricks, pyramids and other configurations that had technical names and had been developed and refined by acrobats over thousands of years. And I found that I could soon recognize each kid's style, every nuance and subtlety of his moving limbs. It was like an action fingerprint. It allowed me quickly to spot flaws and errors, and identify what needed to be done to correct the misperformance.

And I knew the feelings of mastery and exhilaration the kids experienced as they performed their bodily flights. I knew it in my marrow and nerve endings, having executed the same movements myself thousands of times. A special rapport developed between me and these acrobat kids—a kind of nonverbal physical empathy. My communication, even with kids whose English was limited, seemed to improve. Acrobatics was an international language.

Each new acrobatic trick I taught was a creative experience, compelling and satisfying. It was a re-creation, no matter how ephemeral, of an art form that had evolved over the centuries in ancient courts and palaces, marketplaces and circuses.

But it quickly became frustrating. There were too many insistent kids to handle; too many commands to give to allow for individualization of any kind; too many other engaging kids who made me feel guilty when I neglected them to show favoritism to a select few.

Yet I didn't want to give it up. Every time I saw those malleable preadolescents with their infinite possibilities, my stomach tightened. I couldn't give them up. No, I would not give them up.

A plan slowly shaped in my mind. I would take a small group of those kids with exceptional natural abilities and train them on my own time. We would work out during my dinner hour, after work, in Central Park on the weekends and holidays and any other time I could squeeze in. I would develop their acrobatic competence to a high level—not knowing or caring where it would all lead. The prospect excited me.

So for the rest of the year up in my cramped attic gymnasium, I took a long, hard look at the hundreds of tawny, tousled, smelly-footed, dirty-eared, hyperactive, inattentive, disheveled

9

Latin urchins who tumbled, balanced and leaped. And out of a blur of Josés, Juans, Pedros, Angels, Ramons, Rubens, Rauls, Rafaels, Robertos and Carlitos emerged my five mangy prodigies.

2

José Ramos, called Joe by everyone, was a dark, bronzed, solidly built ninety-five-pounder. He was twelve years old, with jet-black curly hair, a big smile and a booming voice that could be heard anywhere in the center. When he first came into my gym area I thought he was shouting, but I soon realized that was the way he talked all the time. Several times, when I was unaware that he was standing next to me, he barked out a string of epithets—"*Chamaco! Carajo! Maricón!*"—which caused me to flinch and cover my ears.

"Joe! Not so loud!" I would say, pained. "Take it easy! Easy! Easy!" Minutes afterward my ears were still ringing. (There was nothing subtle about him. When he entered his house, banging and slamming, his mother would refer to him as *la tormenta*—"the thunderstorm.")

Though domineering and bullying at times, Joe could also be a charmer, a natural leader, genuinely helpful to have around. He was comfortable in giving orders and taking charge—but his diplomatic skills were underdeveloped.

"*Mira! Maricón!*" said Joe to an unruly kid in his self-appointed role as my assistant. "Get in line! *Rápido!*"

"Who says!"

"I say!"

"Who are you!"

"I'm the guy who's gonna mess up your face, you *pato cagón!*"

11

Joe was too restless to be a good listener. His tumbling was erratic; it lacked concentration. But he was well coordinated, fast, powerful, and explosive in his takeoffs.

Joe was the first one to learn to do a full front somersault. Running forward and taking off with both feet, he would go up in the air, tuck up, make a quick forward revolution, open up, and land on his feet. But Joe was inconsistent. Sometimes his arm swing inhibited his rotation; or he opened up too soon, or too late; or he took off flatfooted; or he didn't aim himself in quite the right trajectory. Or he did all these things in combination. But every once in a while everything would come together just right and Joe would go shooting through the air like an oversized cannonball, way beyond his or my intended landing area. In fact, in the cramped places where we had to practice, there usually wasn't any landing room when Joe overshot the mark, and he would go crashing into ring ropes, walls, doors, cabinets, windows and innocent bystanders. Joe got a few scars from this. It was a lethal trick. A karate kick would be a caress by comparison.

Edgar Mourino was almost thirteen years old and weighed almost one hundred pounds. He had white skin, straight light-brown hair, blue eyes and a round, soft face with a ready smile. He was conspicuous among the darker-skinned kids.

Though built like a fire hydrant, he moved almost daintily. He "worked light," as we acrobats would say. He lacked the long, flowing body line that can make well-executed stunts look even better, but he landed on his feet with sureness and without the body-jarring jolts that characterize the inexperienced.

Edgar was especially good on the roller-roller, a three-foot-long wood board balanced on a cylinder, which I kept in the corner of the room for the boys to experiment with. Edgar, standing on the board, could roll himself back and forth right up to the end of the board, where the roller was directly under his foot—always stopping just in time before rolling back to the other end of the board. He never fell or lost control.

12

Edgar was sometimes called "Deditos"—"Little Fingers." He got the name because he was missing the forefinger and middle finger of his right hand. There weren't stumps or anything one could call "little fingers."

"What happened to your fingers, Edgar?" I asked him.

"A gorilla bit them off."

"Yeah, yeah," I said impatiently.

Later I was to find out what really happened to his fingers. A gorilla bit them off. It was true. Back in Puerto Rico, when Edgar was eight years old he played hooky from school to see the traveling circus, which had come to Ponce. He had a wonderful time walking around the menagerie, his hands clasped together behind his back, looking at the lions and tigers. But there was this other kid, who was using his candy cane to taunt Max, a five-hundred-pound untrained gorilla. A cage door had been left unlocked. There were no restraining barriers. Edgar drifted too close to the gorilla's cage and then turned, his chubby hands still clasped behind him. The gorilla suddenly reached out through the unlocked cage door, grabbed Edgar's right arm, yanked him toward the cage and bit off two fingers.

Edgar didn't seem to have suffered from the experience. His remaining three fingers were as strong as steel cables. In fact, Edgar used the fingerless hand to attract attention. A favorite joke was to put his hand against his head, making it look as if the missing fingers were in his ear. He would then feign a struggle to pull them out. Finally, accompanied by a popping sound he made with his mouth, he yanked his hand away, and lo and behold, the two fingers were missing—obviously having broken off and stuck in his ear. It was fun watching new kids see it for the first time.

Edgar learned quickly, listened carefully, practiced religiously, was always ready to try new tricks, and if he had an audience he would literally risk his neck doing stunts. An audience of even one would bring forth a series of handsprings, nip-ups, flips, twisting jumps onto the roller-roller, and never-done-before tricks. He would give the same inspired im-

13

promptu performance for blind people, dogs or cross-eyed retardates. If there were pretty girls watching, I immediately buckled him into the spotting belt (a wide leather safety belt worn when learning a difficult trick), holding firmly to the attached ropes, for fear he would fly away.

Ramon Sanchez, age ten, was called "Chino" by those who didn't know him well, because of his slightly Oriental eyes. Everyone else called him Ray. He had thick, straight black hair, round cheeks, dark eyes, a light-tan complexion, which turned a burnt brown in the summer, and a smooth, seventy-pound body. He was the smallest in the group, but well coordinated.

Although he was as dungareed and sneakered as most of the kids in my little gym, he had a cared-for look some of the others lacked. His clothes were cleaner, the sneakers were replaced more frequently, and his hair, though long, was trimmed around the ears and neck.

When I gave instructions or demonstrated a trick, Ray would listen intently, his brown eyes focused on me, absorbing every word and gesture.

Ray was always at the practice sessions, always on time, always available, always cooperative. He followed me around. I used him and Joe, who also was very dependable, to demonstrate tricks to the new kids in my regular program, which made it easier for me to observe, teach and conserve myself.

Ray got along well with the staff, other kids, and adults in general, but with me there was an instant rapport. From the beginning we understood each other perfectly. There were no culture gaps, no generational conflicts, no communication barriers. Sure, there were things we didn't know about each other. And we had different perspectives and backgrounds. But in some very basic ways we quickly got to know each other well. It was a peculiar chemistry. We had an almost infallible sense of each other. He never compromised me by taking advantage of our special friendship and I never compromised him by ex-

14

empting him from my tirades and punishments that were aimed at the whole group.

By the time Ray was eleven, we were closer to each other than Ray was to some of his peers, or I with the other staff members. Our influence on each other was inordinate. "What do you think, Ray?" I would frequently ask when unsure of my actions. His answers were carefully considered.

Ray was also my most frequently used language teacher.

"Ray, how do you say 'Quiet' in Spanish?"

"*Silencio!*"

"And how do you say 'Get out'?"

"*Vete para afuera!*"

"*Vete parra afuerra!*" I repeated, trying to roll my *r*'s as Ray did.

"And how do you say 'Sit down'?"

"*Siéntate!*"

"*Siéntate!*" I said forcefully, trying to imagine how I'd sound addressing my groups.

As I made progress in controlling my wilder *muchachos*, I broadened my vocabulary.

"Ray, how do you say 'Good'?"

"*Bien!* Or *Muy bien!* which means 'Very good!' "

"Never mind *muy.* Nobody is *muy* anything yet. . . . And how do you say 'Take it easy'?"

"*Cójelo suave!*"

"*Co hay lo swaavey!*" I repeated slowly. That has a nice ring to it, I thought.

"*Cójelo suave!*" I said again to Ray, who nodded approval.

"And how do you say 'Do it again'?"

"*Repítelo!*" . . . and if you want to say 'Do it again, please!' you say '*Repítelo, por favor!*' "

"Much grass," I said, deliberately mangling *Muchas gracias,* "but I'm trying to learn to give orders, not make requests."

When we got to kidding like this, Ray would say "Oh, yeah!" and then proceed to give me a playful pummeling with slow-motion lefts and rights to the head and body.

Ray was a little fearful of new stunts, especially if they were scary or awkward, but he always put forth a concentrated effort, grunting and sweating and forcing himself. During these times, or whenever he was nervous, he had a habit of opening and closing his mouth as though trying to get a kink out of his jaw.

Angel Rodriguez was an anemic-looking twelve-year-old, weighing in at eighty-five pounds. He had a sturdy frame and good musculature, but he was also skinny and unhealthy-looking. From certain angles he resembled Cantinflas, the Mexican comedian, and Alfred E. Neuman, the *Mad* magazine trademark.

His clothes were always ragged and wrinkled. In the middle of winter he wore two or three of the same grimy shirts he wore in summer. Once he came to the center wearing an enormous pair of dirty white sneakers over his shoes. Apparently he was required to have sneakers for gym classes in school and those were all he had and this was the only way they would fit.

Angel always had scratches and cuts on his arms and legs. His stiff, straight, unkempt dark-brown hair stuck out over his big ears, which were always in need of soap and water. He was nicknamed "Orejas," which means "Ears." On Eightieth Street, where he lived, he was also called just plain "Hoodlum," or "Aguja," meaning "Needle," because he was so skinny and because he "needled" other kids into trouble.

A gaping, toothy ear-to-ear grin dominated Angel's face when he smiled or laughed. And what a laugh he had. It was a wild, rippling, gasping, giddy giggle—yet lusty and warm. He laughed with his whole body, rocking convulsively or rolling onto the mats. Each burst of laughter would trigger another, more explosive than the previous one. The sound was so contagious, everyone in the room would be rendered weak and impotent. Decorum, concentration and discipline were obliterated. And the kids' faces, like mine, would involuntarily wrinkle into grins and smiles. I would smile when I heard him, even if I didn't know what he was laughing at. In fact, I seldom knew what he was laughing at. He wasn't often sad or depressed, but when he was, that same animated, bubble-gum sculpture of a face could look pathetically somber.

Angel had a quick, short, ducklike walk, as if he were going to change direction with every step. His center of gravity was low—meaning he had a relatively longer back and shorter legs —which together with his sturdy legs and quick reflexes allowed him to start running at top speed—a very important ability for tumblers, who have to accelerate quickly in small areas.

Angel had a wonderful style of learning. He listened little to my instructions, preferring to see me or one of the other guys demonstrate the trick. He would make a few tentative moves and turns, feeling out the trick, getting a picture in his head. Then he would pull out all stops and go for it without reservation, restraint or a spotter—unless I insisted. He learned quickly.

Israel Gotay weighed eighty pounds and was probably eleven years old. No one knows his age for sure because his birth records were inadequate and confused, a not uncommon situation. Israel was Angel's shadow. They were almost always together. Shy, socially awkward, and with a dour expression, Israel came to life when Angel was around. With Angel he was animated and he would laugh and joke.

Both Angel and Israel were anemic and disheveled. Both were frequently sick with colds, asthma or some other nasal malfunction. Israel's thin nose, which fit his narrow face, was nevertheless big enough to earn him the nickname "Nariz"— "Nose." Some called him "Pinocho," meaning "Pinocchio." An uncle called him "Huesito," or "Little Bony," because he was so skinny.

Israel tried to comb his curly brown hair into a pompadour, the style at the time, but the curls always fell down and stuck out at right angles from the top of his head, like the brim of a hat. Although all five boys had become fluent in English since having come from Puerto Rico, Israel was the only one who still had difficulty with some words. Once when he missed a back somersault by putting his head up instead of down, as I instructed, I said, "You better learn English quick before you break your neck!" At the same time, Israel always seemed to know and understand more than was indicated by his quizzical expression.

Israel had the most elegant form of all the boys. When he did even a simple cartwheel, he instinctively pointed his toes. His limbs would be straight, and the movement flowed. Other kids who saw Israel's cartwheel would say, "Teach me that trick!" and I would tell them they already knew it. Israel made it look wholly different. Loose and relaxed, he would flip and balance using only essential muscles. He seemed to learn by giving the tumbling movements over to his limbs and muscles, as if they had a wisdom independent of and greater than the conception in his head. Stunts didn't have any intermediate stages with Israel. Either he landed limply on his back or there it was, full blown, complete and eye-catchingly beautiful.

Often he would squint and frown, deep furrows forming between his eyes, and he would walk off the mats and sit quietly in a corner. Israel's headaches brought down a curtain of pain over his body, causing him to look whipped and small. The sight of him then made my nerve endings tender.

But when Israel wasn't ailing, and he tumbled in his bare feet with their ever-present five-o'clock shadow of dirt on the heels, in his too-small pants with the breeched fly held together with a safety pin, he was transformed.

Angel and Israel were erratic, exasperating, irritating and unpredictable. They fooled around endlessly. They made each other laugh when I needed seriousness. They were unconscious of time, schedules, plans and appointments. They would disappear for weeks at a time. They could be seen on any random day, even during school hours or past midnight, wandering

18

around Eightieth Street, Central Park, Columbus Avenue or the Planetarium park. They were disruptive with their jokes and clowning. They undermined group morale because they almost never came to practice sessions on time and they undermined me because they missed learning important lead-up tricks but learned the advanced ones anyway.

When they came to the center, it seemed to be by accident. They came on weekends and found it closed. They came five minutes before closing time. They came in the evening, when they weren't allowed in the building. Sometimes they came to the center and got involved in making lanyards, or in a pool game, and forgot to come up for practice. Or they would forget to stay in the center for a dinner-hour practice. It was a fortunate coincidence if they showed up on time to practice with the rest of the group.

Exasperated, I made all kinds of threats. "That's it! You guys are out! Miss one more practice and you can scram! I'm gonna get some other guys to take your place!"

But then these two scurvy-looking vagabonds, after missing three practices, would blithely march in and say, "Hi, Mr. Fred," and with such innocence that my anger would dissipate. I was always relieved and glad to see them. I couldn't imagine building my super acrobatic team without Angel and Israel.

3

Besides participating in my regular sessions of games and tumbling drills in the boxing ring, my five boys were now putting in three extra practice sessions a week. On Tuesdays and Thursdays I would eat dinner quickly and by six o'clock be ready to give the boys a quick workout before the evening session began at seven o'clock, when I was due back on duty in the game room.

Every Saturday or Sunday we would meet in Central Park, on a grassy area under a big maple tree near the Great Lawn softball diamonds, which, if the streets were extended into the park, would be around Eighty-third Street. Here two- and three-hour workouts were common.

The boys enjoyed learning new stunts and increasing their strength and agility, but there were times when the workouts were tiring, grueling and repetitive. I believed a stunt had to be done many times before you "owned it." Ray and Edgar were always ready to do a trick "one more time," but Joe, Angel and Israel occasionally lost their concentration and dragged about. To help sustain their interest, I said, "As soon as we're ready we can give tumbling demonstrations, performances and shows."

"When will we be ready?" asked Edgar.

"As soon as we have a routine," I answered.

"When will that be?" asked Ray.

"That depends on all of you."

"Where will we do the shows?" asked Joe.

"For now, in the other PALs and schools."

"Maybe someday," Israel said, "we can get on the *Spanish Hour*"—a popular but weak variety show, one of the few Spanish TV programs in those days.

"Maybe," I said, "but we have to learn a whole lot first."

"What will we wear?" asked Edgar. "We need costumes."

"Bathing suits!" said Angel.

"To show our muscles," said Israel as he posed with flexed biceps until Joe smacked him on the head and called him *"flaco!"*—"skinny."

"For now, we'll use the PAL T-shirts and shorts," I said, interrupting a flurry of excited, unintelligible Spanish. "Later, when we get real good, we'll get something fancy."

Individually the boys made rapid progress. Two- and three-man tricks and pyramids were much slower. It seemed that someone was always absent—usually Angel or Israel, or both. Of course, when Angel and Israel came to the practices they were brilliant. But they also clowned around and set the others off doing the same. My attempts at restoring order usually initiated a pecking order of recriminations.

But we persevered, and as soon as we mastered a variety of acrobatic tumbling movements and a few simple pyramids, I wove them together into a fast-moving seven-minute routine, which is fairly standard for acrobatic acts. So at each practice session we would now rehearse our routine—our "act"—polishing it, smoothing out the rough spots, getting it ready for an audience. In addition, we continued to practice the more advanced balancing, acrobatic movements and pyramids at the same time the boys maintained proficiency in their basic repertoire.

The first performance was a modest affair in Boylan Center at one of those open-house-for-parents events, with hastily put together crepe-paper-costumed skits, songs, clapping rhythm

21

bands and unappreciated recitations. We dragged three four-by-five-foot mats, ordinarily used in the ballet classes in the kitchen, up the stairs to our game room–auditorium. About ninety young spectators sat on the floor on both sides of the row of mats. A dozen parents and staff were standing or sitting on benches about the room.

I arranged for the boys to go on last. "Acrobats always open or close the show," I explained to Miss Victor. "That's tradition." The real reason I wanted the boys on last was that we had been practicing much more than anyone else and I knew we would have been a tough act to follow.

The boys were nervous and paced up and down like caged animals. I tried to get them to warm up, but they wanted to watch the other kids dancing and doing their skits, so they peeked around the partition in the front room. I knew the boys could do their simple routines well enough. For me, this was an opportunity to try out some tricks and get an audience reaction.

"And now Mr. Johnson's boys are going to show you some of the things they have learned," says Miss Victor. Looking at me in the corner of the room, she asks, "Do you want to tell them anything about what you are going to do?" I shake my head. Ray, being smallest, is first in line. Holding his arm, I can feel his throbbing pulse. He opens and closes his mouth rapidly. Israel is touching his toes, as if he suddenly feels the need to warm up. Except for the children in the center who participate in my top-floor gym program, none of the other boys and girls, staff or parents have ever seen my boys perform their "act."

As soon as Miss Victor steps off the runway of mats, I release Ray's arm and with hushed urgency say, "Okay, go!" and they are off: running, diving, rolling, cartwheeling, thumping the mats with their tumbling feet. Their nervousness speeds up their movements, making it look a little like a silent-movie chase scene. They flay their arms, bounce, grunt, double-roll, and bound in and out of balances. Every so often Angel, Israel and Ray scramble up and stand on the thighs and shoulders of Edgar and Joe, creating human tableaus, the top man triumphantly holding his arms up. Like a bursting bubble, they dismount and are off, running and tumbling again.

By the third pyramid, halfway through the routine, the boys are gasping for breath, their chests heaving. I know their mouths feel as dry as if they had just chewed on a wad of cotton. In their excitement and nervousness they have overextended themselves, putting more muscle and energy into each trick than was required, and they've cut minutes from the routine.

They go on as if by reflex, with their mouths hanging open, gasping and looking desperately uncomfortable. Nevertheless, they make the audience squeal with laughter with their comedy "caterpillar walk" and the "spider walk," which has Ray down on all fours, like a spider, with Israel holding on underneath him. Ray scrambles down the mats, rolls over, and then Israel is on top, on all fours, with Ray slung under him. Israel then scrambles back in the other direction. The turnovers look especially funny because they happen so fast and the direction changes so quickly. Back and forth they go like a circus-size spider, with kids in the audience laughing and yelling.

Joe, Edgar and Angel almost stomp on Ray and Israel as they jump into the next trick. All of them now vault over each other and do a quick front roll, shuttling back and forth so fast the audience can't figure out what's happening. I watch the staff and parents. They are wide-eyed and smiling, following every move, their hands poised in front of them ready to applaud, which they do again and again. Obviously they are enjoying the show, but there's also a faint look of wonder that these street kids, with their bony preadolescent knees and elbows sticking out of oversized green shorts and baggy T-shirts, could have put together such sophisticated patterns and pyramids. I'm surprised, too.

At the end of the routine, the boys quickly line up in two rows, Edgar and Joe on one side, Angel, Israel and Ray on the other, as I, in my regular clothes, make a running dive, high in the air, into their arms. As soon as they catch me, stretched out full length between the two rows, Joe gives the tempo—"And up!" The boys throw me three feet or so into the air and let me drop. I come down on the mat, slamming it loudly for effect. The boys step over me, bow to the laughing, applauding audience as I get up with feigned indignation and chase them off the stage. I put this "cute" ending in, knowing that kids always like to see "teacher" get dumped.

In the front room the boys are breathless, but happily congratulate each other as they look to me for approval. Beads of sweat stream down their necks and temples. They dab their foreheads on the sleeves of their T-shirts. Miss Victor calls them out for another bow and like a cheerleader asks for more applause, which the excited audience eagerly gives.

It was good, I think. Good for everybody. Good to see my five boys smiling, glowing with pride, surrounded by admirers.

"How did you do that thing?" one little boy asks Israel.

"Boy, that was good!" says another to Angel, who acknowledges the compliment with a dignified smile.

"He got muscles!" exclaims a little girl as she touches Joe's biceps.

"That was cool, man!" says a tall, dark boy as he shakes Edgar's hand.

"*Chévere! Chévere!*" ("Good!") says another, shaking the other hand.

The girls in the afternoon program, the eleven- and twelve-year-olds, say nothing, but they watch with coy smiles and circle around, glancing with interest at these guys from "the block," taking a second look at these familiar faces hitherto taken for granted.

A half hour after the show, a whole catalogue of corrections, suggestions, improvements, deletions and ideas welled up inside me and were being edited into a vividly imagined rerun of the new routine. It was going to look great. I couldn't wait to get my hands on the boys again.

4

We continued to perform at these little special events and holiday celebrations at Boylan Center. All the while we practiced and experimented with the routine. Pretty soon the fame of the Boylan Tumblers spread throughout the neighborhood and I was getting requests for them to perform at school assemblies, other PALs, youth centers, playground pageants and community fairs.

We did these shows for the rest of 1954, which boosted the boys' enthusiasm, diligence and, to some extent, even their attendance at workouts.

Although the boys still comported themselves like grim-faced amateurs, we were getting the kinks out of the routine and acquiring experience in performing under pressure.

But I was bored with the basic routine. It was still kid stuff. I had something much more advanced in mind. Busy as I was, I pushed for more practice sessions, longer workouts, and I even assigned homework movements and balances, to be practiced on their own time.

The boys learned almost as fast as I could teach them and their progress made me even more demanding. Every new move mastered meant they were ready to advance. Of course, they still had a long way to go, but there was no end to the possibilities.

Unfortunately, though, I was dealing with five complex little people whose needs, inclinations and orientations, normal as they might be for their age, often conflicted with my desire to create.

Many of our practices involved squeezing in an extra forty-five-minute dinnertime workout. With the time it took to shed unnecessary coats, shirts and other garments, warm up and explain new stunts, there wasn't much room for fooling around. And I wasn't in any mood for it.

And that wasn't all. Joe and Edgar began to develop what would become a deep, heartfelt enmity toward each other—partly due to vying for leadership and partly because their personalities clashed.

The boys weren't a natural group when I pulled them together. Angel and Israel, of course, were very close. Joe hung around with them a lot because they all lived on the same block. Joe and Ray were good friends, but off and on.

When we did shows, a close bond of friendship, loyalty and group togetherness existed. But offstage, Joe and Edgar let their true feelings come out in endless bickering.

It wasn't all aggravation, though. There were times like the Saturday we were practicing in Boylan Center because it was too cold to go to the park. We dragged the mats up from the kitchen to the second-floor game room area.

"Fred, come with me," said Angel, taking my arm and leading me upstairs.

"Sit here!" he said, directing me to a solitary chair away from the mats, but front and center.

Then he, Israel and Edgar lined up at the far end of the old dining room. Intently, Angel sized up the distance to the mats. He moved back two steps, took a deep breath, and with those fast, choppy steps of his, ran toward the mats.

He swings his hands down as his legs swing up and over. He twists and snaps his feet down. His feet kick into the mat and propel him straight up as he swings his arms above him for greater elevation. At the height of his flight into the air, his head goes back as he tucks up his knees, giving himself backward

26

rotation. He is attempting a round-off back somersault, making a complete turn in the air, something he has never done by himself. I had run alongside Angel and the others many, many times, holding the spotting belt as they practiced this trick. At this crucial point I would always yank up on the belt so that Angel could have time to complete his turn, open up and land on his feet.

Angel's head is now pointed toward the mat. He's losing altitude rapidly. Involuntarily my hand jerks upward as if I had the spotting-belt rope in my hand. I wince with body English. But Angel keeps turning, and just in time his toes stab the mat. He is a little bent, but it was a complete back somersault. His first solo flight.

Right behind Angel are Israel and Edgar, who also have never done the back somersault without the spotting belt.

Whap! Israel's feet snap into the mat and he is up and over. He gets out of the way quickly because Edgar's arms are already swinging into his round-off. He, too, snaps down and somersaults up and over, landing flatfooted with a thump that shakes the floor. It was harrowing to watch—but wonderful.

But that isn't all. Joe is now standing on the mat, legs apart in a braced half squat. Ray, pacing like a colt, is several feet away, facing him, his mouth opening and closing rapidly. With short, rapid steps he moves toward Joe and puts his right foot in Joe's hands. As Ray rams his leg straight, Joe, with a grunt and a vigorous thrust, pushes Ray up and away. Ray soars about eleven feet in the air, claps his hands against his tucked-up knees, rotates backward, straightens out, and drops down in front of Joe, stumbling a few steps before letting out a delighted yell. It's a pitch-back—and another solo flight.

5

None of the boys had telephones, so whenever I needed to contact them—which was frequently—I would, during my dinner hour or after the center closed in the evening, just roam the streets near the center. I liked walking around the streets.

"Tell Joe I'm looking for him," I say to a couple of kids I know from the center, as I walk up Columbus Avenue and turn left at Moore's Bar into Eightieth Street.

It's a warm evening. Several men in undershirts are sitting on the stoop of the building where Angel lives, drinking Rheingold and talking rapidly in Spanish. Other people, young and old, are scattered about, talking, gesturing, laughing. A harassed mother drags a squalling infant up the stoop stairs, past a chubby, middle-aged woman with a headful of curlers, who is combing the long black hair of a sparkling-eyed dark-skinned girl sitting on the balustrade. On the next stoop a family is eating from plates piled high with mounds of reddish-orange rice and dark-brown beans. People lean on pillows on the window sills and look out on the comings and goings and talk to the people on the stoop.

A white Mister Softee ice cream truck, with its bells and mambo music, double-parks and several teen-agers wander over. More Spanish music floats out to the street from an open window. Two husky youths pick up the beat, drumming with the heels of their hands on the hood of a parked car. A young man in a dented black Ford guns the engine, screeches the back wheels, races fifty yards down the block, brakes suddenly, blows the horn, calls to a friend, revs the engine, gets out, looks under the hood, and then repeats the process all over again.

A tall, slim, dark homosexual in tight pants walks mincingly down the block. He attracts good-natured jibes.

"Qué polla!" ("What a chicken!")

"Qué linda!" ("How pretty!")

He is obviously a familiar character. He answers with a "Hi, José," "Hi, Sweetie," "Hi, Carmen," all the way down the block.

Near the Amsterdam Avenue end of the block, two drunks argue ineffectually over a wine bottle. Several young men gather around a garbage can, trying to look innocuous, looking all the more conspiratorial. Two nodding junkies draped over the bottom steps of a stoop seem in danger of sliding onto the sidewalk.

Across the street, under the streetlight, lithe teen-agers in sneakers are playing stoop ball. Slim brown arms snake out, like a lizard's tongue, and grab the pink spaldeen.

Four young girls leave their hopscotch court sketched in chalk on the sidewalk and gather round the *piragua* vendor's homemade cart with its baby-carriage wheels and tiny Puerto Rican flag—broad red and white stripes, and a white star on a field of blue. He scrapes the block of ice and puts the shavings into paper cups, then pours flavored syrups over the ice from one of several bottles of white, red, orange and tea-colored syrups, having such names as *tamarindo, frambuesa, coco, china* and *limón.*

The gutters are strewn with old newspapers, candy wrappers, dog shit, remnants of furniture and vestiges of automobiles. Trucks rumbling up Amsterdam Avenue spew exhaust into air already enriched, twice a day, with incinerator fallout.

Near the corner is La Minita, a bodega always crowded with people, boxes, Goya cans and green bananas. In the window, next to the rough brown mavi and yucca roots, is a faded, sun-warped poster of a smiling baseball player endorsing "Cerveza

Shaefer." Young men in short-sleeved shirts lounge around La Habana, the corner bar, which seems to change names every week.

A police car races up Amsterdam Avenue, its siren screaming and turret light flashing. People nonchalantly watch it go. "Eighty-fourth Street," I say to myself. Sure enough, the police car screeches into a right turn four blocks up. Other police cars, sirens wailing, come from other directions and disappear into the block. It's another signal 10-13, for all sector cars to "assist patrolman." A lot of cop-fighters on that block. I could imagine the scene. I had seen it several times. A policeman comes into a block and makes an arrest. The people in the block, remembering past abuses and discourtesies, slowly gather around the alien in blue. Low grumbling escalates to angry yelling. The crowd grows and presses in. The cop, with his prisoner, tries to push through the crowd. Several people pull the cop's hand away as others wedge themselves in front of the apprehended man. Sirens wailing in the distance come closer. The crowd gets more agitated. Someone punches the cop and runs. The cop turns to give chase. A police car speeds into the block, then a second and a third and a fourth. Their red-and-white turret beams going round and round whip the buildings with streaks of light. The cops jump out—guns drawn, clubs poised—and grab the prisoner or those thought to be involved, or just anyone who looks surly and defiant. The cops attempt to hustle the prisoners into the patrol cars. Some resist and are clubbed. One is bleeding. People tentatively and cautiously crowd in again and begin screaming at the cops. Then it starts. Like rain, beer bottles, jars, glasses, soda bottles and dishes are thrown from the roofs and windows, popping and spattering glass all over the street and sidewalk. Some thud on the roofs of the police cars. The cops hunch their shoulders and run for cover. Three of the cops turn and fire several shots at the roofs. People scream and run away. Someone throws a heavy wire refuse basket at one of the police cars as it pulls out, breaking a window and denting a fender, but the cars, sirens screaming, keep going, leaving behind an angry, bitter crowd.

The neighbors call Eighty-fourth Street "Korea." Later, city officials were to call it the "worst block in the city" and neighbors were to call it "Vietnam." Ray lives there.

In a wider circle surrounding the Eightieth Street neighborhood is Central Park and the Planetarium park—a corner of which is home turf for Eightieth Street kids—the Museum of Natural History, apartment buildings and hotels, including the notorious dilapidated Endicott Hotel, which houses over three hundred people, most of whom are welfare recipients, old folks, drifters, discharged mental patients, addicts, pushers, migrants and families unable to find a better place to live. In front of the block-long building, street prostitutes ply their trade. The Eightieth Street kids sometimes come by and watch them. Two blocks west is Broadway, a wide avenue divided by a concrete strip, its sidewalks solid with stores. There are supermarkets and delicacy shops like Zabar's. There is Steinberg's Dairy Restaurant and there are pizza stands. There are bars, churches, garages, a Woolworth's, fruit and vegetable stands, clothing stores, Loews 83rd Street movie house, travel agencies, a secretarial school, jewelry stores and more bars, and the sidewalks are crowded. But Broadway is not really part of the Eightieth Street neighborhood.

"*Qué pasa,* Fred!" says Joe, coming up behind me. "I heard you were looking for me."

"Look, Joe," I say, shaking his hand. "We have to practice tomorrow at two o'clock. In Central Park. Because we're doing a show on Sunday in a community center. I'll tell you more later. Tell everyone to be there. On time! Okay?"

"*Sí*—okay!"

"I gotta go now. I'll see ya. *Cójelo suave!*"

We shake hands. "*Adiós,*" says Joe, a big smile on his strong face. "*Cójelo suave!*"

Cójelo suave—"Take it easy"—had become my favorite Spanish phrase and the one I used most frequently. The boys would sometimes kid me about it or they used it when they wanted

31

to please me. Sometimes they even referred to me as Cójelo Suave. "Where's Cójelo Suave?" Anyway, I liked the phrase.

On those rare occasions when I couldn't get Joe to do the rounding up, I went directly to the boys' homes. As often as not, Israel's father would be drunk and would go into a tirade, mostly in Spanish. The gist of his remarks was: "That's what I want to know. Where is he! Probably he is with Aguja—you know, the one with the big ears. A bad influence, that boy. . . . He's supposed to be home. Tell him that!"

Angel's mother's diagnosis was pretty much the same. "He is going to be punished. He is supposed to be here to take me to the hospital. Nariz is the one—always making my boy go out of the house. Always getting my Angel into trouble."

Getting in touch with Ray and Edgar was seldom a problem. They always checked in with me at the center. But I did have to make regular visits to Ray's home to get permission from his mother to take Ray to shows in other parts of the city and to give advance notice when he would be coming home late.

Ray's mother would see me coming into Eighty-fourth Street from her second-floor window, from which she also watched the daily hostilities down below. She appeared to be in her early thirties, lighter-complexioned than Ray, without his *chino* eyes, a little fleshy in the arms and with faint creases in her face. Her occasionally bewildered expression often gave way to a gruff laugh.

"Here comes the Americano!" she would say to Ray, somewhere behind her in their furnished room. Ray would then poke his head out the window and all three of us would have a conversation, with me standing on the sidewalk amid broken glass, a smoldering mattress and overflowing garbage cans.

Ray's mother was only able to speak and understand Spanish, and maybe a few words of English. Her son was all she had and she was very protective. Ray had to hide the slightest bruise because his mother inspected his body closely, and if she found as much as a quarter-size black-and-blue mark, she would have a fit and forbid further participation in whatever activity caused the bruise. Whenever we returned late from a show, I always took Ray right to the door and made sure his mother saw me, hoping this would lessen her misgivings about letting the boy out in the future.

But Ray's mother never could refuse her only son's appeals to go with me and do those acrobatic things which he obviously wanted so much to do. Nevertheless, she was uneasy. In between Ray's translations, I could make out her mumbled interrogations to Ray about whether I had an *esposa* and where she was.

Joe's mother and the several other relatives who were in and out of the Ramoses' furnished room on Eightieth Street always greeted me warmly, invited me in and treated me as if they had known me for a long time. Joe obviously had given me a big build-up.

I hadn't met Joe's father yet. Most times when Joe mentioned him, it was in terms of being punished severely for being late. He also didn't like Joe's doing tumbling. Joe once quoted him as saying, "You're not monkeys!" Joe felt his father had the wrong idea about his tumbling, so he figured out a way to get him to come and see a performance, something none of the parents, for one reason or another, had been able to do. Joe gave his father, who was a fight fan, a ticket to the PAL boxing championships, being held in the old St. Nicholas Arena at Sixty-sixth Street and Columbus Avenue (later converted to an ABC film studio). Joe's father didn't know that the intermission entertainment was to be us—the Boylan PAL Tumblers.

Because we had a boxing ring ourselves to practice in, I was able to teach the boys some flashy moves using the ring ropes. Midway in the routine, the boys were running and bouncing off all four sides of the ropes, catapulting themselves across the ring, diving, vaulting and rolling over and under each other. It was a maze of flying bodies and it looked as if there would be a crash any second, but it was all carefully timed and precise and soon a couple of thousand fight fans were cheering.

Joe had a prominent role in the rest of the routine. He did his parts especially well.

A few days later Joe reported: "After that show, my father couldn't do enough for me. He gave me money and encouraged me." And never after that did Joe's father say anything against his tumbling.

6

I tried in every way I could to further stimulate the boys' interest in acrobatics. I encouraged them to go on Tuesday and Sunday evenings to the homes of friends who had television sets and watch the acrobatic acts that were always on the Milton Berle and Ed Sullivan shows. Every year the PAL got free tickets to the Ringling Bros. and Barnum & Bailey Circus at Madison Square Garden. I always managed to take the Boylan Center contingent of twenty-five to thirty kids, and Joe, Ray, Edgar, Israel and Angel always managed to be part of that contingent. During the show the boys seated themselves around me and we shared our enthusiasms.

In 1955 I arranged to have photographs taken of the tricks we did. Most of the pictures were still shots of pyramids and balances, but we also caught Joe somersaulting over the others and got a shot of Ray as he was turning over high in the air, doing his pitch-back. I had the photos copied and gave each of the boys a set. I made a scrapbook with acrobatic pictures I cut out of magazines and newspapers, and let the boys leaf through it. I started collecting photos and programs for an album of our accomplishments. One day I brought Smitty, one of my old top-mounters, to the gym, and we gave the boys a demonstration, carefully pointing out that they could expect to do these same tricks if they practiced diligently.

I would have liked to take them to the old Bothner's Gymna-

35

sium, where I had spent many hours learning the trade as a protégé of sorts to Vic Joselyn, of the once-famous vaudeville acrobats Wills and Joselyn. Acrobats, like circus families, don't write books about their trade; they pass on their skills from one generation to the next. Vic Joselyn didn't have a family, so he passed his skills on to me.

I remembered the passion with which I had trained to be an acrobat. It all started when I was recovering from a near-fatal bout with nephritis, a leading child-killer at the time. My twelve-year-old body, which had been robust and tireless, was emaciated. I could hardly walk. With push-ups, calisthenics and weight lifting with homemade barbells, I set out to build myself up. Being young and resilient, I progressed rapidly and was soon again playing baseball and football, running, climbing, and working at odd jobs while continuing with the exercises. I took to reading the body-building magazines and was always intrigued by the pictures of well-built acrobats doing hand balancing. Once there was an article describing a push-up done while in a handstand. A steady, locked-out handstand is not an easy balance, but even on my first attempt I came close. Immediately I sensed I had a "feel" for balancing and my body responded as if programmed. Soon hand balancing and all its variations were the only exercises I was doing, and not knowing anything about training methods, I simply practiced seven days a week, no less than three times a day. Late at night I had to be extra careful to hold my balance or else the thumping noise of my falling body would wake the rest of the family. In school, when students went into the bathrooms to sneak a smoke, I went in to sneak a few handstands.

Being an acrobat also suited my personality. I was somewhat shy and uncomfortable in social situations. Talking didn't suit my style, but action did. I would make my statement by excelling at this physical form of communication.

With single-minded devotion I trained, studied, watched acrobatic acts, and drifted into Y's and gyms in search of other acrobats. Bothner's Gym was my gold mine; a wonderful place.

36

It was a seedy old loft, above the Automat on Forty-second Street, where retired circus people, old vaudevillians and ex-professional wrestlers hung out—and it was where the best acrobats in the world practiced. Here I met acrobats who seemed to relish teaching me. And I was a good pupil; not only did I learn quickly, but I had a proper respect for the art. Here at Bothner's Gym one could see and work out with foreign acrobats who had just flown in to the United States and who would be appearing the next day on the stage of Radio City Music Hall, the Capitol Theater, the Roxy, the Paramount or the Palace. Here the boys could have seen such classy acts as the Wayne Marlin Trio. I sure would have liked Israel to see their top-mounter, Glenn Sundby, work! He had the same kind of toe point. I would have liked them all to see Renald and Rudy ("Poetry in Motion") do their graceful slow-motion hand-to-hand balancing.

At Bothner's they could have seen the Tsilaks, a Hungarian couple, who could do a free head-to-head balance while the husband rode a unicycle and both played violins. And there was Vic and Adio. At one point in their routine, Vic, lying on the floor reading a newspaper, with Adio in a handstand on his feet, does an inside-out roll-around, and winds up on his belly, still reading the newspaper, with Adio still in a handstand on his feet.

I would have wanted the boys to meet Lew Folds, the juggler, who did his act in a high silk hat, tux and cape—on ice skates. He taught me to juggle four balls (he could do seven), and he would have taught Angel a few variations with the juggling clubs. The old-timers would have regaled them with stories about the halcyon days and the acrobatic greats who appeared on the bill with them when they were playing the Pantages circuit. And there would have been interesting guys like the freckle-faced redhead who loved acrobatics and was one of Les Compagnons de la Chanson, a famous French singing group, whose members fought together in the Resistance.

Yes, the boys would have liked Bothner's Gym, though I'm

not so sure some of the old-timers would have wanted kids around the place—much less Puerto Rican kids. When the owner, old George Bothner, died, the place was converted into a second floor for the Automat.

Every so often, on summer weekends, my wife and I and the five boys would pile into my uncertain 1947 Ford, which I had bought the previous year for $125, and drive out to my parents' house in Springfield Gardens, a working-class section of Queens. They had a modest two-bedroom house with patches of lawn and weeds around it. Here my brother and five sisters and I grew up.

On the way out, the Ford would invariably stall because I couldn't shift into gear. I would have everyone sitting in the car lurch forward simultaneously, and as long as the road wasn't uphill, this lurching was enough to roll the car forward an inch or two, which was all that was needed for the gear to slip right in. The boys always got a kick out of the lurching part. Although these trips were billed as an "outing in the country," there was always a one- or two-hour workout on the lawn at the side of the house.

The first time we went out, the boys did an impromptu show for my mother and father and a couple of my sisters. Then my mother fed them fried chicken, rice and trimmings. She, like most mothers, enjoyed seeing the boys eat—and after we convinced them they didn't have to use knives and forks, they enjoyed the eating even more. My mother approved of these visits. She felt this was a good thing for me, her son, to be doing. So did my father.

During my youth my mother was the active parent, and looking back, she did a heroic job in raising all seven of us. My father, when he was home, spent most of his time trying to catch up on missed sleep. He painted the subways for the Transit Authority, and after work he painted the neighbors' homes to earn enough so we children wouldn't have to grow up in the Brooklyn ghetto where my mother and father first settled when they arrived in this country. My father had left his home in Sweden at sixteen to go to sea. For the next fifteen years he was a sort of international citizen, sailing under a dozen flags. Although he seldom spoke of it, we knew he was proud of having sailed in clipper ships around the Cape of Good Hope and Cape Horn, where the great oceans collide and the seas are forever turbulent. In his small talk with the boys he did mention that he had once, in 1923, been to their island, having docked in the port cities of Ponce and San Juan.

After eating, I took the boys exploring in the surrounding swamps. We went thrashing through the swamp reeds, which were over seven feet high in spots, but they were dry and delicate and gave way easily to our stampedes. I had always enjoyed this when I was their age.

We climbed onto the slanted shingled roof of my parents' house and scrambled up to the chimney at the peak, where off in the distance we could see Idlewild (later renamed Kennedy) International Airport, then still under construction. When we became hot and sweaty, we turned the hose on each other and got soaking wet and cool and comfortable as we dried in the sun.

When we left, my parents rather ceremoniously said goodbye to each of the boys, who had been carefully polite and well-behaved all day. It was like a receiving line, with my mother and father by the front door and the boys lined up waiting their turn to shake hands.

7

Throughout 1955 we continued performing in the youth centers and the schools, constantly trying out new tricks, testing audience reaction and rearranging the routine. The boys were getting bigger, stronger, faster. We were doing mature acrobatic stunts now, having cut out most of the modified, watered-down movements.

Joe was doing his front somersault over the other four guys as they did headstands in a row with their legs spread in a V. He also did a "one-arm get-up." Lying on his back, holding Ray aloft on one arm, Joe slowly and dramatically twisted and struggled to his feet.

Edgar did a different "get-up." Carefully balancing Angel, who stood stiff and rigid on Edgar's head, neither of them holding on, Edgar slowly sat on the floor, paused a moment, then muscled his way back up to a standing position. Later, to make the trick more dramatic, we made a flimsy table with pipe legs and Edgar did the same trick, first sitting on the table, sliding his feet under him, and then excruciatingly rising to a stand position on the quivering table—Angel standing all the while on his head.

Israel was becoming proficient in hand balancing. His handstand was really smart-looking. He could point his toes as straight as a ballet dancer's and the bowlike arch in his back made a line worthy of a Calder sculpture. Israel was strong enough to push himself slowly into a handstand. He could do a handstand on the other boys' heads, feet, backs and arms, and on the extended hands of either Joe, Angel or Edgar. He could do handstands on fences, stoops, cars, curbs, a basketball, the roller-roller, chairs, tables and bottles. And he could put the bottles on the table and the chair legs on top of the bottles and do a handstand on that. He could walk up and down stairs and jump off a four-foot platform, all on his hands.

We learned many pyramids, more than we could ever use. Joe and Edgar, with their thick, powerful legs, were still the bottom men, though they weren't any taller than the others now. Angel had grown a little taller, huskier and stronger, but he was still an in-between size, so he was the middle man in the pyramids. In some ways, it is precarious and uncomfortable to be a middle man because you are always standing on or being braced by someone's fleshy, bony body underneath you, while you hold a top-mounter in a handstand or a stand on the shoulders. Or maybe you are upside down, holding someone in a handstand on your feet or ankles—and hoping the bottom man has a good grip on you and the floor. Of course, it can be scary for top-mounters, who stand or handstand on these human structures, which sometimes feel like a stack of giant cooked elbow macaronis in a strong wind.

We learned to do a Jackson, a Camel, and a High San Quentin, a pyramid invented by acrobats in San Quentin Prison. We learned to do a Lean-To with double handstands, a Two-and-a-Half, and other three-, four- and five-man combinations, using bridges, levers, planches and counterbalances. Best of all, we could now top our pyramids with the incomparable Israel handstand.

Juggling wasn't one of my specialties, but I introduced the boys to it, just as I taught them to ride a unicycle and do a lot of other basic acrobatics. Juggling clubs is difficult, much more so than balls, because the clubs have to be spun as they are thrown from one hand to the other. I could remember, years back, spending many frustrating hours learning it myself. After

I showed Angel the mechanics of juggling three clubs, he went off to a corner and practiced. Within fifteen minutes—a mere fifteen minutes—he had the clubs going for six or seven throws.

"Now do it in Spanish!" I said, with good-natured disgust at the ease with which he learned.

Angel looked at me and smiled. "Ha," he laughed, tentatively. "Do it in Spanish! Ha!" He obviously wanted to laugh at what seemed to him like a joke, but he wasn't sure what it was.

Hand-to-hand balancing was my specialty, and needless to say, everyone got a solid grounding in holding and doing hand-to-hand stands. They all learned to do a handstand on my hands. Joe and Edgar learned to hold Ray and Israel on their hands. Angel learned both top and bottom.

Each workout, I would also do some hand-to-hand balancing, using Ray and Israel as top-mounters. This gave the two boys advanced training—while I could enjoy being a bottom man again. Not only were Israel and Ray light as feathers compared to my previous top-mounters, who had been an uncommonly heavy one hundred forty pounds, but they were "clean slates," without bad habits. Experienced gymnasts are often difficult to teach because they are used to balancing themselves and they wind up wiggling, straining, bending their arms and legs, trying to "catch their balance" instead of holding a firm and rigid position and letting the bottom man, or under-stander, do the balancing. Ray was especially good at giving the balance over to me—but then he learned to do hand balancing with me much before he could even do a handstand by himself.

That's not to say the bottom man does all the work. The top-mounter must have finger-to-toe control over the length of his body. He must be able to resist the sometimes almost uncontrollable urge to "break" from the fixed, lock-out position. The top-mounter is helped in doing this by an under-stander who is sensitive to the balance—who gives the top-mounter the feeling that the balance is "alive."

Basically the hand-to-hand balance is a rest position—whether the bottom man is lying down (a "low") or standing (a "high"). The interesting part is seeing how acrobats get in and out of these positions. There's an infinite variety of movements. In some the top man "muscles" or presses himself slowly into a handstand on the outstretched hands of the bottom man. In others there is a "tempo," a synchronized thrust in which the top and bottom men are pushing simultaneously against each other as they go into a handstand; both accelerate and gain momentum. When it is done correctly, the burden felt by top and bottom men is reduced to a fraction. The tempo is the ultimate in coordinated effort. It allows a whole series of complicated moves to be done with exhilarating ease. But a tempo is not easily achieved. Acrobats, for example, can't just say "One, two, three—*go!*" Their timing comes from feeling the rhythm; from an almost intuitive reaction to each other.

To me the tempo is sensuous, just as the one-hand balance is sensuous. Nothing quite compares with the sensation of being in a one-hand stand when you hit the spot just right. Very little strength is required and there is a kind of dynamic relaxation and a heightened awareness of one's body, as if the one-hand balance brings the body into alignments, not ordinarily experienced, that release something akin to electrical radiations, soothing and stimulating to muscles and nerves. And why not! If the yoga headstand is supposed to have such salutary effects on the body and mind, why shouldn't the one-hand balance do the same? But sensuous though it may be, there is nothing orgasmic about it, because control is never abandoned. In fact, the control is so intense that the unwieldy, multijointed human body is disciplined and concentrated to a point of balance centered in the second joint of the fore and middle fingers of the balancing hand.

Within a short time Ray, Israel and I had an extensive repertoire of hand-to-hand balancing tricks. Ray could do a donkey kick (snapping from his hands in my hands to his feet in my hands) and a one-hand stand on my one hand (the same principle of the bottom man doing the balancing applies). Ray and Israel could dive over chairs, and I, lying on my back, caught

43

them in a hand-to-hand balance. With each of them I could do shoots, cannonballs, whip-ups (all tempo tricks). Israel could do hollow-back, stiff-stiff, pike and tuck press-ups in "high" or "low" hand-to-hand stands.

The act was also being professionalized in several important ways. Like all acrobats who work in nightclubs or on the stage, the boys learned to work without mats. This was a difficult adjustment, but it had some positive results. By not being able to "play it safe," the boys had to go all out. They also became more responsible about unobtrusively hand-spotting each other during the more difficult tricks. Joe and Edgar, who had to move around while holding the others, found it easier on the solid floor. Before, their feet sank into the mats and made them feel unsteady.

The boys were becoming more aware of the audience. Although still grim, tense and preoccupied with remembering cues and not missing tricks, they were able to smile once in a while. They were learning to "sell" the more spectacular pyramids and "get-ups" by dramatizing their exertions and building up audience tension before a triumphant finale.

The most important professional touch was costumes. We couldn't afford the real thing, so my wife and I designed a beachcomber/shipwrecked-pirate costume. Using plain T-shirts and white duck pants, we cut jagged, frayed edges on the T-shirt sleeves and the bottoms of the pant legs. We then cooked and stirred these in a big boiling pot of red dye. The result was a reddish-pink color which went well with the boys' varied complexions. We fashioned ropelike belts by braiding strands of heavy white wool. Plain white low sneakers fit the overall effect and gave the boys a good grip on the floor. We were ready. Almost.

We needed a stage name—something jazzy; something that fit. Since I was training the boys almost exclusively on my own time now and we were doing shows independent of the PAL, it was no longer appropriate to keep that identification.

We were doing a summertime show for the children at New

York Hospital, which took place out in a spacious backyard plaza surrounded by tall buildings, trees and shrubs. It was one of the last shows we did in our PAL T-shirts and green shorts. There were many other entertainers. Some were professionals, donating their talent. The master of ceremonies of the Ringling Bros. and Barnum & Bailey Circus M.C.'d the show. He obviously didn't think "PAL Tumbling Team" would do for an introduction, so when it was time for the boys to go on, he took it upon himself to say: "And now, presenting, for your pleasure and entertainment, those daring, dashing, exciting, bouncing, balancing youngsters—the tumbling *Tumbleweeds!*"

"Yeah!" we all agreed. "That's us! The Tumbleweeds!"

One evening a few short months later, we got it all together and launched—unleashed might be a better word—our act on the auditorium stage of Joan of Arc Junior High School. It was an "Awards Night" program for the school's community center and over three hundred parents, students, teachers and spectators were in the audience. They were in a good mood, but as the speeches and presentations dragged on they became restless. Someone wisely decided to change the pace of the program with the Tumbleweeds.

Backstage, I turned on the record player which was hooked up to the loudspeaker system. The music for our act was Khachaturian's "Saber Dance." Gingerly I held the needle arm, ready to set it down on the LP record, which would be our signal to begin.

The houselights are dimmed. A bright fixed spotlight illuminates the middle portion of the stage.

The opening frenzied, throbbing chords of the "Saber Dance" music send Joe handspringing to the middle of the stage as the four other boys charge at him from the opposite side. Joe braces himself in a half squat, his hands locked together, making a foothold. One at a time, in rapid succession, the boys thrust their right foot into Joe's hands and vigorously straighten their legs as Joe, grunting, heaves them high into the air, over his head. In a couple of seconds the stage is full of flying, yelling Puerto Ricans in reddish costumes, frayed edges flapping in the breeze. They slap their legs as they fly over Joe's head, landing behind him with a sharp bump on the floorboards, setting the whole stage vibrating. As they go over they yell:

"*Vivaaaaa!*"
"*Yeooooowwww!*"
"*Arrribaaaaa!*"
"*Marrricoooonnn!*"

Joe, in rehearsal, had spontaneously started this yelling. I thought it added to the excitement and told them all to yell. The only restriction was that they had to limit their yelling of Spanish curse words to American audiences, who I hoped wouldn't understand what was being said.

Second time around now. Here they come, bouncing and running in time to the frenetic music. And up and over they go.

The effect is electrifying. People gasp and sit forward in their seats, too surprised to applaud. Exclamations of wonderment can be heard throughout the audience.

Ray runs and stabs his foot into Joe's hands and does a pitch-back somersault high up near the overhead track of spotlights. Angel pitches over Joe's head and lands straddling Edgar's chest. Both fall, Angel rolls out and Edgar nips up, neat as you please. Israel pauses for a split second, measuring the distance. He moves forward and accelerates as he hits Joe's clasped hands with his foot. He pushes up as Joe gives a long heave, bending backward, following through. Israel is airborne. Ten feet downstage is Edgar, poised to catch Israel in a standing position on his shoulders. This is a trick we miss often in practice. I hold my breath. Israel's feet hit Edgar's shoulders. Edgar stumbles forward, grabs one of Israel's legs at the calf muscle, misses the other leg, frantically grabs again and catches hold. They make it.

This is the first chance the audience has to applaud. But the pace picks up again. As the cymbals crash in the galloping music, the boys, one after the other, somersault, cartwheel, back-flip, handspring, dive, flip-flop, round-off-back-somersault across the stage. Their white-sneakered feet move so fast, as their bodies go over and around, that the illusion is created of a large blurred white tumbleweed rolling across the stage. The audience is pulled forward to the edge of their seats again. In the offstage shadows, I watch the Tumbleweeds and the audience, their eyes wide with fascination, and I have the feeling I am indirectly controlling the people on the stage and the hundreds of people watching. And it is a good feeling—but a strain. I see everything that can go wrong, everything that went wrong in rehearsal, and if everything goes well, as so far it has, then surely something will soon go wrong.

During the more subdued middle passages of the music, Edgar does his "get-up" on the table, with Angel standing like a mummy on his head. Edgar, with controlled strength, slowly stands. As his legs straighten, he and Angel majestically throw out their arms to the audience. The audience applauds. A five-man pyramid is quickly constructed, topped by the handstands of Ray and Israel. The pounding music picks up again as the boys go into their ending, with all of them simultaneously diving, rolling, shuttling over and under each other. They are like juggling balls: as soon as one comes down, the other is tossed up. Then they escalate the action until everyone is jumping, bounding, rolling, yelling, donkey-kicking and somersaulting in a whirling, swirling, cacophonous crescendo of music and color, arms and legs, bumps and thumps.

The music stops abruptly and the boys, right on cue, are lined up facing the audience, panting, sweating, trying to smile. They bow slightly, and the roar of applause rolls toward the stage, intensifying as they trot off.

Backstage, the boys are still breathing heavily as they chatter excitedly about the near-misses, the ad-libbed cover-up moves,

47

and the somersaults that went higher than ever. I feel drained, but happy and proud. The boys see it in my eyes, but I am restrained in my praise. "We can't be satisfied. We gotta go higher!"

8

Motivated by the practical necessity of eliminating impedi-
ments to my developing Tumbleweeds, I became increasingly
involved with other aspects of the boys' lives.

I got tired of seeing Angel hunched and shivering during the
cold weather, goose bumps all over, so I bought him a winter
coat, hoping that no one in his family would be offended. The
only times I didn't see Angel wearing the coat was when Chago
(Santiago), his younger brother by two years, was wearing it. I
was constantly replacing Israel's and Angel's costume sneakers
because they wore them year-round, for school, for playing in
the streets and for workouts.

I encouraged the boys to go to school and admonished them
when they played hooky. I felt school was important, but even
more, I feared Angel's and Israel's truancies would get them
picked up and institutionalized as wayward minors.

Although I didn't realize it at the time, Angel and Israel
stayed home from school a lot because they didn't always have
a white shirt and tie, as was required in the old P.S. 9. Once
Angel tried to slip by in a limp white T-shirt, with a neatly
knotted tie around his bare neck, but they sent him home. He
laughed about the incident later, but I could tell he had been
hurt. Israel once went to a funeral in a borrowed black raincoat,
which he kept buttoned and wore over his undershirt; it was the
most formal outfit he could pull together.

49

Angel and Israel were frequently sick. Besides Israel's headaches, both suffered from asthma, strep throat, sinus trouble, bronchitis, colds and other nasal disorders. They often missed school and our practices. Once when they had to get medical forms filled out for school—a procedure they usually ignored—I took the opportunity to whisk them off to the clinic for checkups. They were free of communicable diseases and not grossly underweight, but they were a little anemic and were cautioned about their diet. The doctor, to his credit, seemed properly embarrassed as he pointed to the brightly colored chart of meats, cheeses, breads and leafy vegetables and said, "Eat some food from each of these basic food groups each day." Angel looked as if he were listening to an explanation of the solar system.

All the guys in my Tumbleweeds were always hungry, but so are most kids during their rapid-growth years. The difference was that Angel and Israel simply didn't get enough to eat. When they looked particularly weak and wan, I would give them each twenty cents, which bought them coffee and buttered toast with a pat of jelly. This was the best buy in the restaurant; preference had little to do with it. But I didn't realize the extent of their hunger, nor how preoccupied they were in their search for food.

Before Israel was old enough to go to school, he would meet his older sister at lunchtime in the cafeteria of P.S. 9 and she would slip him her lunch card. Israel would eat a trayful of food and return home. Later, when Israel attended P.S. 9, his parents didn't come to school to show that their income was low enough to qualify Israel for the free lunch, as they had for Noelia and as Angel's mother had done for him. Angel's girlfriend at P.S. 9, who was a lunch-line monitor, let Israel sneak into the line. Those hot lunches were the most nutritious meals they had all day. But this ended for Israel when he was transferred to the new P.S. 87 and Angel was transferred to P.S. 166.

Angel and Israel pilfered food from delicatessens, supermarkets and bodegas. Angel fashioned a bow and arrow out of umbrella struts, and from a concealed doorway adjacent to the fruit and vegetable stand, shot a sharpened strut, attached to a line of thread, into grapefruits or tomatoes. Thus harpooned, his catch was reeled in carefully. Both of them stole milk delivered to apartment doorsteps. In the winter some people who lived in furnished rooms (few of which were equipped with refrigerators or kitchens) kept containers of milk or pieces of chicken on the window sills. Israel and his brother sometimes fished with a weighted hook from an upper window for these pieces of chicken. Or Angel would lower a rope with a pail on the end to a point just below the milk container. Israel, with a long pole made up of two broomstick handles tied together, would reach down and gently knock the milk container into the pail and Angel would pull it up. Milk was a favorite.

And when the pickings were poor, they went to Central Park and ate those forbidding-looking little purple berries and chestnuts and the hard green bulbs that look like unripe apples.

Most of the boys' families moved frequently, especially Angel's, and always into run-down buildings, sometimes with a hall kitchen shared with several other families. If the kitchen was occupied you had to wait. If you couldn't wait you just had to skip eating or go to a restaurant.

If the electricity, gas, heat and hot water went off, which happened occasionally, life not only became difficult, but you couldn't cook your dinner, even if you had a hot plate in your room. Once when this happened to Angel's family, his determined mother went into the backyard and dragged in two flat stones, remnants of a broken sidewalk. She put these on the kitchen floor, built a fire with old newspapers and splinters of broken furniture, and cooked their dinner rice.

Sometimes the bushy-white-haired Greek proprietor of a tired-looking luncheonette on Eighty-third Street and Amsterdam Avenue would give Angel and Israel something to eat, with the expectation that they would pay as soon as they could. Angel and Israel called him Khrushchev, not because he looked

51

like the Russian leader, but because Nikita Khrushchev had recently succeeded Stalin and was much in the news, and he had a foreign accent, too. Khrushchev pestered the boys for his money and at times they gave him some of the nickels, dimes and quarters they earned carrying packages for people coming out of the supermarket. When Angel and Israel were desperately hungry, they could almost always count on Khrushchev, especially late at night when there were leftovers. For fifty cents, or the promise of that amount, they sometimes got plates piled high with steaming rice and chicken.

After Angel and Israel got to know Edgar through the Tumbleweeds, they had another reasonably "sure thing." At least once a week, sometimes more, they would visit Edgar around dinnertime and Edgar's father always invited them to stay and eat. At least there was always coffee and toast.

Angel and Israel occasionally ate at each other's homes, especially if they knew there was a big pot of something. Their equivalent of "raiding the icebox" produced very little, but they did discover the best method of making coffee using old coffee grounds. Angel's method was to put new water in the pot and boil it. Israel boiled the water separately and poured it over the coffee grounds. Angel conceded Israel's method was superior, especially if it was the third or fourth recycling of the grounds.

But my concern for the boys' well-being wasn't simply a matter of keeping them hale and hearty for the acrobatic act. They were a whole new and heady experience for me. Teaching was wonderfully satisfying. I could step back and look at the boys and say, "I did that; that's a part of me; that's my mark." How many people in this world who toil mightily day after day ever see visible, concrete, identifiable fruits of their labor? There was absolutely nothing like it.

I knew this working with kids had to do with ego, but I didn't think too much about it. My feelings of power were more than offset by my feelings of impotence and frustration at not being able to mitigate the powerful destructive forces that pressed in on their lives.

Far more fascinating than anything in college was being around kids. And Joe, Edgar, Ray, Israel and Angel were unique kids. They had come from small towns on a Caribbean island almost two thousand miles away, with a different language, food, music, culture and history. By late 1955, after a reasonably close association, I had learned quite a bit about the boys. They had been part of the mass migration of Puerto Ricans to New York that began after World War II and reached an average of fifty thousand a year by the 1950s. The boys came with parents or relatives, who, like the rest of the migrants, came to start anew, to join families, to find work. They came carrying all their worldly possessions jammed into suitcases and shopping bags. And though the migrants weren't welcomed by earlier, Old World immigrants, they were welcomed in factories, fields, laundries, sweatshops and assembly lines.

All the boys came to New York between 1947 and 1951 on the economy flights, in the old army-surplus propeller-driven DC-3's and C-46's. After two of these converted military airplanes crashed in the late 1940s, killing more than seventy passengers, some called them "suicide planes." Sad ballads can still be heard on Puerto Rican radio stations about these tragic crashes that wiped out whole families.

The eight-hour flights were overcrowded, uncomfortable, often without ventilation, and bumpy when they hit air pockets. The Puerto Ricans themselves came to call this mode of transport the "cattle car" and it was probably snobbish stewardesses who first referred to it as the "roach coach." An early-day travel agent reportedly called it the "vomit comet."

Joe's father was a barber and he had been working almost three years in a New York barbershop before he sent for his wife, his wife's sister and Joe.

Because of bad weather, their flight was detoured to Bermuda, where Joe, who was only four, vaguely remembered being sprayed with some kind of powder. Apparently Joe had been deloused along with the rest of the passengers because they were foreigners—an experience they wouldn't have in the U.S. because Puerto Ricans are American citizens. When Joe's plane finally landed at Idlewild Airport, he was frightened. Everything was white; no one had explained snow to him.

Joe was still very young when his father was partially paralyzed with some vague disease and his hair turned white. After some cursory dealings with doctors, Joe's father turned to spiritism—a not uncommon practice among Puerto Ricans, especially those from rural areas or small towns like San Germán. The incantations, incense and the burning of special candles, all behind closed doors, mystified and worried Joe. Everybody and everything in the household was subordinated to his father's struggle with the demons of illness.

Joe headed for the streets. Here he could breathe and let loose. Here was a suitably challenging environment for Joe's overflowing energy and restless curiosity. Here Joe learned English as naturally and quickly as he learned the ways of the street. When he started first grade at age seven, he could speak as well as the American kids. He wasn't held back like Angel, Israel and Edgar, and so many other Puerto Rican kids, who, when they started school, were confronted and frustrated by a *no comprendo* language they had to learn before they could go on to the next grade.

Joe lived in several neighborhoods and attended several public schools before settling on West Eightieth Street in a rear-basement furnished room in a brownstone building numbered 160.

Joe's father recovered—who knows why?—from his illness and soon opened his own barbershop, where he worked long and late. Like many barbershops, it became a gathering place for friends and other San Germaneros. Joe's father was an avid sports fan, and pictures of baseball and basketball teams were taped up next to the barbershop mirrors. He once organized a stateside tour of exhibition games for the San Germán basketball team. I didn't see Joe's father very often, but when I did he always seemed very serious. He obviously had his problems.

Four years after Joe came to New York, Luis, Joe's half brother, three years his junior, came from Puerto Rico and joined the Ramos household on Eightieth Street.

Joe was twelve when Georgie was born. Soon after, Joe's mother went to work in a factory as a sewing machine operator. Joe's mother was a quiet, pleasant woman, always friendly and cooperative. She approved of me and of Joe's association with the Tumbleweeds. But Joe used me at times, especially as he got older, whenever he needed a quick excuse to go carousing on the streets: "Gotta go to tumbling practice," or when sneaking in late at night, bleary-eyed: "We were doing a show." Yet she indulged Joe and very early on he became the "man of the house," because his father spent so much time in the barbershop.

When Edgar's father decided to leave his little restaurant in Ponce and go to New York, Edgar elected to go with him. Eventually an older sister and two older brothers would come, but they stayed with relatives or started families of their own. One brother returned to Puerto Rico many years later. Edgar's mother and a younger sister didn't think they wanted to leave Ponce—and they never did. Much later the younger sister attended secretarial school in New York for several months, but immediately returned.

Edgar was ten when he arrived in New York in 1951. He was shocked by the cold. He was even more shocked when the other Puerto Rican kids in the neighborhood treated him like the blue-eyed, light-brown-haired, white-skinned gringo foreigner he seemed to them to be. In Puerto Rico the kids knew him and took his fair complexion for granted, but not here in Manhattan. Puerto Rican gangs threatened to get him. After all, who was this "American" kid to casually roam all over their "turf." With the American kids it was no better. Edgar couldn't speak to them or understand them, and anyway, to him they were foreign-looking.

But Edgar was outgoing and irrepressible and he made friends, even though sometimes it was a hassle going into a new class, a different building, a strange block, or even a community center.

Edgar and his father, after living briefly with his father's sister and other relatives, sublet two bedrooms of a five-room apartment on Eighty-fifth Street, between Columbus and Amsterdam avenues. The primary tenant of the apartment was a woman with a very young daughter. They lived in the third bedroom. All of them got to be close friends and soon Edgar was calling the woman "Mama Rosa"; the daughter was like a little sister. They shared the whole apartment and meals were done cooperatively.

Edgar stayed home a lot. His father didn't want him wandering around while he was working at the bakery, and Mama Rosa also kept a lookout so Edgar wouldn't be led astray. The boy was reasonably comfortable with this arrangement.

Although Edgar was put back a grade when he started school, he did well. He learned English quickly and he was artistic. He participated enthusiastically in most things and sought approval from the teachers.

After meeting Edgar's father, I never really worried about Edgar. Eusebio Mourino was a soft-faced man, about fifty, with intelligent eyes, who spoke English well. He seemed sensitive and solid. He was appreciative that I was teaching his son worthwhile things which he assured me his son enjoyed a great deal.

Edgar was also a pretty steady guy. As on the roller-roller, he swung back and forth, between occasional silliness and responsible behavior, most of the time keeping himself, like the rolling cylinder, within the two extremes.

Because Ray and I were good friends in addition to our Tumbleweeds association, I got to know more about him than the other boys and was more involved with his life. I gave him my old bicycle, which was his first. I attended his graduation from P.S. 166 and I went to his birthday parties.

"Where's your wife?" asked Ray's mother when I arrived for Ray's thirteenth birthday party in a rear-basement furnished room on West Seventy-eighth Street. She had moved here recently to escape Eighty-fourth Street.

"She's home with our baby," I answered, confident I had said something reassuring to Mrs. Sanchez, who was still a little uncertain about me and the kind of influence I was having on her son. And she was right to be concerned because, for better or worse, I was influential. Between the Tumbleweeds' practices and Ray's daily attendance at the center, I spent more time with him than even the most conscientious parent.

"Next time I'll bring my wife," I said. Ray's mother raised a skeptical eyebrow, smiled and nodded. She introduced me to Paula, a hefty, dusky, shapely woman in a tight green silk dress, who appeared to be in her early thirties. She was Ray's mother's friend and neighbor. She had helped put up the decorations, buy the refreshments and the frosted birthday cake with thirteen candles. Ray quietly informed me that Paula was a B-girl who worked the clubs and fancier bars in the Times Square area. Her claim to fame was having once entertained a well-known irascible major-league baseball manager.

Paula was nice and she obviously enjoyed making a fuss over Ray. He had that kind of effect on people. With his *chino* eyes, his innocent but handsome face and quiet good manners, he was an engaging kid. He evoked motherly instincts—and fatherly ones, too, I guess.

There were about five other women, two men, and seven or eight of Ray's schoolmates in the room, all dressed up, dancing and chattering gaily, trying to hear each other over the *"Cha, cha*-cha-cha-cha *cha, cha*-cha-cha-cha . . ."

Ray's birthday was a big event for his mother. Each year she threw a party and invited friends. I think she came to associate birthday parties with being a good mother. Or maybe she was compensating with Ray because she felt bad about her younger son, Jaime, who remained with her mother in Rincón. Rincón, which means "Corner," is a very small coastal town in the northwest corner of Puerto Rico. Here Ray was born when his mother was sixteen years old. The next year Jaime was born.

Ray's father worked as a seasonal sugar-cane cutter, a withering, low-paid job. *Se defienden*—"defending themselves"—is the cane worker's phrase for the struggle of making a living, and working in the cane is *bregando*—"doing battle" with it.

When Ray was five years old, his father left Rincón for New York to find a good, steady job, with the understanding that he would save enough money to send for the family. He never did, and a little over a year later Ray and his mother flew to New York. Ray's mother immediately went to work as a sewing machine operator in a factory where she stitched together plastic covers for furniture and clothing.

The plan was for Jaime to join his mother when he was old enough to go to school all day, like Ray, while she worked. In the meantime Jaime was to remain with his grandmother. But Jaime was the only boy-child remaining in the family and he and grandma became very close. When he was old enough to go, he didn't want to—and grandma wanted him to stay.

Six years passed before Ray saw his father again. His father was conciliatory and friendly, but his life had changed. It had begun to change soon after he arrived in New York. Everything had been so different. He had a new wife and children now and he had moved to the Bronx. Later he would move to New Jersey, where he worked as an assembly-line mechanic in a factory making cardboard boxes. He tried to make up with Ray by taking him out for ice cream and soda, but Ray was unresponsive, and angry. Visits were infrequent after that, but Ray's father never completely broke off his contacts and inquiries.

During the party I had *palitos* (shots) of Seagram's Seven with the adults, and danced the merengue like a "Rican," as Joe would say. Ray had taught me. I talked with the other kids I knew from the center, ate birthday cake and had a good time.

The Tumbleweeds in 1956. From top:
Joe Ramos, 14; Edgar Mourino, 14; Israel Gotay, 12;
Ray Sanchez, 12; Angel Rodriguez, 13

Mentor and author in two characteristic poses, 1959

The Tumbleweeds in a pyramid

Ray and Fred

From top: Ray, Joe and Fred

Mayor Robert F. Wagner and Joey Adams, president of
AGVA (far right), officially thank Edgar,
Israel and Angel after a Youth Board show, 1960

Earning the money for his college education, Ray teaches acrobatics to a delighted group of children, 1961

From top: Israel, Angel and Edgar in a television performance, Mexico City, 1972

Twenty Years Later

Ray Sanchez, social welfare
executive, Department of Health,
Education and Welfare

Edgar Mourino, instructor at
The Gym, exercise salon

Joe Ramos, community center director, The Goddard Riverside Community Center, New York City

Israel Gotay, parking lot attendant, New York City

Angel Rodriguez, manager of the Mail Department, American Brands, Inc.

The Tumbleweeds reunited in 1974: Left to right, Angel, Edgar, Israel, Joe, Ray

Parents were often a little self-conscious when I visited and there were profuse apologies for the humble fare, which was often unusually tasty, or apologies for the run-down building, the peeling paint, the dripping faucets and the urine-ammonia smell of the bathroom in the hall. They thought of me as a government official or teacher of some kind.

"*El* party *es mucho bueno,* Mrs. Sanchez," I said to Ray's mother. "*Mucho bueno!*"

"Milagros!" she said. "*Me llamo*—you call me—Milagros . . . my name!"

"Okay, Milagros, but then you call me Fred. *Me llamo* Frred." I tried to give it a little accent.

"Okay, Frred," she said, smiling.

During the rest of the afternoon I had the feeling Milagros was sneaking glances at me to see how—or if—I looked at or danced with the women.

Milagros was proud of Ray and he was a constant source of satisfaction. He was bright and enthusiastic. He brought honor to the family. The year before, he had been selected as one of the all-round outstanding PAL kids from Boylan Center, for which he received, in a public ceremony, a plaque from Mayor Robert Wagner. I didn't influence his getting the award in any way except to vote with the majority of staff who made the selection.

But in spite of Ray's accomplishments, Milagros was worried. New York City was a rough place, full of addicts, gangs and bad influences. One of her major concerns was not being able to afford anything bigger than their single furnished room. The twenty dollars a week rent she now paid took a big chunk out of her thirty-eight-dollar weekly take-home pay. Milagros wasn't sure it was good for Ray's development for them to share the same room. A boy needs a man around to influence his growing up, to inculcate *machismo.*

Machismo was as important to Milagros as it was to Puerto Rican men. It was behavior that normal, healthy, happy men developed and it was behavior that Puerto Rican women understood and expected. How was Ray to learn this *machismo* when his teachers were women, most of her friends and neighbors were women, and his friend Frred was an Americano and who knew what else?

Not many more birthdays were to pass before Milagros more or less arranged for Paula, the B-girl, to make sure—absolutely certain sure—that Ray was developing normally.

The bitter cold stung the legs of seven-year-old Israel Gotay in his short pants as he walked down the airplane ramp at Idlewild International Airport. He shivered so much his nine-year-old sister, Noelia, who had accompanied him, bought him a hot cup of coffee, which he promptly spilled on his lap, nearly scalding himself. Soon older Gotays, who had come years earlier, arrived to take Israel and Noelia to the Bronx.

Israel was the youngest of the nine Gotay children (one died in infancy). His mother had a child every year after she was married at age fifteen to Israel's father, who was about twice her age. Before coming to Eightieth Street, Israel lived on Fox Street, in the infamous 41st Precinct in the Bronx, and for a short while he lived in Brooklyn and East Harlem.

In their first-floor furnished room on Eightieth Street, the Gotay family consisted of Israel, his mother and father, Noelia, and an older brother, Juan. The beds ringed the room and a curtain hung in front of the parents' bed in a corner alcove. They had a small refrigerator, a sink and a hot plate. The bathroom was in the basement.

Israel's father, the only wage earner in the family, made belts for Rudy's Leather Goods. Four older Gotay brothers, who had households and families of their own, also worked there. All made at least the minimum wage at the time: seventy-five cents an hour.

Israel was twelve when his mother died. It happened very suddenly. Israel was walking to the store with her when she said she felt sick. They went to Israel's brother's home on Seventy-seventh Street and his mother lay down. Israel was sent to get a doctor. He ran to the doctor's office near Riverside Drive and Seventy-ninth Street where his mother had recently got some pills, but the doctor wasn't there. He ran around frantically, looking for a doctor. He couldn't find one. He rushed back. Other brothers and sisters had arrived, and he sensed instantly that it was too late. Israel ran out and rode the subway until two in the morning, when exhaustion forced him to return home. His mother was only thirty-seven.

Tragedy seemed to stalk the Gotay family. Manolo, who was said to have the potential to be "a great baseball pitcher," lost a major-league contract because of his drinking. Manolo was very upset at his mother's death and soon after died of double pneumonia. Roberto, another older brother, who had a wife and five daughters, was soon to die of something "cerebral."

Israel's father deteriorated after his wife died. He began to drink heavily, and occasionally went on binges, spending extravagant sums on prostitutes. He was often sick and his asthma attacks were so severe that Israel had to take him regularly to Roosevelt Hospital for shots. But mostly he would come home from work, eat and then sit before the TV, hypnotized, watching professional wrestling for the rest of the evening.

He wasn't a man with many resources or much resiliency. In Puerto Rico he had been an unskilled "maintenance" worker at the airport. He never learned to write his name. Israel later told me: "The only time my father even tried to make a pot of coffee was to get the grounds to put in a sock to put on my head to help my headache." And then, with warmth in his voice, he added, "It was the only thing that ever worked. It stopped my headache."

Noelia and Juan tried to hold things together, but they were on the threshold of leading their own lives and busy with school and their jobs and the search for suitable marriage partners and a future beyond Eightieth Street.

Israel learned to fend for himself. Sometimes he cooked simple dinners of rice or chicken for himself and his father. Occasionally he had to rescue grocery money before his father spent it all on booze. Often things just drifted and Israel would buy junk food from the bodega, or skip meals altogether.

Israel's life drifted more and more into the streets, where he could always find his best friend in the world, Angel Rodriguez.

9

Angel was very young when his father separated from his mother and went to New York City. Angel was still only four when his mother sent him to live with a woman neighbor and left with Angel's baby brother for New York to join her three older daughters and oldest son.

Angel came to think of this neighbor as his mother and expected to stay with her always. But one morning two years later, relatives came to get him. His mother had sent a plane ticket and that afternoon Angel was put on the plane, never again to see the neighbor, who had been his mother for a third of his young life.

By the time I got to know Angel, all his older siblings except Rosa had married and moved away. All had common-law marriages, which is traditional for the rural poor in Puerto Rico. Angel lived with his mother, Rosa and Chago, his younger brother, whom I knew from the center. Chago was a funny-looking, effervescent kid, but wild, like Joe's half brother Luis, always getting into trouble. Although I hadn't met Reynaldo, Angel's older brother, who was in his late twenties, everyone in the neighborhood knew him to be a notorious dope pusher, thief and hustler. Most of the time he was in jail.

Rosa was the only member of Angel's immediate family who worked with any regularity. She was a sewing machine operator, but she had plans for a more glamorous life as a chorus girl

63

with one of the Latin bands. Angel's mother did piecework at home for a short time, gluing costume jewelry, but gave it up when the glue began to hurt her eyes.

When Angel saw his father again, many years had gone by and there was nothing between them. His father had another family and was a self-ordained "hallelujah" minister in a store-front church. Angel had never had the chance to develop any feelings for the man.

I wanted to find out more about Angel, who, along with Israel, was my biggest worry, so I decided to make a home visit.

One cold January afternoon, I plodded through several inches of snow on my way to the center. I had just emerged from the Eighth Avenue subway and was nearing Columbus Avenue when I saw Angel on the sidewalk headed uptown. He was pulling a sled loaded with cardboard boxes. Piled on top of the boxes was a bundle of dresses and other garments. The wire hangers that were sticking out the end of the bundle of clothes kept falling into the snow, and Angel occasionally picked one up, all the while holding a brown table radio, with the cord trailing in the snow, under his arm. Strung out in front of and behind Angel were other members of the Rodriguez family, struggling with and partially hidden by boxes, furniture and bundles of clothes draped over arms and shoulders. I thought Angel might be embarrassed if I stopped to talk with him now about a visit, so I avoided letting him see me.

The very next day, in the very same spot, I saw the same parade of Rodriguezes loaded down with clothes and furnishings—going in the opposite direction. Angel was in the lead, pushing a baby carriage precariously loaded with bulging laundry bags and pots and pans and dishes. This time I stopped and grabbed a long-stem floor lamp which Angel carried in one hand but couldn't keep from banging into the spokes of the baby carriage.

"Let me help," I said, taking the lamp. I shifted my briefcase to my left hand and held the lamp upright in front of me like a torch as I led this heavy-laden band of pilgrims back to their Eightieth Street home.

"We're movin' back," Angel said. "My mother didn't like the landlord in the Endicott." With only the slightest edge of exasperation, he added, "That's the way she is!"

"There's a gymnastic club out at the Jamaica Y," I said. "They're putting on an amateur circus two weeks from now. My friend Gene Cron, who's organizing it, wants us to be in it. The only trouble is we will be out very late Friday and Saturday nights. If it's all right with you, I'll come over some night and tell your mother about it so she won't worry."

"She lets me go."

"Don't you think it would be better if I told her about it?"

"Sometimes she's busy."

"I'll come sometime when she isn't busy."

Angel still seemed reluctant, but he didn't oppose the idea. "Come at night. That's better."

"Okay—*bueno!*"

At ten o'clock Friday evening a week later, after the center closed, I walked to Eightieth Street and found Angel playing stoop ball under the streetlight. It was a mild, foggy night. Angel saw me and said hello. He had forgotten about the visit, but he told me to come home with him and meet his mother.

"Are you sure it's not too late?"

"Are you kidding!" he said, smiling. "They should be just getting started."

Angel led me up the stoop stairs of a brownstone into a first-floor furnished apartment. The contrast of the bare-bulb kitchenette light with the dim lights in the living room made me squint, but I immediately recognized the shapes of beds, stuffed chairs, worn linoleum on the living room and kitchen floors. The television set near the curtainless front windows added a little light and much sound.

Otherwise the place was surprisingly uncluttered. They don't stay long enough to accumulate things, I thought. A couple of cockroaches were making their way up the wall over the stove, where a big pot was being tended by Angel's mother.

As far as I could make out, Angel's introduction, in Spanish, emphasized my being a teacher of sorts. Angel's mother was a really beat-up-looking woman, her hair in disarray and her clothes wrinkled. Her wide cheekbones were like Angel's, but the expression was angry. Under one eye was a yellowed purple bruise—the latter stages of a black eye. She nodded pleasantly to me, but then let out an angry stream of words. The man she was talking to—or yelling at—was introduced by Angel as his "father-in-law." He was short and scrawny, and looked half the age of Angel's mother. He shook my hand, but ignored me as he yelled back at Angel's mother with elaborate *macho* gestures of defiance.

In the living room, seated deep in a gray upholstered chair, was Angel's older brother Reynaldo, the dope pusher. He was sullen-looking, clean-shaven and pale. Prison pallor, I thought. He seemed to be ignoring the proceedings in the kitchen, yet I wasn't sure he was watching the TV. For a few seconds I was hypnotized by the blurred snow and flashing streaks moving across the television screen, waiting for those electronic distortions to organize themselves into recognizable shapes. I shook my gaze loose and moved toward Reynaldo. He had the same Rodriguez features, but I couldn't imagine that face summoning up an Angel grin or laugh. I assumed Reynaldo had heard the introductions, so I made a few innocuous remarks about the weather. Reynaldo, with unexpected friendliness, agreed it was foggy but not cold.

"Angel is a good athlete," I said.

"Which Angel?" he answered, without turning his gaze from the blurred images on the TV screen.

"This Angel," I said, pointing at Angel and smiling, not sure if he was kidding.

"He's a good acrobat—and he can run, too. Very fast! Why don't you come see him at the center sometime?"

"Which center?"

Our scintillating conversation was interrupted by the entrance of two young women, who had come out of the room just off the kitchenette. One was Angel's sister Rosa. She was dressed in a short imitation-fur coat, high heels, strong perfume and a short, tight skirt outlining a slim, shapely body. The Rodriguez facial characteristics almost looked good on her, but her studied seductiveness and wet red lipstick spoiled the naturalness of her smile. She was very friendly, but even her small talk had a teasing quality.

Hilda, the other woman, plopped herself down in Reynaldo's lap. He didn't move. Hilda was chunky, but well-proportioned. Though a little cross-eyed, she was not unattractive. She looked at me curiously and chatted away in Spanish to no one in particular. The irritating sounds of domestic squabbling in the kitchen were becoming a monotonous drone, as was the frantically loquacious TV announcer with his *"Tremendísimo! . . . Extraordinarioso! . . . Magnífico!"*

Rosa was on her way to a dance. Pausing by the door, she said coyly, "Maybe I will join the community center also."

"Er . . . that would be nice," I said, trying to sound as noncommittal as possible.

Angel whispered to me that Hilda was his brother's "woman." As soon as Angel said that, I remembered where I had seen her before. She was one of the regulars who patrolled Broadway around the bars from Eightieth to Eighty-fifth Street. So Reynaldo was her pimp, I thought.

It was difficult for me to find things to say to Hilda and Angel had to translate, though I felt Hilda, like so many Spanish-speaking people, was afraid to struggle with the English she did have. Nevertheless, she was the only one who seemed willing to talk.

"I'm like a teacher or coach of different sports," I explained. "Do you play any sports?" As soon as I said it, I wished I could rephrase the question. But Hilda answered enthusiastically in passable English.

"In school in Puerto Rico, I play bolleyball. *Me gusto*—I like

67

that game. I could jump high." She put her arm up and snapped her wrist forward as if hitting a volleyball over the net. "Once our girls' team beat the boys," she added with animation.

She interrupted herself to reach down and pick up Reynaldo's limp arms, wrapping them around herself. She bounced a little on his inert body and wiggled her behind into his lap. Getting no response, she threw his arms apart, got up and went toward the kitchen.

I decided to try and talk to Angel's mother, wishing at the same time that I could get someone to turn down the goddamn television. Angel's mother interrupted her domestic dialogue. "You have a beer?" she asked me.

"Yes, have a beer," added Angel's "father-in-law" as he opened the refrigerator. There was none. "Angel," he commanded, "go get a six-pack." He found his own pockets empty. After five minutes of bickering and badgering among the people in the kitchen and living room, a dollar bill was secured and Angel went out to buy the beer.

In a motherly tone, Angel's mother said to me, "Angel is a good boy." I nodded agreement. Now we were going to get into the subject, I thought.

I was distracted by a large conga drum edging its way through the front door. The bearer was dwarfed by the drum and as he hugged it in front of him the drum looked as if it were walking into the room on short little legs.

It was Angel's younger brother, Chago. A dark, curly-headed kid was with him. Chago was wearing one of those narrow-brimmed fedoras, which looked as if it had been rammed down on his head so hard it pushed his face into an exaggerated grin.

A cheerful "Hi!" and Chago moved to the bed against the wall, braced the drum between his legs and started beating out a mambo.

Expressionless, the dark kid banged along with a spoon against an empty beer can.

Angel returned. He passed me a cold can of beer and said, "That's my brother Chago."

"I know! I know!" I said, feeling very aware of Chago's presence.

Hilda turned up the sound on the television. She complained she couldn't hear her *novela,* but I noticed she never stopped tapping her foot and bobbing her head slightly to the mambo drumming.

Father-in-law banged his fist on the kitchen table to punctuate his shouted ultimatums. Angel's mother talked angrily to herself as she scraped and stirred the pot with a vengeance.

There was a twinkle in Angel's eye and he was smiling at me.

"Let's go, Fred," he said as he opened the door.

Right, let's go! I said to myself with relief. Limply I gestured that Angel and I were leaving.

"Muchas gracias. . . . Adiós!" I said several times, trying to acknowledge everyone in the room, at the same time suppressing a wave of exasperation.

Feeling flushed, bewildered and numb, I shuffled after Angel. The beer on an empty stomach had made me feel light-headed. Angel started to laugh. A muffled giggle at first, his laughter gathered momentum. The heavy front door banged shut behind and he exploded into a roaring crescendo of laughter, an arpeggio of giggles.

By the time I reached the sidewalk, Angel had disappeared into the foggy darkness. But I heard his laughter clear and loud down the block, reverberating in the concrete canyon of Eightieth Street, dominating the street sounds. Side-splitting, eye-watering, gasping-for-breath wails—one after the other—like the sound of Olympian jubilation. The vibrations of the sound set my body shivering and ears ringing. I felt a big, silly grin crease my face. Another roll of his laughing thunder and I began to feel giddy. My stomach muscles contracted fitfully. Shrill, gigglish sounds welled up in my throat and involuntarily forced their way out. Once more Angel's beautiful, unsettling laughter echoed up the street, and triggered an answering burst from me, a little too high-pitched and nervous at first, but improving in tone as the tension drained. I took a deep breath and the guffaws rolled up from deeper in my gut, heartier, less inhibited.

I bounced along as I walked, swinging my arms. I swatted a garbage-can cover, causing it to clatter along the sidewalk. Angel's laughing continued—cascading, joyous, abandoned, paroxysms of hilarity. My own laughter followed his as if independent of my control. Under the white-orange streetlight moons, we howled into the foggy asphalt night.

10

The Tumbleweeds began receiving requests to perform at various functions and benefits outside the youth center/school circuit. We accepted all invitations because no matter how smoothly the boys performed in the park or gym, it meant nothing until they could do it before an audience, under the sometimes blinding spotlights, on postage-stamp-size stages, and under the worst condition of all—the too low ceiling. Most of our tricks now were high; pitches went up over ten feet in the air and some pyramids over fifteen feet. Although we were always assured we would have enough ceiling height, we often arrived at new locations an hour before show time and found we had to modify and adjust half the routine because the ceiling was too low.

Sometimes, if we had no rehearsal, we misjudged the ceiling height. Once Angel was up on top of the other guys and as he stood up his body disappeared behind a front-stage curtain. The audience could see only the bottom of his legs. Angel just reached down, lifted the curtain, bent to the side, peeked out from under the curtain and gave the audience a winning smile. He got a big laugh for that. After a while we developed a special routine for low ceilings.

The Christmas show for the children at Mount Sinai Hospital made a strong impression on the boys. They were to remember it vividly years after. The Tumbleweeds were part of a short

71

program of entertainment: a clown, a folk singer, a magician and a Santa Claus. We started on the ninth-floor ward. An aisle separated two long rows of beds and wheelchairs occupied by eight-, nine- and ten-year-olds in wrinkled pajamas; autographed plaster casts covered a few little heads, arms, chests and legs. In between the beds were crammed crutches, oxygen tanks, chrome trays, rubber tubes and plasma bottles.

The other acts did appropriate children's routines, not much different from what these kids saw on TV each day. But the Tumbleweeds were different. They turned that polished linoleum aisle into a five-ring circus and every kid had a front-row seat. The boys threw in every knockabout slapstick comedy trick they knew. Every kid they landed near or narrowly missed got a personal performance. The boys talked to the kids. They hammed it up. They even invented stuff, inspired by the cheering and laughing. Even the Santa Claus integrated himself into the Tumbleweeds act. The boys caught him, dropped him, set him up for pratfalls. They really stirred up the place.

Afterward the boys were sweating and puffing more than usual—and smiling more, too.

"Hey, Fred," Angel said. "Did ya see the kids? They really liked it!"

But that was just the beginning. There were five more floors of children's wards, which meant five more performances. In the best tradition of show business, every floor got the full treatment—the whole noisy business was repeated again and again with the same fervor that had marked their debut on the ninth floor.

This was the first time the boys had such a close, personal experience with an audience, where they could see the reactions and hear the expressions of appreciation. They had a clear sense of doing something for someone else. They felt good about it—better than the applause of a "full house" made them feel.

The Tumbleweeds made their first TV appearance in early 1956 on *Ted Mack's Original Amateur Hour*, a corny show with Geritol commercials, but TV nevertheless. Viewers sent in postcards to vote for the act of their choice and whoever got the most votes won a prize and a professional booking.

The boys were excited. They knew their friends would be watching and they enjoyed being behind the scenes with all the cables, headphones, glass-paneled sound booths, stage managers, directors, rolling cameras, props and bright klieg lights. During several hours of rehearsal, the boys had to go through their routine and individual tricks several times as the director tried out camera angles and marked in chalk on the stage the exact spots where they were to begin, end, and hold their pyramids.

Also for the first time, the boys had makeup put on them. Ray and Joe didn't need much, but the anemic Angel and Israel and light-skinned Edgar came out of the makeup room looking pasty pink.

"Hey, Fred, look at me!" said Israel, for whom even washing, teeth-brushing and other basic grooming were sometime things.

"Yeah, I see—but just make sure you all wash that stuff off before you go out on Times Square, or you'll have trouble!"

They all walked around stiff-necked until show time, so as not to mess up their makeup.

The boys performed well, but we were limited to three minutes and had to cut out good parts of our routine. We didn't win the contest, but scored very high. We rationalized, with some logic, that whoever can mobilize the biggest postcard-writing campaign can win.

Each performer on the Ted Mack show got ten dollars for carfare and meal money. When I gave the boys their envelope containing fifty dollars, they were delighted. To them it was not only a lot of money; it was, in effect, the first pay they got for performing. Their faces reflected pride and satisfaction at this concrete recognition of their talents.

Later, after they had finished dressing, Angel came over to me and handed me a ten-dollar bill.

"Here's your share of the fifty, Fred."

"Thanks, Angel," I said. "That's very thoughtful and I appreciate it a lot, but that money is for each of you. But," I added, signaling for everyone to gather round and listen, "now that money has entered the picture, let me clarify something—now and forever. Any money you earn is yours. If you someday have an agent, you have to pay him ten percent of what you make. My pay is I enjoy doing this." And that formalized our contract.

None of us had eaten for hours and we were feeling really hungry. We walked out of the theater toward Broadway. At Forty-third Street I stopped in front of a fairly new Hector's cafeteria. It was a big place and with its shiny chrome-trimmed façade, its plastic flowers in the window surrounded by soft pink fluorescent lights, and its mahogany wallpaper, it looked more appetizing than the usual seedy short-order restaurants in the area.

"Let's eat here," I said. The boys looked at the cafeteria and then, with dubious expressions, they looked at me to see if I was serious. Seeing that I was, they sidled over to the large plate-glass window and heavy glass doors and tentatively peered in, squinting, trying to be as unobtrusive as possible. Then they milled around me, frowning but not looking at me.

"That's too fancy," said Ray in a weak voice. The others, somber and subdued, nodded agreement. "We would feel uncomfortable in there," added Ray.

"Too expensive!" said Israel, shaking his head from side to side.

"Let's find a hot dog stand," said Joe.

"What!" I exclaimed incredulously. "This is nothing but a crummy cafeteria. You take a tray and wait in line." Angel and Edgar went to take another look in the window. The others followed. With skeptical expressions, they unenthusiastically shuffled away from the window to take up their places slowly orbiting around me.

"Just a hamburger is all I want," said Edgar.

"Or we can buy baloney and a loaf of bread," said Joe.

"Okay by me," mumbled the others.

"Now wait a minute!" I said with an exasperated laugh. "The food here is no more expensive than a hot dog stand—and it's probably better. And they have anything you want to eat—even baloney sandwiches!" With that I said, "C'mon," and walked in through the heavy glass doors up to the pile of trays. As I picked up my silverware, I looked behind me. Trailing me in a single file were five uncomfortable-looking adolescents.

"Get a ticket and a tray and follow me," I said. I helped them find food they were familiar with and helped them order, but I also kidded them.

"You guys are real *jíbaros*." As I used the word, it meant "hicks, hillbillies, greenhorns." "And there's plenty of other Puerto Ricans here, too," I added. "See them back there in the kitchen, washing the dishes?" They smiled weakly.

After the boys finished the most conventional sandwiches and soda, they began to feel better about the whole experience. They had come through it all right. The place wasn't so forbidding now. No one had embarrassed them. And I realized that they had never been in a cafeteria before. It was really a new experience.

We went to Newark to perform on the Channel 13 *Spanish Hour*, hosted by the glib, mustached Don Passante. During rehearsals we were so cramped in the corner of the set that every time Joe did his front somersault over the four headstands, he sent stagehands, cameramen, prop men and technicians with wires attached to them scurrying to get out of the way of this human cannonball.

The live show, which I watched on the monitor, had some of the weirdest camera angles I have ever seen. Some close-ups were head-on shots which made it seem as if the boys were going to jump right into the TV screen. Other shots looked like on-the-scene TV coverage of a saloon brawl, with bodies hurtling out of nowhere, in and out of the cameras' view. The cameramen, unable to keep up with the action, only caught up with one or another of the boys after they landed. Then they went chasing after the next body flying through the air.

The Tumbleweeds performed on the auditorium stage of Washington Irving, the oldest high school in the city, and on the modern and multicolor-lighted stage of the Fashion Institute of Technology. They performed in the Swedish Methodist Church, the Seamen's Institute, the Henry Hudson Hotel, the Carlton Terrace Ballroom. They took a special ferry out to Riverside Hospital, a detention facility for adolescent addicts on North Brother Island in the East River, where the recidivism rate was almost 100 percent; it closed soon after.

We did shows at the city's youth houses, which are detention centers for kids too young for regular jail, meaning sixteen years and under. At the Youth House for Girls, the very presence of the boys set many of the inmates screaming like groupies at a rock concert. The girls, predominantly black and Puerto Rican, many of whom had been incarcerated for months, were completely segregated from boys. And many were deprived, excitable and prone to acting out, which had got them in trouble in the first place. The result was an audience of a couple of hundred boisterous girls.

"How about doing some tricks with me, baby!" teased a big girl in the front row of the auditorium.

"I like the one with the big chest," yelled another voice, "and the big"—the next word was drowned out by raucous laughter.

The boys were shocked by the girls' aggressiveness. Israel was visibly uncomfortable in the dressing room. The other boys reassured him.

"They're gonna rape you," said Ray.

"If they get you," said Joe, "they'll keep you here and make you do it with all of them."

76

Our act also got us into some posh places. We performed at a "Boys Club of America Annual Meeting," hosted by tall, tuxedoed Gene Tunney, the ex-heavyweight champion, which was held at the exclusive University Club on Fifth Avenue. During the performance, a cherubic-looking old man with a benign grin, sitting at the head table, watched the boys effortlessly balance, tumble and build pyramids on the thick, soft maroon carpets.

"Boy!" said Joe afterward in the dressing room, as he changed into his street clothes. "We performed for a President of the United States."

"Yeah?" said an impressed Israel. "Hey, Mr. Fred, that right —there was a President out there?"

"Yup," I said.

"What's his name?" said Angel.

"President Hoover," said Joe. "It was printed on the program. Didn't you see the old man with the white hair and red face sitting at the middle table?"

"That right, Mr. Fred?" said Israel.

"Yep, that was President Hoover. He's the honorary president of the Boys Club, or something like that. That's why he was here."

"Never heard of him," said Israel.

"Well, he wasn't a very popular President," I said. "Roosevelt took his place. You heard that name?"

"Sure, Roosevelt Hospital!" answered Israel with a laugh.

The boys tumbled and did pyramids in the middle of Broadway in the annual Macy's Thanksgiving Day Parade, during which they were almost stomped by a phalanx of amazon-size high-stepping majorettes, marching close behind them.

In the Puerto Rican community we performed for political groups such as the Movimiento Por Representación Proporcional—MPRP. Israel arranged for us to do that show. Well, "arranged" is not quite accurate. Here's how it happened.

Angel and Israel were now in Haaren High School and it was just another one of those days when they induced their girlfriends to play hooky with them and go to Israel's empty furnished room, his father and brother being at work and his sister Noelia in school.

Israel retired with his girlfriend to the alcove behind the flimsy makeshift curtain which had once afforded his parents some privacy and now was used by Noelia. Angel waited in the front part of the room, near the windows overlooking the street. His girlfriend was expected soon. When Angel heard a knock on the door, he opened it without hesitation, feeling sure his girlfriend had finally arrived.

But lo and behold, standing there in the doorway is the uncommonly tall, mustached Mr. Ortiz, the attendance officer at Haaren High. He asks to come in. Angel, disarmed by Mr. Ortiz's friendly manner, holds the door open. Too late, Angel is aware that Mr. Ortiz can see some of Israel and his girlfriend behind the ineffective curtain.

The next day in Mr. Ortiz's office, Israel has a rough, rough time.

"You weren't in school yesterday, so I visited your home."

"I was sick."

"Oh, what was wrong?"

"I had a headache."

"What did you do for the headache?"

"I went to bed. I was in bed."

"Yes, I know. I saw you." There's a heavy silence as Mr. Ortiz pauses. He continues: "There was a girl with you."

"That was my cousin."

"What was wrong with her?"

Israel's hands are sweating, his face is warm. He squirms in his seat. He feels trapped. "Nothing," he answers. "She was minding me." As soon as he says that, he knows what is coming —the cat is going to pounce.

"Minding you!" says Mr. Ortiz incredulously and impatiently.

"Minding you! With her legs wrapped around you!"

Israel throws up his hands as if in surrender. "Okay, okay! I give up! I played hooky! I wasn't sick! No excuse! No excuse! . . ."

As it turned out, Mr. Ortiz was an officer in the MPRP and a very decent guy, who took an interest in Israel. When he found out Israel did tumbling and acrobatics, he invited him to bring his group to perform at the MPRP anniversary meeting.

After the show, which had gone very well, we were all corralled into a group photograph, which appeared in the centerfold of *El Diario*—the Spanish-language newspaper—the next day. The boys *("los jóvenes acrobatas")* in their costumes sat, with me, in the front row and eight people, including Mr. Ortiz, other officers of MPRP and guest speakers, stood behind us. The photo caption was: *"Exhibición de acrobacia."* We certainly couldn't complain about our billing in that show.

Over the years I appeared several times in photos with the boys in *El Diario*. I always wondered what Puerto Rican readers thought when they saw the names Mourino, Rodriguez, Sanchez, Ramos and Gotay, and then, always at the end, an inexplicable Fred Johnson.

For a few years in a row, Joe Moratta, an old song-and-dance man, called us to join his annual benefit show for Lechworth Village in upstate New York, a sprawling institution for retarded children that resembled a college campus. Joe's son was there and that's how he got involved. After a three-hour ride in a bus full of entertainers through some pretty, green country, we would do an afternoon and an evening show. Between shows we ate in the cafeteria and walked around the grounds, amid the trees and the clean gray buildings.

At first we couldn't tell the patients from the maintenance men, grounds keepers and other staff. The first time we went to the cafeteria, the young woman who piled Joe's plate high with food said to him, "Do you want to go out with me?" Joe was flustered and flattered, but noncommittal. Later it was explained to us that most of the kitchen staff, laundry and bowling-alley workers, and others in jobs requiring minimum skill, were retarded patients who functioned reasonably well. Joe felt he had had a narrow escape.

Initially Angel and Israel privately mimicked the genial, affectionate Mongoloids, with funny faces and silly grunts, and they did it well and it was funny and we all laughed among ourselves. But later we saw many more retarded people, some with gray hair, old enough to be grandmothers, who had probably been here, or someplace similar, all their lives. We saw others who had to be fed by attendants, who mechanically shoved spoonfuls of food into their mouths. We saw some who stared dumbly and rocked back and forth, and we heard of the hundreds in the hospital section who couldn't do anything for themselves and literally rotted away. The boys became very subdued.

During the performance, held in the auditorium, the audience of several hundred retarded people watched, talked and applauded, some at inappropriate times. Before and after every act, Joe Moratta, who M.C.'d the show, came out and told the audience to give the performers a "big hand," and they did as they were told.

Once we wandered past the cottages where the mildly retarded teen-age girls lived. Somehow one of them slipped Angel a crumpled note, which he later showed me. In a rough scrawl it said: "Take me with you." Not knowing what to say, I just nodded.

Every summer we toured the city's playgrounds with the New York City Youth Board, which was trying to keep the ghetto kids cool, distracting them from gang fighting with evening dances, rock-and-roll concerts, and entertainment. These shows usually meant lousy lights, a noisy, shifting, moving audience, public bathrooms as dressing rooms, and the roughest kind of concrete as a stage—not to mention the ubiquitous shards of broken glass. I have a theory that the hostility in a community can be measured by the pervasiveness of broken glass. A certain amount can be attributed to a normal accident rate. Beyond that, when bottles get heaved into playgrounds, shattered against buildings; when youngsters go rummaging through the garbage for bottles to slam into curbs, stoops and sidewalks where children play and old ladies walk—that's hostility. In some neighborhoods one can see much evidence of hostility.

But these shows, difficult as they were, made the boys sharp and adaptable. Israel's dive and roll became, in my opinion, as good as any in the world. In the routine, Israel dived over Angel's almost upright body, and he had to land on his hands but quickly duck his head and roll on the back of his shoulders. He had to time his tuck just right or he could take a nasty jolt on his hands, head or the back of his neck. Israel would come out of these dives with such precision, with such softness, one was never sure he touched the ground. One second he is stretched out, toes pointed, arms extended, sailing up and out in a soft arc; the next second he collapses his body in a rolling tuck and melts into the pavement. As quick as the blink of an eye he emerges standing, relaxed as could be. I have the most excruciating memories of Israel at these shows, floating over Angel's head, out of the dim circle of light into total darkness, but never failing to reappear, unscathed, in the spotlight.

It's amazing how few injuries we had: hardly more than a few sprains and sore feet from tumbling on hard surfaces. We did try to have mats at these playground shows, but we weren't very successful because the staff responsible for bringing the mats too often forgot them. Or they only brought one five-by-five mat, too small to be of use. Or the mats they did bring were so torn, lumpy and corroded with dirt they constituted a hazard. Mats are very expensive and buying one the size we needed would have cost several hundred dollars.

There were a few mishaps that could have been dangerous. Angel once fell off Edgar's head as Edgar was standing up on the table. Angel hit the table sharply with his back before Ray and Israel, who were spotting, could catch him. A leg broke off the table and the next morning when Angel awoke, his back muscles were so stiff he thought he was paralyzed.

Once Edgar was doing a series of flip-flops (back handsprings) at an amateur circus in the Brooklyn Y and as he threw his arms backward, gathering momentum, doing one back handspring after the other, he lost track of the distance he had before the brick wall in the gym. All he remembered was seeing the wall as he whipped his head back and in a split second realized he was on top of it and would have no room to swing his arms backward. He checked his arm swing but he couldn't check his body, which was already on its way to propelling his head into the mat. Edgar probably got a mild concussion from that—Joe had to keep telling him what the next trick was.

At another amateur circus, the program blurb read: ". . . a tumultuous explosion of human energy featuring the whirlwind routines of The Tumbling Tumbleweeds." In this program the boys were asked to participate in some special tableau displays after they did their act. In special costumes, they did their highest pyramid on a decorated plywood pedestal. When Israel finished his handstand on Angel, who was standing on Joe and Edgar, he lowered his legs slowly and jumped clear of the rest of the guys. From that height he was coming down with considerable force. He crashed right through the pedestal. Everyone agreed it was a smashing ending. Luckily Israel got only a slight sprain.

The most frequent casualty was the costumes. Quick, violent tumbling movements put great strain on seams. Once Israel split his seat seam, right up the middle. He did the remainder of the routine without turning his back to the audience—nor did he spread his legs or bend over. He moved and pivoted like a silent-film Chaplin. It was a potential comedy routine.

Another time a young woman with a friendly face in a front-row seat caught Joe's and Edgar's eyes as they were holding a pyramid. The woman gestured awkwardly to them, pointing to an area just below her navel.

Edgar, seeing her, said to Joe, "Oh, boy, I got me a woman!"

"No," said Joe. "She's giving *me* the signal."

As it turned out, the woman was giving Edgar the signal. His fly had ripped open.

11

One afternoon toward the end of the summer of 1956, I got a phone call from PAL headquarters. They were offering me a job as director of the Miccio PAL Youth Center in Red Hook, Brooklyn. Although I had been doing well at Boylan Center, having been promoted to assistant director, I was a little surprised at this offer because Miccio was a much bigger center, with a staff of fifteen and twelve hundred kids registered. At twenty-four, I would be the youngest director in the whole PAL. I was pleased.

Yet I had reservations. Going to Miccio Center in South Brooklyn would take me far away from my Tumbleweeds. The thought of not working with them anymore never occurred to me. We had been together three years. Ray and Israel were now thirteen years old; Angel was fourteen, and all three weighed about ninety pounds each. Joe and Edgar were fifteen and each weighed a husky-looking hundred and fifteen. To me they were full-size people now, even though they all hovered around five feet, three inches in height. Three years of training had made them quicker, stronger and more agile. They could bounce higher and pitch and throw each other around with greater ease. And they were growing fast. Each pound of muscle and each inch in height gave them a new potential. Difficult tricks that couldn't be done one month were easily learned the next. All the little-kid tricks were being eased out of the routine and advanced stunts that had been scaled down were now practiced in their original form. Everything was developing better than expected. I hadn't realized how involved I was in the boys. I also hadn't realized that we had become such good friends. I would have missed them even if there were no Tumbleweeds.

But it was too early in my career, and I was too ambitious, to start turning down promotions. Besides, I now had a two-year-old son, Conrad, and my wife and I were in college, so the extra money that went with the director's job was very much needed.

The evening after I accepted the Miccio Center job, the boys and I had a meeting at the Steinway Restaurant, a tired-looking all-night cafeteria frequented by old people and insomniacs, on Broadway at 103rd Street. Here I figured we could talk as long as we wanted without being disturbed.

Ray was quiet. I had told him the news beforehand. I was feeling downright distressed and the other boys sensed something was up. Ordinarily we would have disturbed the melancholy mood of this place with our joviality. Now, feeling depressed, we blended right in.

I bought a round of coffee and toast. I just had coffee and wished it were scotch. My voice was a little scratchy as I began to talk, so I cleared the lump in my throat and started again. I told them of the new job in Brooklyn, letting that message sink in for a second, before adding that I wasn't ready to let go of the Tumbleweeds and hoped they were not either. Then I leaned forward and looked around the table at each of them, fixing their attention.

"Here's my plan," I said in a steady, hopeful-sounding voice and, I imagine, with the beginnings of a gleam in my eye.

"I'll give you carfare to come to the Brooklyn PAL center twice a week and we'll practice like we do now—during the dinner hour. And every weekend we'll meet in Central Park—just like we do now."

I leaned back to let them think that one over. Ray was expressionless. He had already settled it in his own mind—one way or the other. Joe and Edgar pursed their lips and wrinkled their

85

faces into a very tentative expression of "I'm not sure it'll work, but keep talkin'.'' Angel and Israel were quiet and avoided looking at me. They had listened, but they seemed to be almost uninterested. To an extent, they probably weren't interested in plans and promises. Their reality was here and now, and that was enough of a strain.

"But, Fred," Joe said, "what happens if we need to get ahold of you? Now all we do if something happens is go to the center and you're there."

"I'll give you the phone number of the new center and you have my home number. Just call! Anytime."

"Will you come with us when we do shows?" asked Edgar.

"Most of the time, but sometimes you might have to take care of yourselves. You don't need me to do a show. Right?"

Miccio Center was on Union Street between Henry and Hicks in an old Italian neighborhood whose borders were becoming fuzzy as blacks and Puerto Ricans moved in. It was a traditionally tough area, but now it was also full of teen-age fighting gangs and racial conflicts. The center reflected them all.

The husky sons of "Tough Tony" Anastasia's longshoremen came to the center, as did his niece, who informed me of her uncle the first day. Some of the brighter Italian kids graduated from the center into the Gallo mob, which had its headquarters just around the corner on President Street. Albert Anastasia, Tough Tony's brother, whom the *New York Times* referred to as the "Master killer for Murder Incorporated, a homicidal gangster troop," occasionally met his brothers (the third one is a priest) in Frank's Luncheonette nearby, where Al Powers, my assistant director at Miccio, and I ate dinner. On October 26, 1957, a year after I came into the neighborhood, Albert caught five assassin's bullets while sitting in a barber's chair in the Park Sheraton Hotel in Manhattan. Altogether it wasn't a neighborhood in which my boys could be expected to feel comfortable.

So it was a bit of a surprise when they all showed up for the first workout. Up the stairs they came, each carrying a piece of equipment. Although they complained of the forty-five-minute subway ride and the fifteen-minute walk from the station, they seemed pleased to have found their way successfully. Joe, especially, was proud because I had given him the major responsibility to get everyone there. We all felt good seeing each other. It proved we could keep together.

Miccio Center was a dreary, run-down converted firehouse, but the ceilings were high and there was plenty of running room for tumbling. It wasn't the best arrangement, but it was going to work. We were back in business.

The twice-weekly subway rides were a drag, but the boys made the best of it—and sometimes the worst of it. They fooled around a lot. Although dimly aware of what was going on, I tried to put out of my mind the bits and snatches of information I picked up about their shenanigans. With everything else, I couldn't handle it. The least damaging picture that seeped into my consciousness went something like this:

Pooling their thirty-cent round-trip fares, they bought a few cans of sardines, stole two loaves of Italian bread and made sardine sandwiches, pouring the salty oil over the foot-and-a-half length of bread. After sneaking into the subway, they used the subway poles and handholds to perform various gymnastic planches, levers and flying-ring routines. Often Angel would sit on one side of the car and entertain the others. Mostly he would mimic people, always focusing upon some distinct characteristic—a walk, an expression, an article of clothing. At times he must have been obnoxious—like when he would go over to someone sleeping and yell, *"Hey!"* in an ear. When the person awoke, usually with a start, Angel would be standing nearby, singing benignly, "Hey! Get your cold beer. Hey! Get your ice-cold Ballantine beer."

Whenever the boys traveled with me they were models of propriety—or else! I was especially severe with any behavior that might reflect the attitude "We're Puerto Ricans and it's all right if we behave this way." When traveling to "American" communities I demanded extra-good behavior. Any fooling around or silliness on the subway or backstage would result in my giving them a fierce look or an equally fierce squeeze on the arm or back of the neck, followed by an admonishment: "If you make a bad impression, then the people who see you will have a bad impression of all Puerto Ricans."

When the boys occasionally did shows without me, Joe was more or less in charge. He took his responsibility seriously. He planned where and what time they would meet and what subways they would take. He was the spokesman for the group. The arrangement broke down when Joe tried to make decisions beyond what the others perceived as his responsibilities. Edgar, for example, vehemently challenged Joe's frequent and gratuitous observations about his inadequacies. And Joe couldn't do anything about Angel's and Israel's stealing whatever wasn't tied down in their dressing rooms or backstage. Candelabras, picture frames, ashtrays, rolls of toilet paper, soap, light bulbs, cold cream, cigarettes, coat hangers and clothes would go into Angel's and Israel's costume bags.

Most times Ray, Joe and Edgar were too timid or conscience-stricken to steal, or just not interested. In fact, they were embarrassed by Angel's and Israel's blatant banditry. Of course, if there was something worthwhile, like cold soda, ballpoint pens or warm-up jackets, they all joined in.

But it wasn't that simple. There was an evolution to their stealing. When Angel and Israel were younger, they took bikes, gloves, toys, money and candy from younger, middle-class kids in Riverside and Central parks. They were mini-muggers, no question about it. As they matured, got caught, or didn't enjoy their ill-gotten gains—developed fear or a superego or got religion—they changed, and their stealing was governed by discernible rules. Roughly these rules boiled down to this: stealing from friends or people who treated you decently was wrong; stealing from other poor people was wrong, unless the situation was desperate, in which case one stole only from those one didn't know or didn't like. There was little onus attached to stealing hub caps, the figurines and emblems mounted on the hoods of automobiles, or from impersonal corporations or wealthy strangers. Of course, the pattern only applied to their teens and evolved further as they got older.

But far more prevalent and pronounced than their stealing was their generosity. They shared everything. They enjoyed being able to do someone a favor. In their dealings with me, I trusted them all completely and never had reason to do otherwise.

12

I had been working at Miccio Center a year when my family and I moved from Queens to 74 West 90th Street. Besides being closer to where the boys lived, it was easier for me to get to Miccio Center and to New York University in Washington Square, where I was finishing my last year. My wife had just graduated from Queens College and had finished a summer season as an "Aquadorable," a member of the water ballet in Eliot Murphy's *Aquashow* at the old World's Fair grounds in Flushing. We had no further ties to Queens. We both wanted to move to Manhattan. We liked the big city.

Our new apartment was one block away from Central Park, which made it much easier to get to weekend tumbling practices. Every Saturday and Sunday, weather permitting, the boys and I would meet at our regular spot. We brought the juggling clubs, the spotting belt and sometimes the unicycle and roller-roller.

After running through our regular act a couple of times, we practiced new tricks and did other stunts just for fun. When I wasn't spotting or teaching new tricks, I worked out also, using Ray and Israel as top men, or I was bottom man in pyramids. My wife, a fair acrobat herself, occasionally joined in.

Morrie Moritz, a young ex-professional acrobat, famous for his one-arm planche and his flexible backbend, sometimes worked out with us, as did Ray Gill, a fine all-round acrobat, who taught the boys some of his specialty tricks.

These Central Park workouts became a kind of tradition. Strollers in the park came to see us regularly. Fathers brought their children. Lonely-looking older folks became familiar figures in the background. If we skipped a day, someone usually commented on our absence at the next practice. Camera bugs found us a popular subject. Sometimes there would be over a hundred people watching, but I didn't encourage big audiences because I didn't want the strain of entertaining people. After all, these weekends were also supposed to be my days of rest.

The boys became regular visitors to our small apartment. We usually had such economy dishes as spaghetti, meat loaf, baloney or cheese sandwiches, and Kool-Aid. Meat loaf was their favorite. For them, it was an exotic "American" dish. My wife, Gretchen (whom Israel called "Retch"), delighted in telling the boys about all the unappetizing stale bread, leftovers and meat scraps that she said went into the meat loaf.

We never wanted for baby-sitters. They came in teams; usually Joe and Ray, or Angel and Israel. For Angel and Israel it was a particularly attractive deal. They could eat anything they could find in the refrigerator and they could take showers—long, hot showers.

Showers were a really big thing with them. After all, they were like most adolescents, sensitive and self-conscious about their bodies and intensely embarrassed about being dirty or smelling bad. Washing in their own homes was often discouraging and frequently unsuccessful. We had difficulty getting any of the boys to accept even a token few dollars for their baby-sitting services. But my wife and I insisted. "It's an American custom," we said.

For a while Ray had a regular after-school job of picking up our four-year-old son, Conrad, from the day care center at 3 P.M. and taking care of him until five-thirty, when my wife came home from work. This way our son didn't have such a long day in the center. Ray was highly regarded in our home. You could set your clock by him.

Increasingly, I would informally drop in at Joe's or Ray's home when I was in the neighborhood, or to pick them up to go somewhere or to attend a party or talk business. I did this less often with the others, but some holidays we all wound up at the same party at Joe's or at Angel's sister's home or the home of a friend we had in common, like Angel Cruz or Abe Rodriguez. And each New Year's Eve at the stroke of midnight there would begin a string of phone calls wishing my wife and me "Happy New Year!"

Although the boys still gave me plenty of aggravation, they were also a source of unlimited satisfaction. I was always glad to see their familiar, friendly faces, hear about their escapades, talk acrobatics—and I think we all felt good about being part of the Tumbleweeds. The malaise of urban alienation never touched me. I had an instant antidote—five of them.

But I also worried over them and occasionally exercised a degree of protectiveness. One evening after a show, we were walking down Columbus Avenue. The boys were carrying the table, roller-roller, juggling clubs and costumes. A police car pulled up to the curb and the cop next to the driver said to the boys, "Where ya goin'?"

I didn't like his snotty tone, but okay, I thought, it was their job to check and see if these guys were going to a gang fight or if they had stolen goods.

"These kids are with me, officer," I said. "They use that equipment in their tumbling performances. We just performed at P.S. 163, around the corner."

The cop looked skeptical and I couldn't understand why. I certainly looked official enough to vouch for the boys.

"Tumbling, heh! Well, let's see you tumble," the cop said to the boys.

The boys looked at me.

"They can't tumble here at night, on the sidewalk, with the bits of broken glass," I said, feeling a blush of irritation.

"Well, simulate tumbling!" said the cop, with a thick surliness.

These were the days of rampant police brutality—before a

civilian review board; before the restraining influence of the civil rights movement; before outraged citizens demonstrated at station houses. And these were the kind of cops who slapped kids around with impunity. It happened all the time. This was just another incident reflecting the attitudes of many policemen.

"Simulate it!" the cop repeated. He kept addressing the boys, ignoring me. The boys looked at me again. Down deep I felt the stirrings of my stubborn, hard-headed, inflexible streak. Usually I suppressed this aspect of my character because it invariably made me intemperate. But now, in this confrontation, I just let it come up. It was as if my ever-present rational, conscious self had packed its bags and said to those visceral rigidities, "The place is yours!" In a deliberate tone of absolute finality, I said to the cops, "They ain't gonna tumble!" With that, both cops jumped out of the car, stood in front of me and berated me for talking back to police officers.

I had won that one and the cops knew it. They got back in their car and drove away without another word to the boys or even a look at them.

"Nobody's gonna mess with my boys!" I muttered to myself as I marched off angrily down the avenue, with the boys skipping along beside me, trying to keep up.

They had become "my boys." I called them that. "Have you seen my boys?" Others called them "Fred's boys." Bullies hesitated picking on "Fred's boys." And I knew that when Joe took the Tumbleweeds out to face the world in foreign parts of the city, he would march into the establishment where they were going to perform, put down the equipment he was carrying, ask for the person in charge, gesture with a sweep of his arm to Edgar, Angel, Israel and Ray behind him, and say, "We're Fred's boys!"

13

For two years, through sweltering summers and freezing winters, the boys made the dreary trek and walked through hostile territory to Miccio Center. Then in 1958 I became director of the East Harlem Children's Center, a branch community center of the Childrens Aid Society, on East 101st Street between Park and Lexington avenues, in the middle of Spanish Harlem, also called El Barrio.

Now the boys had only to take a short bus ride to meet me for dinner-hour practices. The East Harlem Center was also easily accessible on weekends when the raw, muscle-stiffening cold weather drove us out of Central Park.

As it happened, 1958 was also the year our daughter, Gretchen, was born and I graduated from NYU and we moved to a larger apartment on Riverside Drive at West 119th Street.

And 1958 was the year we read *Dr. Zhivago*, listened to Leonard Bernstein's *West Side Story* and watched the coronation of Pope John XXIII on television. Eisenhower was into his second term and second recession. Senator Joe McCarthy had been dead a year and Vice-President Nixon toured South America and was met by angry mobs, unappreciative of our foreign policy. College students were called the "silent generation" and "military advisers" were just beginning to be sent to Vietnam.

It was the year the Supreme Court ruled against Governor Faubus's anti-integration maneuverings in Little Rock. The contact lens was introduced and the Nautilus submarine crossed under the North Pole. It was the year of the first "Negro air stewardess," the first woman director of a stock exchange and the first passengers to fly in commercial jets.

Nineteen fifty-eight was the year Castro pledged "total war" against Batista and Russia launched Sputnik III. Water skiing became popular and the baseball Giants moved West. *The $64,000 Question,* a TV quiz program, became a scandal and Sherman Adams was compromised by Bernard Goldfine. Floyd Patterson was the heavyweight champ and the Yankees beat Milwaukee in the Series.

But there was yet another event in 1958: a very significant one for me, gone unheralded all these years. In the total scale of things, the event was of little consequence, but for me, a minor actor in the drama of history, it symbolized my "finest hour"—the grandest achievement in all my twenty-six years on earth.

It was on a cold Saturday afternoon in that empty, cavernous, incongruously silent East Harlem Center gym that the boys, after many months of my prodding, exhortations and instructions, finally succeeded in doing our highest and best pyramid. The "Big Five," I named it. It was my own invention, although it combined elements of other pyramids. It was, as far as I know, never performed until that particular day in 1958. And for me, what a day it was!

Angel, Israel, Joe, Ray and Edgar are dressed in sneakers and a variety of washed-out, worn, torn T-shirts, sweat shirts and shorts. None of them are necessarily "up" for this attempt. It is just another try at building the human pyramid, hoping this time to take it a little further, a little higher, than the last time.

Edgar and Joe stand side by side. Angel and Israel climb up on them. Ray climbs up even higher. I watch intently, hoping to pinpoint our problem. Ray and Angel, standing on Joe and Edgar, join hands, their arms extended, reaching up and out as far as they can go. On this delicate, seemingly untenable pinnacle Israel puts his hands, and he lifts his body until he is suspended in the air. Then he slowly curls up his body and begins the slow, agonizing push toward a handstand. Higher and higher Israel goes, his ballet-pointed toes tentatively poking their way toward the high, screened ceiling lights. The four-man foundation shivers and Israel's upward progress is halted, but he holds his hard-won position in the air space. The tremors pass and Israel continues, slowly . . . slowly . . . until his arms lock out, completing the handstand. They hold it.

So subject to sudden collapses in so many practices, the structure now looks solid. Yet it is also delicate, fragile—and majestic! Five sets of arms and legs precisely arranged, the weight distributed evenly. The torsos arched and angled with mathematical precision. Every man integrated, blended into one symmetrical configuration.

One has a rare physical sensation when striking a balance such as this. It's difficult to describe, except to say that when everything is aligned just right, to the hair line, there is a weightlessness, an absence of exertion. It's as if the combined weight were less than the sum total of its parts. I'm sure there's some architectural principle to that effect. At the same time there is a feeling of control; the bottom men feel, in the soles of their feet, the balance of the top man, even though they are not touching him. Everyone can almost relax. Tensed-up limbs extend and lock out. Bodies lean back, confidently, like a flower opening its petals to display its centerpiece.

One might say the experience is also spiritual. By pushing gravity to the very edge of its tolerance, one has an intense feeling of transcendence. For fleeting seconds one's sensibilities are elevated.

For me, the lone spectator, this is the ultimate creation. An impermanent monument, to be sure, but forever fixed in the mind's eye. Let it be known, at this moment, by whoever may record such things, that I am the artist of record—the creator of this authentic original. And as sure as Rodin chipped, filed and molded his materials of wood and stone, so had I molded mine. Mine being all the more difficult, for I worked with the most unstable of elements—the mercury of adolescence!

14

If I hadn't known Joe, Edgar, Ray, Israel and Angel and I had seen them, developed in body as they were, on the beach or in the gymnasium, I would have guessed them to be acrobats. Besides their lean, symmetrical musculature, I would have noticed the swelling of their triceps muscle, above the elbow, on the back of their upper arm. And I would have watched as they straightened their arms to see if this swelling concentrated itself into a larger-than-ordinary, horseshoe-shaped bulge. This well-defined bump of the triceps muscle is a characteristic of those in our trade. Just as the thick neck identifies the wrestler and calluses the laborer, the acrobat's unique trademark is a shapely fold of muscle riding up and down the humerus bone, as the arm bends and straightens.

The triceps, even for those who haven't developed it, makes up the greater mass of muscle in the upper arm. Its function is to straighten the arm, as opposed to the biceps, which bends it. Although the biceps is flaunted in Mr. Universe contests, and is considered by the uninitiated to be a barometer of strength ("Feel my muscle!"), the biceps is largely cosmetic, having comparatively little strength (even when developed), and a limited range of function in sports or physical labor. The triceps is naturally stronger than the biceps and it is the primary muscle, working in conjunction with shoulder, chest and upper back muscles, that acrobats use in pushing or pressing themselves into a handstand, or in holding someone else on their hands. It's the muscle that holds one's arms straight as the body cartwheels, handsprings and tumbles. It's the muscle the boys used when I had them lie on their backs with their arms up and I tested their strength and control by doing a handstand, with my one hundred eighty pounds, on their hands—something they could all do now.

But there was nothing excessive or grossly overdeveloped about the boys. Acrobatics, because of its enormously wide range of movements, had given them very balanced physiques —yet they still had their distinctive body types. They had all gained over ten pounds during the two Miccio Center years, mostly from just growing. While Joe, Edgar and Israel were near their maximum height of a little over five feet, four inches, Angel and Ray were still growing and were already almost an inch taller than the others.

It was a combination of increased size, strength and skill that made it possible to add a couple of big new tricks to our routine.

Edgar put his roller-roller on the same pipe-leg table he used for his "get-up" with Angel standing on his head. While he rolled back and forth, Angel slowly and agonizingly climbed up Edgar's back and stood on his shoulders. The table shook and the roller movements became jerky as Edgar struggled with his added burden, all of which made the whole thing look suitably precarious—and high. Israel then threw the three juggling clubs up to Angel. By the time Angel got the white-enameled clubs spinning and flashing in the spotlight, the photographers in the audience would rush forward to snap pictures. This trick and a few other high pyramids really set the flash bulbs a-popping.

Joe, in his role as bottom man, had been doing most of the pitching, lifting and supporting of the others and had become exceptionally powerful. And he was one of the fastest runners in the neighborhood, Angel being a close second. Joe was generously endowed with chunky, sinewy, thick muscles. He was the classic mesomorph. He would have been strong and fast even if he did little exercise.

Once I saw Joe watching bigger, older weight lifters picking up a two-hundred-pound barbell. They used technique, getting down under the weight, taking advantage of hydraulic principles. Joe went over, lifted the barbell a few inches off the floor, realized it was heavy and set it down. He adjusted his grip, lowered his hefty hindquarters and heaved; no technique, bad form, but he pulled the barbell to his shoulders, the cast-iron plates rattling, without even moving his feet.

And he had an appetite to match his strength. After eating a heaping plate of *arroz con pollo con habichuelas con plátanos* and seconds of the *arroz y habichuelas,* he would proceed to wash down a loaf of French bread with a quart of water. I decided to put Joe to the test—to see just how strong he really was.

It was a rainy Saturday afternoon in the East Harlem Center. All week an idea for a new encore or ending trick had been knocking around in my head. The trick hung on Joe. He would have to carry almost four times his own weight. After we rehearsed our regular routine, practiced basic tumbling, did some hand balancing, and were thoroughly warmed up, but not worn out, I explained the new trick briefly and said, "I'll tell you what to do as we go along."

Edgar sits on Joe's shoulders. "Now brace yourself, Joe, because Angel is going to sit up on Edgar's shoulders." Ray and Israel help Angel up. Angel locks his legs around Edgar's back and Edgar locks his around Joe's back. Stacked up as they are, three high, they look like a totem pole.

"Now, Joe, put your arms out slightly because Ray and Israel are going to link arms with Edgar up above and pull themselves up and sit on your arm."

They get in position. "Okay, Ray and Israel, together now . . . Up!"

Edgar pulls and Ray and Israel give a little jump and they

hold on to Edgar. The whole thing sags heavy around Joe's neck. He's holding all four of them now. He resists and forces his head back. He grimaces and grunts. His fingers dig into the thighs of Ray and Israel on either side of him.

"Terrific!" I say. "Hold it one second, Joe, because I want to get a look at it from front and center." Quickly I run back and there is Joe with a gigantic human wreath going around his neck and hanging down to his knees. "Angel, hold your arms up and out. . . . Israel and Ray, do the same with your free arm!" This gives it a pointed-star quality. It looks especially good, because Joe is no taller than the others and here he is holding all of them—a total weight of about four hundred and fifty-five pounds. It was going to be a neat ending trick.

Then I did something on impulse—which I ordinarily never do. Without any further explanation or practice, or the usual few weeks of building up to a new movement, I say, "Okay, Joe, now turn and . . . walk off the stage!"

Joe's eyes tell me he senses the challenge. Slowly he begins turning, sliding his feet a few inches at a time, making faint scraping, squeaking sounds with his sneakers on the varnished gym floor. I can see the bulge of his thigh muscles stretching his trousers.

"Careful now! Small steps . . . shuffle steps! That's right!"

None of the other boys say anything. They are preoccupied with the strain of holding on. The broad pyramid swings around with the agonizing slowness of a drawbridge, until Joe is sideways. Here he seems stuck. Turning was one thing: he could do that by rotating his body slightly. Walking forward "off the stage" is another matter.

I can see Joe give an ever-so-slight tilt forward. Too much and he will buckle; not enough and he won't be able to move. His sneakered feet shuffle and squeak again as he struggles for the correct tilt. The pyramid waves slightly and Joe quickly shuffles back two or three inches. He moves forward again, but there is too much lean, and he frantically scrapes his feet forward until he catches the balance. He steadies himself and then, with

101

stuttering, mincing steps, he moves forward again, firmly in control now, as if he has conquered this beast and is now going to drag it for several more feet as a final assertion of his dominance.

After struggling inch by inch for almost twelve feet—a herculean distance for a first try—everyone just melted safely in a heap, still holding on to each other.

When we did this ending trick on the stage, we got into it quickly, with Edgar doing a round-off and bouncing up in the air so Joe could duck under him and catch him in a sit on his shoulders. Almost simultaneously Angel was pitched up to sit on Edgar's shoulders. Then Ray and Israel quickly tacked themselves on. Audiences applauded vigorously as Joe carried the four boys off the stage, but they applauded even louder when they all came running back to take a bow.

Joe was still doing this trick when he weighed only one hundred thirty-five pounds and the combined weight of the others was over six hundred pounds.

Strong Joe. *Fuerte! Fuerte!*

As the Tumbleweeds began to realize my predictions of acrobatic virtuosity and as they got deeper into their adolescence, our relationship became unexpectedly strained. To the casual observer, I'm sure the boys looked quite normal, hardly distinguishable in their adolescent idiocies from other American kids. But for me it was different. Everything the boys did I felt impinged on their functioning in "the Act." It became increasingly difficult to separate their everyday behavior—typically teen-age though it was—from their functioning as members of the Tumbleweeds. So I sounded off, forcefully and regularly.

"What are you guys doin' to your hair? . . . Edgar! What's all that gook and the stocking on your head for? . . . Israel! What's wrong with curly hair! . . . You're like a woman, Angel, with all the time you spend combing that pompadour!"

Whenever Angel or Israel got any pocket money from delivering groceries or from a relative who hit the numbers, they would treat themselves to a restaurant meal and then buy clothes. They never saved. They bought the latest cheap, flashy styles, which couldn't stand rough wear or washing, or they wore their new garment every day, everywhere, until it got unbearably dirty or ripped and then it disappeared, unless it was rescued by a sister or younger brother.

"Save your money," I would say, "until you have enough to buy better quality, something that will last—instead of that cheesecloth you're wearing."

Edgar was generally more practical about clothes, although he, too, had his fits of indulgence. Joe was becoming very conscious of clothes and he earned enough from his after-school job at Remy's Radio and TV Repair Shop to buy his preferred conservative Ivy League fashions. He had good taste in color and style. When he got dressed up, his pants were always creased, his collars starched and his shoes shined. Joe did much of his own washing, pressing, altering and mending. Ray wore practical dungarees and his Sunday suit only on special occasions.

One time the boys started wearing sunglasses: indoors and out, winter, summer and nighttime. It was a fad, having to do with affecting a movie-star image or something like that. When they wore sunglasses indoors, I was especially annoyed. "You guys do extraordinary feats of skill, but you're gonna break your asses tripping down the steps because you can't see them."

"Aw, Fred!" said Edgar. "It's the latest thing."

"Fred, you got to be modren," said Israel. "You got to be cool —be sharp!"

"Maybe," I said, "we should call ourselves the Five Blind Mice . . . or the Stumbleweeds."

"Fred, you're getting old," said Angel, "and we're young."

"We can't be square like you," said Ray. Joe laughed, patted me on the back and called me *"Viejo"*—"Old man."

They were having a good time "sounding" on me, but my irritation was showing. "You guys are just like immigrants. The first things you pick up in the new country are the worst habits."

Angel was clever. He was always getting ideas. Some probably deserved consideration. Like his idea for dealing with the problem of the perpetual and embarrassing holes in his socks by cutting the tops off his socks and sewing them onto his sneakers. Other ideas he had were clever—but stupid. At age fifteen, when he was convinced that his latest girlfriend, Saucy, was to be his everlasting love, he tattooed her name on the fleshy part of the back of his left hand, between the thumb and forefinger. Angel devised his own tattooing equipment. He surrounded a sewing needle with four toothpicks and bound up the ends with thread. The point of the needle protruded about a quarter of an inch. When he dipped the instrument into regular blue-black ink, the thread binding the toothpicks held the ink, which ran down the needle as he poked a series of holes close together in his hand until he had written out in flowing lines—he tattooed in script—his Saucy's name. The result was an excellent tattoo —very clear, very legible and very permanent. And very *estúpido*.

"The people who call you 'spics' are stupid, but its also wrong to say Jews are cheap and colored guys are bad! *Comprende!* . . . Pay attention—and turn that radio down. . . . Joining the army to get out of school or the neighborhood is dumb, and a dead end. . . . If you get into trouble and get a police record, you wouldn't be able to get some kinds of jobs. . . . *Mira!* Don't go outside sweating like that! . . . Are you eating that garbage again? . . . Pay attention! . . . Don't eat anything right before a show or a workout—and wash those costumes tonight! . . . Stop fooling around! . . . Be quiet for a minute! *Mira!* . . . *Por favor,* your attention, *por favor!* . . . Stop picking at your face—and cut those fingernails before you slash someone's wrists! . . . Quiet! *Cállate!* . . . Listen! . . . Hold the singing, please! . . . Stop moving around! . . . Listen! . . . Take your fingers out of your mouth! . . . . . . Stay out of trouble! . . . Go to school! . . . Get enough sleep! . . . *Mira!* . . . Quiet! . . . Pay attention! . . . Turn that radio down! . . ."

104

The potential for getting into trouble, getting hurt or getting arrested was ever-present. Once Israel was walking along Columbus Avenue with Lydia, Edgar's girlfriend, when three tall young blacks lounging in front of a laundromat made a crack about her. Israel went to Eightieth Street to get Angel's help in avenging the slight on Lydia's honor.

When Angel saw the size of their antagonists, he told Israel, "Forget it! They're too big and too many."

"No, man," said Israel. "I'm gonna hit 'im! He got fresh with Lydia."

"They might have knives or zip guns," warned Angel. "Let's get outta here."

"No, man. I'm gonna hit 'im!"

Angel tried to make the impending altercation less suicidal. "Push 'im through the window. I'll try to keep the others away. Then *run!*"

Stubborn Israel disregarded the plan and went for a conventionally chivalrous punch in the jaw. He jumped straight up and bopped the black guy with his fist.

By then word of the initial incident had spread on the Eightieth Street grapevine (which just as often created inflammatory rumors), and about twenty guys and girls converged on the scene and chased the black guys. Later Angel laughingly told about the incident. "When Israel hit 'im, the guy snapped his head back like he was shakin' off a pesty mosquita."

Other times they weren't so innocent. Angel learned to jump the wires on Chevrolets and start them without an ignition key. He began taking Israel and other friends for joy rides, sometimes returning the car to the same parking spot in the evening so the owner wouldn't realize his car had been borrowed. He went joy riding many times without incident, but once, near the end of his car-stealing career, just past his sixteenth birthday, he took Israel, Edgar and three other friends for a ride and a cop stopped them near Idlewild. Angel said he was picking someone up at the airport. The policeman apparently got suspicious because Angel looked young and there obviously wasn't room in the car for the person they were supposed to be picking up. He asked Angel for his license and registration. He also asked Angel to open the trunk—for which Angel had no keys.

The owner of the car refused to press charges, so Angel, Israel, Edgar and their friends only had to spend one night in the Tombs.

The late 1950s were the peak years of teen-age fighting gangs. It was the time of the Dragons, Buccaneers, Latin Gents, Red Hook Dukes, Playboys, Viceroys, Royal Bishops, Golden Guineas, Chaplains, Untouchables, Enchanters, Enforcers, and many more. It was the time of "rumbles," "bopping," "stomping," "japping," "zip guns," "switchblades" and "turf." Newspapers carried stories about a "100 percent rise in juvenile delinquency" and banner headlines like COPS DECLARE WAR ON GANGS, and these were followed by more stories, about "coddling criminals," letting the cops use their night sticks, the social causes of delinquency, and the formation of youth boards, task forces, youth clubs, squads, commissions, committees, councils, clearinghouses, departments, and inquiries on youth.

Although my boys may have had some insulation from the pervasive gang culture—by dint of their involvement with the Tumbleweeds and the community centers—they weren't immune. Once Joe was arrested along with a group of about thirty kids at the corner of Seventy-ninth Street and Columbus Avenue. They were charged with "disorderly conduct"—a blanket charge used interchangeably with "unlawful assembly" in situations deemed to be incipient gang fights. Joe, of course, protested his innocence, and it may have been as he said: "How could I be planning to fight? I was all dressed up on my way to a party. I stopped to see what was going on."

My appearance in court was always welcomed by the judge because he could then dispose of minor offenses, such as Joe's, with a recommendation—and sometimes a mandate—that the offending youth join a community center, where he or she will receive "proper supervision" in "constructive leisure-time activities." I did this court scene for many of the kids from the center. On this particular day the judge chewed out Joe and the others and then "dismissed" all charges.

But Joe wasn't always a victim of circumstances. He wanted to be near the action—no matter where or what it was. He was too much a part of the street scene, too gregarious, too much the leader, to stay away from gang intrigues.

Joe once got himself into the position of negotiating with a leader of the Buccaneers, a notorious East Side gang. This task is usually relegated to a "war counselor," a gang member whose role is to discuss differences, clarify misunderstandings and if necessary arrange for a fight of one sort or another with the rival gang. Joe's diplomatic talents were such that the representative of the Buccaneers immediately declared war on Joe by breaking a beer bottle, and with the jagged edge of the neck of the bottle, aiming a jab at Joe's face. The Buccaneer missed Joe's face but caught him in the side of the shoulder. Joe got a profusely bleeding laceration, which eventually healed into a blister of scar tissue three inches in diameter.

Ordinarily this would have meant big trouble, because retaliation was part of the code—an honor-bound duty. But Joe, not liking his role in this drama, arranged to get lost for a while, and a Youth Board street club worker stepped in to try and bring down the curtain on that scene.

I should have known the boys were courting trouble when they bought red sweat shirts with big white felt letters spelling TUMBLEWEEDS sewn on the back. Although they intended to wear the sweat shirts backstage, during workouts and for casual walking around, it was inevitable that the shirts would be mistaken for a gang uniform—the "club colors."

Once the boys were all wearing their red sweat shirts as we were on our way to do a show at Booker T. Washington Junior High School. We walked serenely along 108th Street to Columbus Avenue and did the show. Everything went smoothly until we were leaving and we saw a dozen or so kids loosely, but menacingly, lounging around the school exit. Joe quickly learned from one of the admiring girls who had been in the audience that the Spanish Knights waiting outside had seen the red-sweat-shirted Tumbleweeds walking through their block and thought they were coming to use "their" school community center. After all, "turf" included the neighborhood institutions.

I sensed that the Spanish Knights were also jealous of their girlfriends' enraptured response to the Tumbleweeds' performance—and presence. In any event, Joe, Ray, Angel, Israel and Edgar's reaction wavered between "They better not touch me!" and "I'm not going out there!"

Having always been impatient with all that chicken-shit gang stuff and confident of my ability to handle tough teen-agers, I said, "Relax! Let me handle this!" They weren't reassured. Joe handed out the pipe legs for the table. Angel, feeling the heft of a juggling club, handed one to Ray, who looked as if he wasn't sure he wanted to commit himself that far. With pipes and clubs in their hands, stubborn looks on their faces and a defiant bracing of their legs, they looked like most kids ready to fight— scared.

It was late and I wanted to get going. Knowing most incipient gang situations are full of bluster, with nothing developing, and still confident I could handle things without a fuss, I said, "Okay, but no one swings until I do." Agreed, the boys tucked away their weapons. We walked out without incident. The Spanish Knights probably thought I was a plainclothes cop—and an angry-looking one at that. And probably they were scared, too.

Girlfriends of the Tumbleweeds occasionally came to practices and sometimes accompanied the boys when they did shows. Because of the turnover, I never got to know many of the earlier girlfriends very well, although they all struck me as self-possessed and pretty. We enjoyed their company. They never distracted the boys in the gym or at shows. Outside it may have been different.

The boys knew their popularity with the girls was enhanced

by their being Tumbleweeds. As far as I was concerned, this reinforced their commitment to the Act. I always tried to make the girlfriends feel welcome.

I never got into any sex education with the boys. As far as I knew, they were all experienced—from early adolescence. Yet they harbored a monumental ignorance of women and sexuality, and were hung up in varying degrees with the *macho* myths. Besides feeling uncomfortable with the subject, there was little I felt I could tell them about the basics. "Don't get the girls pregnant!" was my dominant theme.

It was Angel's and Israel's frequent association with homosexuals that gave me some concern. I wasn't worried about their sexual inclinations, because I knew both were scandalously promiscuous with girls. And they expressed the usual taboos about homosexuality with a full repertoire of scurrilous epithets and snide jokes. (This was well before any of us were enlightened by Gay Liberation.) Nevertheless, despite their disparagement of homosexuals, Angel and Israel did have these friends on Eightieth Street. Among them was Orlando, a stocky, tan-skinned Puerto Rican in his thirties, who was a medical technician. Although his outward appearance was "straight," he apparently made no secret of his homosexuality. When Angel and Israel introduced me to him, I felt he was sensitive and articulate, but a little embarrassed.

Angel and Israel visited Orlando's apartment at random hours to drink his soda and beer and eat any food they could find in his refrigerator. They also watched his TV and took showers.

"Don't you think you are confusing this guy?" I said to Angel and Israel. "Doesn't he expect a boyfriend/girlfriend kind of relationship?" Angel and Israel jokingly accused each other of taking care of that.

Then there were the Fitzpatrick brothers, two blacks in their twenties, who shared a furnished room a few doors away from Israel's home. Although the Fitzpatricks had less to offer in the way of material goods and facilities, they were warm, friendly, outgoing and generous. They were irrepressibly pleasant and seemingly without any self-consciousness about their homosexuality.

"Sonia Fish" was another homosexual friend of all the boys, but more so with Joe, Angel and Israel because they all lived on Eightieth Street. Sonia Fish was a derisive nickname (he swished like a fish's tail) which stuck and eventually was used by all who knew him, with more affection than ridicule.

Sonia Fish was an older man: tall, slim, walnut brown in complexion, and quite overtly feminine. He bleached his black curly hair an orangy blond and occasionally walked around his apartment in women's clothes. He was a "character" on the block. Everyone knew him, and although he was known to be temperamental, he was most often friendly and effusive in his greetings to children and adults. He would put a little American flag in a stand outside his window, which faced the street.

"La alcaldesa [the mayoress] is home!" Joe would say upon seeing the flag. Sonia Fish was the unofficial mayoress of Eightieth Street.

Once Joe, Angel and Israel, along with other guests, attended Sonia Fish's wedding to another homosexual. The wedding was held in Sonia Fish's apartment and he wore a long white wedding gown. The wedding, I guess, was also unofficial.

Sonia Fish was talented at making clothes and the boys went to him to have their costumes and even their school clothes repaired—and to drink his soda, eat his food and take showers. At one point I called their actions "blatant exploitation." Angel and Israel shrugged it off. "They don't mind." And apparently Sonia Fish, Orlando and the Fitzpatrick brothers didn't mind.

But once Angel got himself into a situation that wasn't so easy to handle. He was working as a temporary messenger for a midtown corporation when he was approached by a tall, distinguished-looking man (and a fairly prominent public figure, though Angel didn't know that then), who offered him a job, ". . . paying twice what you get now." Angel took the job. He worked with a crew of men tearing out the seats of Carnegie

110

Hall in preparation for renovations. The distinguished-looking man sought out Angel's company and even invited him up to his Sutton Place apartment to work out with his barbells and pose for muscle pictures. Angel never returned to the penthouse and my guess is that Angel and the distinguished-looking man discovered some basic incompatibilities. But the man was persistent. He began showing up at Carnegie Hall and on occasion came to Eightieth Street. Angel was beginning to feel uncomfortable. He wanted out. I asked Angel if he wanted me to talk to the distinguished-looking man. Angel said he thought he could handle the situation. He quit the Carnegie Hall job, avoided the man and somehow discouraged him, and that ended the affair. For a short while the distinguished-looking man then courted Israel, but nothing came of it.

Over the years I gradually learned that there were Eightieth Street homosexuals whom the boys avoided, because they were pestered with sexual advances. I also learned that Sonia Fish, Orlando and the Fitzpatrick brothers set no conditions on their friendship with the boys—although they were undoubtedly sexually attracted to them. They were warm, accepting human beings, coincidentally homosexuals, to whom Angel, Israel and sometimes the others could turn when they had troubles or needed help—when they were hungry or dirty or when they wanted a brief respite from their own homes or the turbulent streets.

Strangely enough, the one thing I don't remember ever chiding the boys about is drugs—not even "glue-sniffing," which was popular for a while with the younger kids. Although they were growing up before the heroin "plague" of the sixties, hard drugs were readily available on Eightieth Street. We all knew many addicts and junkies there.

Except for Joe, Angel or Israel's having an occasional experimental joint, drugs were never a problem. Ray never even smoked regular cigarettes and didn't have his first drink of liquor until he was near the legal age. Edgar was equally abstinent, although he did smoke tobacco cigarettes for a few years before quitting. Being Tumbleweeds undoubtedly helped. There was considerable pressure on each of them not to get messed up and let the others down. They also got a degree of status and recognition by doing shows. They didn't have to retreat into a dream world to feel good about themselves. Israel had an aversion to drugs because he once had a very sick, nauseated, half-knocked-out reaction from a drink that had been doctored with some kind of drug without his knowledge. Angel frankly said, "I don't want to be like my brother." And they were interested in developing their muscles, attracting girls—and they knew that if they touched hard drugs I would break their ass.

15

By early 1959, Ray and Israel were sixteen years old. Angel was seventeen, and Joe and Edgar eighteen.

As Tumbleweeds they had performed all over New York City and some surrounding areas. They had done repeat performances at almost all the social welfare institutions and youth agencies—in effect, making enough "field visits" to warrant a semester of sociology credits. They had been to several ethnic neighborhoods and had met all kinds of people. They were capable of exuding charm and sophistication when they wanted to impress someone. This was especially true of Joe and Edgar —much less so with Israel, who was more comfortable standing behind the others.

Although at times still quarrelsome among themselves, they were very professional in setting up for their act. They knew when to stand by, what instructions to give the musicians, where their equipment should be placed, and they knew how to adjust the routine to fit the limitations of ceiling height and running room. And there were times when they performed with such panache they had the audience in the palms of their hands.

They had performed in a few of New York's most elegant establishments and in a great many of its grubbiest. They toured the ghettos, performing on the asphalt and concrete of streets, schoolyards, playgrounds and housing project plazas. They had got their pictures in newspapers and many thousands had seen them on television.

They were also learning something about teaching tumbling and acrobatics. Occasionally I had the boys teach along with me in the community centers where I was working or where the boys performed. We even ran a few workshops for the adult gym instructors from several centers. One such "Tumbling Clinic" was judged by the program director of the Childrens Aid Society to be "the best of its kind I have ever seen." Of course, there weren't many of its kind. The Tumbleweeds were most effective when they would first do their act for the younger kids and then move onto the mats to teach them a few basic tricks. And then, just for fun, the boys would flip the younger kids as I used to flip them. Joe would lie on his back and the kids would run at him, put their hands on his knees, jump up and roll, and Joe would catch their shoulders and give a push so they would land on their feet. Ray would have the kids lie on their backs with their feet up, then he would grab them by the ankles and yank them up and let go and Angel or Israel would be there to make sure they landed right side up. But best of all, the boys knew or remembered the basic teaching techniques with the proper progressions so that in an hour or less they could teach a few simple moves a kid could master or learn on his own with further practice. We left a trail of these budding tumblers all over the city.

For many ghetto kids the Tumbleweeds were the biggest "stars" they had ever seen in person. The boys were transformed by the adulation. They became mature, sensitive and worthy models of emulation. And in the Puerto Rican neighborhoods there always seemed to be some youngster who would summon up his courage and ask the boys questions. Like the cinnamon-colored kid with the thick black hair falling in his eyes who drifted over to Joe.

"Are you Spanish?" he asked timidly, but with great interest.

"No," said Joe. *"Soy puertorriqueño!"*

"Yeah?" said the youngster with a look of pleasant surprise.

114

"We're all Puerto Ricans!" added Joe, pointing to the others.

"Yeah? Wow!" exclaimed the youngster, looking at Edgar, Angel, Ray and Israel.

"And you?" asked Joe.

"Soy puertorriqueño también!" said the youngster, holding himself a little straighter.

Only with girls was their teaching somewhat disappointing. Although the girls seemed to enjoy the attention, there was altogether too much lifting, helping, holding, supporting, touching and spotting of behinds instead of lower backs.

But it was Joe and Ray whom I increasingly relied upon to assist me with teaching tumbling. They were motivated, interested and available more often than Angel, Israel or Edgar. And they had talent.

Joe was especially good at controlling groups and moving them through the exercises with dispatch. He compelled their attention with his decisive commands and propelled them with his forcefulness. He had a booming voice and never lacked for words. He could cut through the noisy hubbub of shouting, laughing children with a piercing whistle that emanated from between his front teeth. And he had a stern, "break-heads" look that could cower even the most defiant youngster. Although he wasn't very tall, his husky, muscular body made him look imposing, and although he preferred charming, cajoling and praising the children into desirable behavior, any rowdiness would bring forth one ferocious Joe Ramos.

Ray had a more low-key, individualized approach, which was also effective, even though he wasn't as strong as Joe in controlling boisterous groups.

Because Joe and Ray were so extensively exposed to community centers, they were also learning to conduct group games, coach sports, run tournaments, supervise dances, game rooms and lounge programs; and they were learning, in their own halting, self-testing, exploring ways, how to relate to kids—not just as softball players or tumbling students, but as complex, dynamic, unpredictable little human beings.

In addition to the experiences with me, Joe and Ray were volunteering and hanging around the Goddard-Riverside Community Center, then on West Seventy-seventh Street (Boylan Center had closed), where they were beginning to be noticed by the staff. Joe also took on a once-a-week volunteer job teaching tumbling at the Duncan PAL Center on West Fiftieth Street.

All the Tumbleweeds, except Ray, were nearing the end of their high school careers. Joe was to graduate in the spring from Aviation High School in Queens. He had been a mediocre student. Reading, theory and abstractions perplexed and frustrated him. It was more a matter of style and tolerance than lack of intelligence. But Joe managed to pass, just as he had passed the not-too-easy entrance exam for Aviation High in the first place.

Joe was genuinely interested in airplanes and mechanics. He thought he might someday work on jet engines. His father wanted him to make a career in the U.S. Air Force. Joe claimed he deliberately failed the Air Force exam because of his commitment to the Act and because I had spoken out so strongly, so many times, about not joining the armed services to escape one's situation.

But Joe did distinguish himself during his school career—as he did in most places. In junior high, for example, he used his gregariousness, aggressive charm and take-charge qualities to corner the best monitor jobs. He operated the movie projector, the stage lights and curtain, the visual aids, the mimeo and ditto machines, the hole puncher and pencil sharpener, and he erased the blackboards. He issued supplies and sports equipment. He seemed to have got control of the storerooms. The only one in the school who carried more keys than Joe was the custodian. Joe ran errands when he wasn't sending others in his "service squad." He built scenery for the pageants and fairs.

Sometimes he brought the Tumbleweeds to perform, which further enhanced his position.

In high school he joined, organized and provided leadership in a host of clubs. He ran on the track team and would have been involved much more if he didn't also have a part-time job in Remy's Radio and TV Repair Shop and another part-time job in the grocery store and if he didn't play weekend softball, juggle girlfriends, and tumble with the Tumbleweeds.

Joe was a dynamo, always in motion. He was well known and well liked in school and the neighborhood—except, of course, by those few, and there were a few, to whom he appeared as an overbearing, autocratic know-it-all.

Joe's parents separated just before he graduated from high school. Joe elected to stay with his mother. His younger brothers, Georgie, now six years old, and Luis, now fifteen, went to live with his father, far out on Long Island. Apparently there were second thoughts about the arrangement, because soon after the separation, when Joe's father went on a trip to Puerto Rico, Joe traveled out to Long Island and fetched Georgie to his mother's home.

Edgar was soon to graduate from Haaren High School. After two years at John Brown Vocational High School, which is a big boat (a converted freighter) anchored in the Hudson River, he had transferred to a general course at Haaren. He left John Brown because he felt his boat-building shop courses (they were still using wood) weren't going to prepare him for any job he knew of. Because of his missing fingers, Edgar was eligible for tuition assistance from the State Division of Vocational Rehabilitation. Edgar had seen a lot of job ads in the paper for keypunch operators, so he registered for a seven-month IBM keypunch-operator training program at the Monroe School of Business.

Edgar was artistic and skillful with his hands. He did well in all shop work. He built sets for the school theatricals, made sketches and for a time painted in oils. Edgar had other interests, too, none of which flourished in high school, none as compelling as being an acrobat.

Ray was a sophomore at Charles Evans Hughes High School, in an academic course. Ray's mother and I had differences over where Ray should go. Milagros, unfamiliar with the schools, understandably wanted her son to go to a vocational high school, to "learn a trade and get a steady job." I vetoed this, not thinking or caring much about my right to interfere. But my reasoning was sound. Most vocational schools were like Edgar's John Brown—obsolete. Ray had proved in junior high, where his record was "above average," that he could handle academic work. With an academic diploma Ray had the option of going to college. If he wanted a trade, the academic diploma was just as good, and maybe better than a vocational one. My position prevailed, mostly because Ray thought I was right and Milagros, by now, wasn't so sure I was wrong—or queer.

Angel was seventeen and Israel sixteen when they started Haaren High School. They were still seventeen and sixteen when they dropped out.

For Israel this final exit was probably the culmination of a process that began way back in elementary school, when Mrs. Moran grabbed him by the neck and forced his nose into a book, saying, "Read. . . . Read!" Israel remembered the incident vividly and the hurt could still be heard in his voice. "I couldn't read and I was ashamed. I ran out of the room."

Angel and Israel avoided going to school and when they were in school they avoided teachers, texts and tests. They were promoted along, in accordance with the policy in those days. Yet both learned to read before entering high school. Israel learned mostly on his own with comic books, *Daily News* funnies and discarded primary-grade readers. Angel, who learned more and learned more quickly, helped him.

But their learning—their whole growing up—was at times

incongruous. For example, on the same day that Angel and Israel played hooky and invited girlfriends to Israel's home for a little sex play, Israel might spend the next hour, under Angel's tutelage, practicing reading. "See Dick run! See Jane run! See Dick and Jane run! . . ."

And there was the time Angel drove downtown to perform with the Tumbleweeds in the citywide Youth Board Delinquency Prevention Show—in a stolen car.

Angel's tale of his first day at Haaren High is a classic beginning—of the end. "I was put in Miss Weaver's class. She was the biology teacher and she had animals all over the room: guinea pigs, snakes, goldfish, and a chicken named Chester who just roamed around the room. I wasn't that interested in school, so I sat in the back of the room with the big colored guys who threw chalk and goofed around until they were old enough to quit. When I sat down, I felt something messy on the seat of my pants. The chicken had taken a crap and I sat in it—in my new pants. I was a mess.

"Later, when Miss Weaver went out of the room, this colored guy sitting next to me asked me, 'Do you want to get back at the chicken?' I wasn't sure what he meant, but I said, 'Yeah!' 'cause I was mad. This colored guy watches the chicken comin' down the aisle. When the chicken gets next to him he grabs the chicken by the neck and flings it across the room and it hits the blackboard. The chicken squawks like crazy. It's laying on the floor in front of the teacher's desk, when Miss Weaver walks back into the room. I'm standin' there laughin', chicken feathers on my head. The colored guy never got out of his seat and he's hidin' in a book.

"So I got blamed and had to go to the office. My punishment was to copy the whole front page of the *New York Times*. I never finished. It was too much."

Even if Angel and Israel had been borderline successful, which they weren't, there were other pressures to leave school.

Israel got little support from home to stay in school. None of the Gotay children stayed in school beyond the age they could go to work. Israel began working weekends as a delivery boy in the Chicken Inn, a short-order, take-out store. They had a full-time place for him, beginning immediately, if he wanted it. There was also a place for him at Rudy's Leather Goods, with his father and brothers. Here he could punch holes in leather belts, and he could begin Monday morning if he wanted to. Israel could earn almost forty-five dollars a week at either of these places. The family needed more money to pay bills. Israel needed some clothes, a pair of shoes, a few bucks in his pocket. He needed to be free of asking his father for carfare and lunch money. He needed to feel he had a place in society—one that he understood; one that those around him and those closest to him understood.

When Israel finally told the woman in the office of Haaren that he was leaving school, she said, "If you feel you have to go, we don't want to see you back here later."

Angel made many trips to the Amsterdam Welfare Center, acting as interpreter for his mother, who was never deemed eligible for welfare. There were too many adult brothers and sisters in the family, whom Welfare expected to provide support. Angel's mother's story was always the same. Her children did not give her enough money.

On one particular trip to the welfare center, everything went as it had before, only this time the welfare worker, pointing to Angel, said, "What about him?"

So Angel went to work as a messenger for CBS at forty-six dollars a week. From then on, he was the sole support of the family.

Shortly before Angel and Israel dropped out of school and Joe and Edgar graduated, there was a show that was to become a "showdown" for the Tumbleweeds.

The boys had become seasoned performers. The routine was sharp and polished. We were ready for a tryout in the big leagues. And that meant: could we get paid for doing our act?

120

There was no such thing as "amateur" acrobats, gymnastic competitions, olympics, varsity teams or AAUs for us. Ours was the world of vaudeville, variety, circus, the stage, novelty acts, show business, the entertainment industry—and booking agents.

Brad Reeve, an agent whom I had known slightly, came at my request to the East Harlem Center gym and "caught the act." Reeve had a smooth superficiality; he was the kind of person who casually signs off with: "Let's have lunch sometime."

Reeve liked the act. I could tell by watching his face. We talked about the possibility of breaking in this summer with some club dates, fairs, or weekends in the Catskills—shows the boys could do without having to leave school or give up their jobs. We talked about having music written for the act, the maximum amount of "time" we could do, and getting another kind of costume. During this technical talk, Reeve dropped the names of well-known variety artists, letting us know he was a pretty big impresario. The boys were impressed and encouraged by Reeve, but I was a little let down by the lack of specificity in his parting: "I'll give you a call if something comes up. . . . Let's have lunch sometime!"

I was surprised when, about two weeks later, Reeve called me at home. He sounded urgent. "Tomorrow take your boys to the Broadway Theater. They're auditioning for a show called *Gypsy*—about burlesque. We'll pass your boys off as an Arabian acrobatic troupe. There were a lot of them around during burlesque days."

"They might as well get used to 'passing,' " I said facetiously.

"Listen, this is big-time. If they get into a show like this, the boys would get over a thousand dollars a week to share. And if the show is a hit, that's steady work."

He was right. It could be a good deal. One show a night, a matinee or two, union rates, no travel costs, no major dislocations in school or work.

It was late afternoon on a cloudy, balmy winter day when we entered the Broadway Theater, near Fifty-third Street, dressed in our best suits, each of the boys carrying a piece of equipment.

Edgar carried the re-dyed costumes, clean and pressed, in a plastic costume bag, over his shoulder. We were more nervous than usual. For the first time we would be competing as equals with other professionals.

The houselights were dim, but the stage lights brightened the whole front of the theater. Long-legged women in scanty costumes were standing on stage and in the wings, fussing with their makeup or practicing shuffling dance steps. Comedians, jugglers, contortionists—the kind of novelty acts that might have appeared between burlesque strip-tease numbers—were also spread around, preoccupied with equipment or warming up. Sprinkled throughout the first few rows of seats were the production, casting, directing people, and theatrical agents.

"Go back there to the dressing room on the side of the stage," I said to the boys. "I'll see about when we go on."

Single file, they disappeared through the door on the side of the stage. I went looking for the stage manager. A family tap-dance act started to audition. With only the piano accompaniment, they seemed a little flat.

Five minutes couldn't have passed before I saw the boys coming out of that same side door, single file, somber-faced, still dressed, carrying the equipment.

"What's the matter?" I asked.

Joe, in an embarrassed whisper, said, "There's all women dressing back there. Most of them got no clothes on. There's only a curtain on a string to stand behind. And the women are all walking around."

Apparently the great numbers of women auditioning overflowed the dressing rooms.

"That's okay," I reassured them. "That's the way show people are with each other. They don't mind as long as you're one of them. . . . Now go!" I added, gently turning them around and steering them back toward the dressing room.

Casually dressing together may have been the way of show people, but despite the lack of privacy in their own homes, it wasn't the way of my boys—or, I guess, of most teen-agers.

When I joined them in the dressing room, Israel was standing behind Ray and Edgar, who were holding towels, and he was putting on his jockstrap over his underwear. Joe and Angel were also behind this screen, with towels tied around their waists, squeezing into their costume pants. They started to put their street clothes on over their costumes.

"Stop it!" I said. "You'll get wrinkled."

I went back out to the stage area to see how many more acts were still before us, but I got involved talking to an old acrobat friend and it was almost an hour before I returned to the dressing room. This time they looked more relaxed. In fact, they had a cat-that-swallowed-the-canary expression on their faces.

"Having a good time?" I said suspiciously.

"Oh, we're just juggling," said Israel.

"Juggling?"

"Let me show you how we juggle," said Angel. He flipped the clubs around a few times and deliberately dropped one. As he bent down to pick it up, he peeked under the curtain at the women dressing on the other side.

"Well," I said officiously, intending to snap them back to the serious business at hand, "I hope you're all warmed up." A second too late, I realized that wasn't quite the right word.

"Oh, yeah, Fred, we're reeeaaally warmed up! . . ."

All things considered, the piano player did a good job during the Tumbleweeds' audition. He approximated drum rolls and cymbals clashing, and the boys were stimulated by his fast beat. Everything went well and the routine looked good, even from the wings, where I was. When they finished, chorus girls and other performers praised the boys warmly. This camaraderie of show people was one of the nicer traditions of the business, I thought. A good beginning experience for the boys. Breathing heavily, sweat beginning to form on their foreheads, the boys strained to smile as they gasped their thank yous. They were elated, but also relieved.

The dressing room was almost empty now. By the time the boys were knotting their ties, Reeve came in, his eyes shining, rubbing his hands enthusiastically. We gathered around.

"I talked to the producer and he liked the act, but he's looking for an acrobatic act with a girl in it. But—out there in the audience was another producer. And he wants you guys to go on tour with his circus—for fifteen weeks at five hundred fifty dollars a week."

The boys squealed with delight. "Wow!"

"*Chévere!*"

"Man, oh, man!"

"*Coño!*"

"We're in the money now!"

They shook hands all around.

One hundred ten dollars each a week was a lot of money for teen-agers in the late fifties for doing glamorous work. I could see they were already buying clothes, presents for mothers and girlfriends, restaurant meals, and maybe even a car.

Reeve was really building it up. . . . "And who knows where that will lead? You become known and before you know it—the big time!" The boys hung on every word. Reeve was making real what had never been more than a vague dream. Five years ago they were five obscure Puerto Ricans, lost in the multitudes. Now they could see the marquee lights spelling out TUM-BLEWEEDS.

Then, as if the lights suddenly dimmed, the boys realized I wasn't sharing in the jubilation and they knew that was ominous. They turned to me.

"We have to think it over," I said to Reeve. "The boys are still in school."

"We can hire a tutor to go with them," said Reeve.

The boys mildly murmured their agreement with Reeve, but they trusted me and that took the steam out of their protestations.

"We'll have to think it over," I said again.

"This is a great opportunity," said Reeve, beginning to get a little anxious. "You can't start out by turning down bookings."

"But," I said, "we talked about weekends and summers; nothing about going on the road."

"Well, I don't see . . ."

"We'll have to think it over," I said, interrupting Reeve as gently and as apologetically as possible.

When Reeve left us, I explained my position to the boys. "Once a contract is signed, Reeve doesn't have to do anything more. You join the circus and he sits back and collects his ten percent every week. So remember, he really wants you to sign. If you go on the road it's hard to get back to school. The tutor idea is completely unrealistic.

"Now, I know some of you may not finish school anyway, but some of you definitely will. In terms of the future, it's important to have as much education as possible. Being an acrobat in show business can be rough. Fifteen weeks is good. Some acrobats feel lucky if they work fifteen weeks in a year. But what happens the rest of the year? . . . Other years?"

They didn't like to hear this, but like a bitter medicine, they took it because the doctor said it was good for them.

In the back of my mind I had known a situation like this could arise. At some point I must have mulled over the alternatives, for I had a plan ready to propose. I knew Angel and Israel were hanging by a thread at Haaren and Edgar would soon graduate from Haaren and was planning on taking a short course at the Monroe School of Business. Ray and I had agreed he would be going to college. Joe had a couple of prospects. College was vaguely under consideration, but Joe really wanted the neighborhood settlement house to hire him full-time to teach tumbling and acrobatics.

"Let's make a three-man act," I said, "with Angel, Israel and Edgar. You guys will be the most free in the near future. Then if you get the same kind of circus offer, you can take it."

16

In the summer of 1959, I was selected along with some twenty stateside social agency executives and supervisors to attend a five-week Social Welfare Workshop in Puerto Rico, sponsored by the Migration Division of the Commonwealth of Puerto Rico. The workshop was designed to help welfare supervisors, foster care and family social workers, housing project managers and youth workers like me to work more effectively with our Puerto Rican "clients."

Joe and Ray had been expecting to visit their grandparents in Puerto Rico this summer, as they did every few years. My wife and I tentatively arranged to meet them in their home-towns when we went into the interior on field trips we had planned.

As our four-engine Constellation approached the Aeropuerto Internacional in San Juan, everything suddenly appeared in technicolor. The bright blue of the sky and ocean contrasted with the white of the clouds and the beaches ringing the island. Several shades of green were splashed over the low, steep hills. The matchbox homes in the developments surrounding the airport looked like dabs of pastel yellow, orange, fuchsia, pink and purple. As we got closer I could see the leaning palm trees and the bright red-flowered flamboyan trees. Getting off the plane, I hesitated to breathe the air "straight," it smelled so sweet and clean. The tropical balmy warmth of the trade winds pressed gently against me. Excited though I was, I felt my New York City alertness draining away. I felt friendly, and so, it seemed, did everyone else.

The workshop had a full schedule of lectures, discussions, field trips and just plain sightseeing. I saw high-rise apartments in San Juan, plush tourist nightspots in the Condado section, old Spanish stucco and iron grillwork in old San Juan. Simple wood houses on short stilts or cinder blocks dotted the countryside. Over sixty thousand people lived in some ten thousand tightly packed squatters' shacks on the edge of the Martin Peña Canal, one of several *fanguitos* (shanty town slums), which have continued to grow despite government efforts to replace them with sprawling developments of relatively low-cost compact concrete houses with tile floors. Every town I saw had a baseball field, many with lights for night games.

I visited agricultural co-ops and factories and learned that manufacturing had recently overtaken agriculture in the island's economy. I visited housing projects, water purification plants, a solar energy installation, schools, markets, public health stations (most Puerto Ricans receive free medical and dental care—largely because they can't afford any other kind), and many quaint and beautiful plazas, where in the early evening, colorfully dressed, coy young *señoritas,* accompanied by *chaperonas,* boyfriends or dark-eyed smiling children, strolled and chatted.

I went to a *gallera* (cockfight arena), supervised by the government's Recreation and Parks Department. I learned that the Health Department checked the few prostitutes, who were mostly in the tourist sections of San Juan. The government wanted to phase out both these activities because, as one official said, "They are not progressive."

Each day in the *San Juan Star,* an English-language daily with a circulation of several hundred thousand, we read short items about small numbers of San Juan teen-agers getting into trouble with drugs or gangs. According to the reporter, these Puerto Rican youngsters had grown up in New York, where they had

127

got into the same kind of trouble; they had resolved their problems with the juvenile authorities there by returning to Puerto Rico.

I visited the town of Loíza Aldea, where most of the inhabitants are black, the descendants of slaves. Puerto Rico freed its slaves peacefully, years before the States did. But there is de facto segregation in Puerto Rico because most blacks were held back by centuries of slavery. Blacks hold the lowest-paid, most menial jobs, have the fewest graduates from high school and in general have fallen behind.

During the lectures, readings and discussions we attended, I learned that Puerto Rico had a population of two and a quarter million people on an island thirty by sixty miles, giving it a population density eleven times that of the U.S. mainland. Another 600,000 Puerto Ricans lived in New York (in 1959); more than in the capital city of San Juan. (By 1970 Puerto Rico had a population of 2.8 million and well over 1.5 million Puerto Ricans were living on the U.S. mainland.)

I learned that Puerto Rico, despite its having the highest living standard in all Latin America, a rapid rate of development and a growing middle class, was still very poor. Yearly per-capita income in 1959 was below $700, and if the several hundred thousand adults and young school dropouts, who are not in the labor force, are included in the unemployment statistics, the rate would be 30 percent, comparable to our own ghettos. Although the unskilled Puerto Rican migrant is at the bottom of the economic ladder in New York City, he still earns an average of three times what he could earn in Puerto Rico. (During the recession years, prices in Puerto Rico exceeded those in New York. Undoubtedly, U.S. surplus foods kept some Puerto Rican families from starving.)

But I already knew it was the availability of jobs that provided the impetus for migration. I didn't have to learn that. And I knew that the mothers, fathers, older sisters and brothers of my boys went to work the Monday after getting off the plane. Jobs are the central economic fact of life for the Puerto Rican. When the U.S. job market shrinks, migration falls off, welfare applicants increase and family life deteriorates.

I learned that in Puerto Rico, when the boys were born, in the early 1940s, the yearly per-capita income was $118; and health conditions were so poor, life expectancy was forty-seven years. Out of 200,000 Puerto Ricans called for military service in World War II, 78 percent were rejected for physical reasons. Two people in three were illiterate. Neither Angel's nor Israel's parents ever attended school, nor did Ray's mother. Joe's and Ray's fathers and Edgar's father and mother didn't go more than a few grades in elementary school. Only Joe's mother finished high school, a rarity in those days. Two of Angel's older sisters are still illiterate.

I learned something about the commonwealth status which evolved under Governor Muñoz Marín. Although Puerto Ricans have been citizens since 1917, they do not vote in U.S. elections unless they reside on the mainland. They elect their own governor and local legislature, but have no vote in the U.S. Congress. They pay no federal taxes, but are subject to the military draft. Puerto Rico is economically tied to the U.S. mainland through a multimillion-dollar tourist industry and U.S. subsidies for education, public housing, highways, hospitals and welfare. Puerto Rico's "Operation Bootstrap" gives ten-year tax exemptions to mainland corporations that open factories and plants on the island, thereby creating jobs. The Independentistas, among other things, feel that commonwealth status makes Puerto Rico "dependent" upon the United States. The pro-statehooders, among other things, feel statehood would bring even more economic benefits to Puerto Rico.

Some observers said the Puerto Rican government is paternalistic toward its citizens, and that could be so, but I liked the attitude expressed in the sign over the front gate of El Oso Blanco Prison, which said, in effect: "Hate the sin, but never the sinner." And I liked hearing "La Borinqueña," the national anthem, which is neither martial nor marching, but more a ballad extolling Puerto Rico's serene beauty. I also liked the humor of the people in one of the worst slums, who named their *fanguito* "Buenos Aires"—"Good Airs." And I liked finding out that Puerto Rico had one of the few governments in the world spending one third of its budget on education—which hasn't, by any means, ensured quality education, but has secured for every six-year-old child a seat in a school, a khaki uniform and, if needed, transportation to school, financial assistance and shoes.

On one of our field trips to the interior, my wife and I went to San Germán. Several miles from the center of town we met Joe, his grandparents and many relatives. Several of Joe's relatives ran grocery stores of various sizes. One uncle had a small business making guava candy. The guava fruit was cooked up in an enormous kettle, like a witch's cauldron, over a wood fire in the uncle's backyard. Joe's grandmother made delicious meals, especially the *zurullo* (made with corn meal), goat steak, *bacalao frito* (fried codfish) and *sancocho* (stew). We picked and ate wild *guanábana*, mangoes and coconuts. All the women in the house, which included Joe's grandmother and two aunts, seemed to spend the day in the kitchen. Immediately after breakfast they cleaned up and started preparing lunch and dinner. They worked leisurely and chatted gaily all day long.

Although their home was of wood, it was more substantial than the omnipresent wooden shacks and had a small porch. It was serene and peaceful sitting there looking out at the mountain in front of the house. But it takes getting used to. There was no TV, movies, magazines, books, nightclubs, beaches, athletic facilities, pedestrians or traffic, and pretty soon Joe, my wife and I felt compelled to climb that mountain.

Two days later we met Ray in Rincón, an even smaller town in the northwest corner of the island. Ray did his best to reassure his grandmother (Milagros's mother) that I was just a friend and not a big *jefe* (chief) from New York. She was a wonderfully pleasant woman and although I couldn't speak Spanish very well, she communicated easily with her smile, her perceptive eyes and her withered but graceful hands.

Their house, a more typical plain wooden house on short stilts, was surrounded by low hills with high grass and knobby trees, about a hundred yards from the palm-tree-lined ocean-front. Chickens and goats roamed freely in the yard, keeping it clean by eating all the food scraps and garbage. We pumped our own cold well water to wash, used the *latrina* and slept under mosquito netting.

Each day Ray's grandfather, who was in his eighties, trekked down the road to cut some grass for their cow. This took him the entire morning. After lunch he walked the half mile to town and bought a loaf of bread, one of the few commodities not obtained from their own land and livestock.

We spent much of our time lolling in the ocean while Ray's brother, Jaime, up in an overhanging mango tree, threw mangoes out to us in the water. I'll never forget that taste of sweet mango pulp with salty sea water on my lips.

In the evening, grandfather, Jaime, a young cousin and Ray sat around the kitchen table, under the bare electric light bulb hanging overhead, and played dominoes. The old man teased the young folks and they teased him back. I enjoyed watching, even though I understood very little. Outside, the stars blanketed the sky, bright and clear, from horizon to horizon. It was only nine o'clock, but everything was quiet, except for the chirping sounds of the tiny tree frog, the *coquí*.

I returned to New York with a new interest in everything Puerto Rican. I read books and journals about the history and culture. I listened to Puerto Rican music, intensified my study of Spanish, perused the Spanish newspapers, and took a graduate course on Puerto Rican migrants.

I went with the boys to Puerto Rican restaurants and nightclubs, and once we even went to the "Villas," near Plattekill, New York, the Puerto Rican resorts in the Catskills. Joe showed my wife how to make *biftec y tostones* and rice *con sofrito*. Each year we watched the many thousands of Puerto Ricans marching up Fifth Avenue in the Puerto Rican Parade, proclaiming that they, too, are good Americans, like the Irish, Italians and Germans before them.

I pumped the boys for information about their lives, especially Angel and Israel. To me they were the most authentic *jíbaros*, country people—people of the land. They represented the poor from the *campo*, the rural agricultural *barrios* that could no longer support the overflowing population. This group constituted the majority of the migrants. Even those coming to New York from the big-city slums of San Juan, Ponce and Mayagüez had their origins in some rural *barrio*.

Angel and Israel claimed they remembered little because they left when very young. "You probably know more about Puerto Rico now than we do," said Angel. "We never traveled anywhere either. Just to the airport and then to New York."

With a little prodding, Angel and Israel sketched in a vague picture of simple wood-frame houses, many people sleeping in one room (Israel's family had ten members, Angel's seven), wood-burning or kerosene stoves, eating rice every day (the only utensil being a spoon), often with beans, less often with chicken, drinking well water, climbing trees and picking *quenepas*, mangoes, coconuts and bananas, going shoeless most of the time, living almost completely outdoors and wandering anywhere at will.

They remembered the hurricanes and storms because their flimsy wooden homes, resting on cinder blocks, had to be tied down with cables going over the roofs. They remembered corrugated tin roofs flying off houses in storms. Angel once saw a latrine get blown off its foundation and ending up on a neighbor's roof down the hill.

Israel remembered the "rock fights" where he lived. According to Israel, it was like a Hatfield and McCoy feud, only in this case it was the six Gotay brothers versus an equally large family of Gonzalezes up on the hill. Every Friday evening it started. The two families would throw rocks at each other. Israel's job was to collect stones in a bucket for his bigger brothers. Israel remembered the stones pinging and thudding into the corrugated tin roofs and how he used a tough palm frond, as big as himself, for a shield.

Nobody got seriously hurt, but once some rocks landed on the "rich man's" (he had a gun, a jeep, and folding money in his pocket) house, situated in the middle of "no man's land."

"The rich man," said Israel, "shot off his gun and said, 'Stop or I'll kill you!' " Everyone stopped and Israel was very afraid. But the rock fights continued. Israel remembered his father once saying he wanted to go to New York to get away from all the fighting.

Many years later Israel ran into one of the Gonzalez brothers in New York and they greeted each other like old friends from home, which makes one wonder whether Israel's rock fights weren't, in part, a kind of rough rural recreation.

Angel's and Israel's faint memories of Puerto Rico kept shifting to their more vivid memories of New York. One minute Angel talked about how profusely the roof of his house in Puerto Rico leaked when it rained and how they just moved the beds away from the cascading drops, and the next minute he jokingly related this to his complaining to the super about the leaks in his Eightieth Street room. "Here," he said, "the super tells you, 'What are you complaining about? You wanted running water!' "

The boys regularly kidded each other about acting like *jíbaros* and they made fun of Puerto Ricans who looked as if they "just got off the boat," dressed in old-fashioned styles unsuited for New York weather and carrying bulging shopping bags instead of suitcases. If one of the boys did something dumb or naïve, the others would say he was from Jayuya, a small town in the central mountains of Puerto Rico, representing the ultimate in provinciality—the equivalent of the Ozarks. Or they would say he was the kind of person who, when it rained, took off his shoes and carried them around his neck to protect them from getting wet or muddy (as probably most poor country people do). Or they accused each other of locking the front doors of their furnished rooms with a *tranca*—a two-by-four dropped into hasps on each side of the door, similar to what is used in log cabins or barns.

Joe worked up an "immigrant" routine: "Fi jears I bean een dis cuntree en all I lairn ees de forrking baad worrds!"

And there were corny self-deprecating jokes that sometimes reflected an element of reality.

"Why do Puerto Ricans wear pointy shoes?"

"I don't know—why?"

"So they can step on the cockroaches in the corners."

17

On Sunday, August 30, 1959, at fifteen minutes after midnight in a West Side playground, two teen-agers were brutally stabbed to death and one was wounded. The newspaper headlines called the killers the "Cape Man" (because of his "Dracula-like appearance") and the "Umbrella Man" (because he stabbed with a sharpened umbrella).

These killings came in the wake of several very recent teen-age homicides. Mayor Wagner and Governor Rockefeller called "emergency meetings" to plan how to deal with "the crisis of youth violence." Fourteen hundred extra policemen were deployed. A dragnet started pulling in suspects in the "Cape Man" murders. Joe and almost every other kid on Eightieth Street were taken in for questioning. The *New York Times* reported developments in the case on the front pages. Four days after the killings, on September 3, I was stunned to read: "Last night, detectives arrested Santiago Rodriguez [Angel's brother Chago], 15. . . . Inspector Frederick M. Lussen said the youth was one of those sought for homicide. Rodriguez was charged with juvenile delinquency and unlawful assembly." The next day's *Times* reported: ". . . And in Children's Court, Santiago Rodriguez, said by the police to have acted as a look-out near the playground, was adjudged a juvenile delinquent by Justice Charles Horowitz and committed to the State Training School for Boys at Warwick."

It's a warm Friday evening in the middle of September. I walk down to Eightieth Street, as I do occasionally on my way home from East Harlem. Joe, Israel and Angel are there, as they usually are. We sit on a stoop in the middle of the block and talk and watch the passing scene. Joe goes to La Minita for beer.

People are everywhere: chatting and arguing on the sidewalks, eating, playing dominoes, listening to portable radios on the stoops. Laughing, yelling caramel-colored kids run in and out of the street. Several kids stand on tiptoe and look in a first-floor window at a blaring television which has been turned to accommodate them. Looking up the sides of the buildings, I can see chubby-armed women leaning on pillows on the window sills and men in undershirts looking out at the panorama of life below. There's no air conditioning to be seen and windows and doors are opened wide. The street noises blend with the inside sounds of a crying baby, crooning bolero music, spirited voices and the barely audible bumping and scraping of crowded inconvenience.

Funny, I think, how my perception of this block has changed since I first saw it. Although it was never a forbidding block, much of what I initially saw was overcast with the gloom of everything I read about "slums." That's not to say there weren't desperate social problems then and now. But to write it off as a slum and that's all would be to deny its diversity; to see only the surface; to see only the bickering and quarreling when the real wonder is that so many people live close together with monumental tolerance.

The block is alive. It's where the action is. It's the plaza, the playground, the promenade. It's compelling and distracting. How, I think, do Angel, Israel or Joe ever read, study or do homework with all this going on? How does anyone wind down or shift gears?

Tonight the block is festive. It's Friday and there are paychecks and parties, dancing, drinking, eating and open house, for few have to get up early tomorrow. There's also a pervasive rough sensuality in the air, full of promise and tension. Prostitutes and homosexuals cruise through the block, heading for Broadway. Lonely men, waiting to send for their families, visit lonely women whose husbands never sent for them. Other men, on the stoops, groan quietly as women in soft summer dresses walk through the seductive streetlight shadows. A young woman whose husband is in jail glances discreetly at us as we stroll by. "Cool" guys lean against the fenders of parked cars and "cool" girls in dungarees lean against the guys.

At other times of day this same block can look completely different. Seeing Eightieth Street on an early Monday morning, for example, as the sun begins to streak into the block, is like watching a newsreel about "America on the March." Out of each building comes a steady parade of clean-shaven men in work clothes and women in starched bright blouses and sheer stockings, who step gingerly around the flotsam of garbage. The subways, like vacuum cleaners, suck them in and carry them "downtown" to factories, sleek office buildings, restaurants, laundries, hotels and hospitals where they will operate sewing machines and switchboards, load and unload, file, study and type, drive taxis, trucks and elevators, carry mops and packages, bedpans and syringes.

Angel and Israel tell me of having once attended a séance in a third-floor apartment. "Right up there," says Israel, pointing to the upper floor of a brownstone. Lydia, Edgar's girlfriend, had been the "medium." She was thought to have special *espiritismo* talents, so she studied and practiced and became qualified to perform rituals which help people communicate with deceased loved ones, fend off evil spirits, cure diseases and maybe revive a failing romance. Sometimes she used herbs, potions and incense purchased from *botánicas*. All the parents of the boys were exposed to or practiced spiritism in Puerto Rico and New York. Edgar's and Joe's fathers, at one point in their lives, did it extensively. Lydia, on this occasion, was going to help cure Angel's asthma and rid Israel of bad dreams. There were candles, a crystal ball and incantations. Angel was given

137

a special cigar and instructed to light it and puff furiously, "Deep! . . . deep!"

Israel was instructed to buy flowers, take off his clothes, stand in the tub, hold the flowers over his head as someone poured hot water over the flowers, letting the water run down his body. Without washing, he was to dress and take the flowers to some obscure, never-to-return-to place and throw them away. Israel claimed his unwanted dreams diminished somewhat. Angel's asthma still plagued him. Neither Angel nor Israel ever returned to the séances.

Almost every adult on this block bets twenty-five to fifty cents a day, hoping to hit the number. The boys' parents play regularly; for a while Angel and Edgar collected numbers, as did one of the boys' parents and several older brothers.

Walking down the block, I feel surrounded by familiar faces. I must know the names of at least a hundred people here, most being kids whom I met at Boylan Center several years ago.

It amazed me to see how many "potential delinquents" made good—settled down to conventional, law-abiding lives. A few even became street-corner preachers. "Let Jesus come into your life," I once heard one of the reformed delinquents say, "and you will be saved." Some said this was just a different kind of addiction.

At the same time it depressed me to see how many bright, personable kids got lost. The kid who at seventeen was an enterprising go-getter, delivering groceries, is suddenly twenty-two years old and still delivering groceries.

Sometimes on my visits to Eightieth Street, kids ask me for advice about jobs, legal problems or where they can get treatment for sores that don't seem to heal. Always there is a smile, a greeting or a friendly handshake. Even most of the junkies, thieves, muggers and pimps are friendly—so like "normal" people. Yet I know they are cruel and exploitative. Still, it's difficult to work up one's disgust and reject someone you see so often, someone who appears so human. I expect it's the same for many of the people on the block.

"There's Abe!" I say to the boys. Abraham Rodriguez is a close friend of the Tumbleweeds. He was to spend the next four years in the Marines instead of a university. "Don't call him," says Angel, laughing. "He'll talk our ear off."

"Señor Johnsohn!" says Abe as he crosses the street, coming toward us. *"Qué pasa! Cójelo suave!"* He shakes hands, grabs arms and shoulders, and proceeds to dominate the conversation until he returns to his dominoes game.

Angel, Israel, Joe and I stand talking in front of the last stoop on the block, near La Minita. Eddie, a tall black homosexual in his mid twenties, with startling green eyes, whom Angel and Israel are always pestering to tell them stories, comes over. He's friendly and likable, and often has a faint marijuana high. He tells of his latest escapade. He had been in jail for the past thirty days and had served his time on Hart Island digging paupers' graves. He tells us how the plain numbered boxes came over on the ferry and how he and the other prisoners carried the boxes with the corpses of unclaimed, sometimes unknown derelicts inside. The boxes seemed light, but had "a feel" of a human body inside. With ropes they lowered the crude caskets and shoveled dirt on top.

"That's all there was," he says, frowning. Then, seeing he has made us all silent and sad, he opens his eyes wider, and the corners of his mouth begin smiling. He gives Israel an affectionate punch on the arm and says, "Now let's talk about us!" We all laugh, but Israel and Angel are already at him: "Tell us about the time . . ."

Across the street I see Josephina, with her fine features, cocoa-brown skin, and a voice so high-pitched it embarrasses her. She is growing up and will probably get fat, but now, at fifteen, she is stunning.

And there's Lola, a tall, dark-eyed Eurasian-looking beauty whom I had "given away" at her wedding to Tony Arroyo, a left-handed pitcher on the Goya team. Walking down the aisle of Holy Name Church with her warm hand on my arm, she all pink and white, four months pregnant, no father on the scene and a mother who was trying to repair her own life, she seemed so vulnerable. It ached me to see innocent seventeen-year-old high school dropouts start out in life with so little going for them.

The Lolas and Josephinas, of whom there were many, also caused another kind of ache, which I learned to dull by reminding myself that these same distractingly beautiful young girls could also be gum-snapping empty-heads, surrounded by comic books and cacophonous rock music.

And here's Torry coming up the block, smiling sardonically, as he often does, with one side of his mouth. Mike Torrance is a husky, freckled Irish kid, a leftover from the Irish exodus from Eightieth Street when the Puerto Ricans started moving in. Sully fought with everyone, regardless of race, color or sexual proclivities. Although I didn't share his feeling that he and I were fellow Americans, lonely survivors surrounded by a sea of alien "Spanish," I couldn't help responding to his friendship.

In 1960 I entered the Columbia University School of Social Work. On my application I had said something to the effect that I wanted to learn more about working with kids.

18

PAL TUMBLING ACT BOUNCES INTO BIG TIME, headlined a sizable back-page story in the *New York Post* on July 28, 1960. "Edgar Maurino, 19, and Angel Rodriguez and Israel Gotay, both 18 [Israel was actually 17], are three Puerto Rican boys, Island-born, who constitute what is now an acrobatic team called Los Andantes."

The article went on to summarize their careers: how they started with a group called the Tumbleweeds, and how they performed at dances and on the *Spanish Hour* and the Ted Mack show, and worked the Macy's Parade, and how two guys from the original five dropped out—one to go to college and the other to work in a community center—and how "Fred Johnson told us that if we kept practicing, we could be good enough to be professional."

The article was full of human interest: "They are looked upon as neighborhood heroes by many of the boys. . . ."

Edgar is quoted: "A lot of guys in the block, even the ones who are supposed to be bad . . . they ask us all kinds of questions, like what food we eat, what hours to sleep, what exercises to do. Then they want to know if they could get in our act. It's a funny thing. A lot of times we automatically go around the corner to see all the guys we know. And we're afraid, because we might get into trouble with the crowd."

Angel is quoted as saying: "It's a pull, you know. It's hard to keep away from it."

Then Edgar concludes with a little contortion of the truth: "But we've never been in trouble."

The "big time" in the headline referred primarily to a television appearance on the *Paul Winchell Show*, for which Angel, Israel and Edgar shared $550 (less 10 percent for the agent), the union rate in those days for a variety act performing on TV.

It was relatively easy for the boys to break in the new act, because the routine was essentially the same. The four- and five-man pyramids were replaced by three-man pyramids and a short hand-balancing solo by Israel. In everything else they just took on the extra work of doing Ray's and Joe's parts themselves.

The first things Angel, Israel and Edgar bought with their money were twenty-five-dollar olive flannel suits with vest, long-sleeved white shirts, black shoestring ties and new pairs of plain white sneakers, which looked like summer white shoes. These became their new costumes. Soon after, they went to register the name of their act, but found it was already being used, so they changed it to Los Antinos, for no better reason than that it sounded like a stage name.

A month later, after they had done several tune-up benefit shows, I met the boys for a late practice at the East Harlem Center. Edgar excitedly showed me their new contract, specifying that Los Antinos would get seven hundred dollars for one performance on the *Caravane* TV show in Quebec, plus round-trip air fare.

"Very good!" I said. "Very good! You should try to be at your best."

"That's what I tell these guys all the time," said Edgar, gesturing to Israel and Angel. "We have to practice more often, until we are perfect."

"Canada's a foreign country—right, Fred?" said Israel.

"Right. It should be interesting for you."

142

The boys were mostly on their own now. Our association had been gradually moving into a new stage. It was no longer appropriate for me to exercise such control over the decisions in their lives—if it ever had been. In my mind I still thought of them as "the boys," but I was very aware that they were young men who now held jobs or studied very hard. Angel completely supported himself, his mother and Chago.

The boys handled their own business with booking agents, arranged rehearsals, auditions, practices, bought or made their costumes and equipment, and for the most part, did it very well. My role was more that of an elder statesman. But I still worried.

"Call me at home, collect, if you have any problems in Canada," I instructed.

The day after I expected their return Edgar called. They had done the show, but just realized they had no return tickets.

"Go to the check-in counter of the airline you went up on," I said, "and see if they are being held there for you."

I had been right about the tickets and the next day we got together so they could tell me all about their adventures.

"This is our biggest payday," said Edgar, beaming, as he held up the check for seven hundred dollars.

"Make a copy," I said, "and we'll put it in our album."

"There were at least a thousand people in the audience," said Israel. "And man, those lights were hot."

"Ben Dova was there doing his drunk act on ice skates—with the swaying lamppost," said Edgar. "And there were other big acts, too."

"The show went great," said Angel, "but they kept us nervous. Before the show, they said, 'Stretch the act to eight minutes,' then as the show ran late they told us to cut. We kept putting in and taking out tricks."

I asked them detailed questions about the routine and how specific stunts went over with the audience.

"Hey, Fred, listen!" interrupted Angel with a big smile on his face. "On the plane going up—and remember we were first class, real fancy—the stewardess asked if we wanted lunch. We didn't know if you had to pay extra and we only had a few dollars between us because we expected to fly back the same day. I looked at Edgar. He showed nothing on his face. We didn't want to act like we were dumb Puerto Ricans, so I said, 'No, thanks,' and Edgar said, 'I'm not hungry.' And we were all really starvin' 'cause we didn't have time to eat anything except coffee and toast and that was hours ago. And then," Angel added with a pained, amused expression, "we had to watch the other people eat ham and eggs and hash and *batatas fritas* . . . ohhh! Later we found out the food comes with the ticket."

Wandering around the streets of Quebec after the morning rehearsal, Angel and Israel were fascinated to hear the people speak French. Israel mimicked them by jabbering away with nonwords in a heavy French accent. Edgar complained that this caused people to keep looking at them. But the French language wasn't a subject for humor when they went to lunch, because the menu was in French. How would they order?

"I thought I found the solution," said Angel. "On the menu there was a picture of a hamburger. I pointed to the picture, smiled at the waitress and nodded my head. I thought the waitress would nod back that she understood, but no, she just turned to Edgar and said just like any New York waitress, 'Do you want the same?' "

"And, Fred," said Edgar, "on the way back to the airport, after the show, the 'runner' who was driving us made so many stops to take care of his other business, he made us miss our plane. And there were no more flights until the next day, so we asked the runner to take us to a cheap hotel."

"The rooms were so small," interjected Angel, "if you sat on the bed and bent forward you would hit your head against the other wall."

"I think the place was for prostitutes," said Edgar. "There was a woman at the end of the hall who collected two dollars from everyone using a room. And downstairs there was a burlesque show and music blared all night.

"Anyway, we go to our rooms and after midnight I have to go to the bathroom. I open my door and here's this guy"— Edgar chuckled and pointed to Israel—"tiptoeing down the hall, in his underwear, with his mattress under his arm."

"Israel squeezes in my room," said Angel, picking up the story, "and says, 'Can I sleep here? I don't like to sleep alone.'"

Angel and Edgar laugh and I smile at Israel, wanting to convey some sympathy, at the same time feeling that the picture described of Israel in his underwear, with his mattress under his arm, stealthily slipping into Angel's tiny room in the middle of the night, was pretty funny.

"I don't like to sleep in a room alone," said Israel, looking misunderstood. "I just roll around. I can't sleep."

Afterward I realized that Israel, in all his life, probably never, until this Canada trip, slept in any room, anywhere, with fewer than four other people.

The money from their first big payday didn't last long. Mostly they bought clothes for themselves. Angel bought a chair and other things for the house. Israel paid back money he had borrowed and spent. Some money went to their parents to buy groceries and some went for restaurant meals. They enjoyed being generous to family and friends. And they enjoyed letting people know that they were in show business. Edgar, especially, was increasingly heard to drop lines like: "Sorry, can't make your party. Have to do a show . . ." and "Yes, we're appearing at the Coliseum." And there was talk about "bookings" and "contracts" and "our agent," "auditions" and the size of "the house."

The Antinos needed an ending trick: something spectacular, like the Tumbleweeds ending with Joe walking off the stage carrying four guys on his shoulders.

After a burst of diligent practice, the boys learned a "three-high," with Edgar standing on the ground and Angel standing on his shoulders and Israel standing on Angel's shoulders, in a single column. In most theaters, this left Israel up near the guy

145

wires, curtain drops and ceiling lights. Climbing up is all part of the stunt, and this human column waves unsteadily as Israel shimmies up Angel's body in making his final ascent. As Israel stands, he raises his arms with a cautious flourish, signaling he is up and standing free. The audience applauds, but it is not over. Edgar, on the bottom, turns sideways, and ever so slowly the column, by design, begins to fall forward. The boys must remain rigid during the fall. They can't buckle, bend or jump free until the last second. The three-high column must look as if it is going to fall flat on its three faces. The drum roll gets louder and faster as the falling column gains momentum. Israel, up on top, must be especially disciplined in holding his position. His eyes bulge as he sees the floor closing rapidly. The almost overwhelming compulsion is to bend one's legs and jump, but Israel has to stand fast and aim his landing over fifteen feet downstage—the length of the column. When the trick is done correctly, the column falls until it almost reaches a forty-five-degree angle. Just as it looks like a "splat," pancake landing for sure and the audience is provoked into muffled screams and gasps, the boys jump free and simultaneously roll out of their fall. They come up with a flourish, smiling, arms raised, bowing expansively. Tension relieved, the audience sighs and applauds.

The San Juan Theater is in a big drab building at 165th Street and Broadway, in the middle of a large Puerto Rican community. Its spacious interior, large stage, boxes and rococo balcony railings are now grimy and worn. The adjoining building is the Audubon Ballroom, where, a few years later, Malcolm X was assassinated. Across the street is the mammoth complex of Columbia Presbyterian Hospital. Spanish movies are shown at the San Juan Theater, and sometimes there are live shows. It's to the upper West Side what the Apollo is to Harlem.

The Antinos were booked in the San Juan Theater for a run of seven days, two performances a day, and three each Friday, Saturday and Sunday. Then the show was to move to the Broadway Theater in Brooklyn for another three-day weekend of three shows a day. For the ten days they were to receive $475. The show was a "Spanish Circus Extravanganza." Included among the regular circus acts—lions, tigers and trapeze artists —were Gaby, Fo Fo and Miliki, popular South American comedians, comparable to our Marx Brothers. Although the Spanish language was used by the M.C., the singers and the comedians, not all the acts were Spanish. Some just had Spanish-sounding names. And some, like the three trampolinists, made no pretense of being anything other than "The Kelroys." Of course, some acts were from Spain and Portugal. All were white, without a shade of color. None, except the Antinos, were Puerto Rican. But the audience was Puerto Rican —100 percent Puerto Rican. I was there opening night along with a full house of Puerto Ricans—factory-working, subway-riding, beer-drinking, baseball-watching, tenement-dwelling, rice-and-beans *puertorriqueños*. And they were here for a little respite from this sometimes alien city.

To fit in with the general circus theme, the Antinos had bought new costumes of white baggy-sleeved shirts and black trousers.

Willie Chevalier, the ebullient master of ceremonies, kept up a machine-gun chatter between the acts. The only clue I had that the boys were next was the words *"saltos mortales"* (equivalent to death-defying somersaults) in the introduction. And then Chevalier, with ringmaster intonations, said, ". . . *y ahora . . . les presento . . . Los Tres Antinos!"* The orchestra brassed forth with a throbbing, foot-tapping mambo as the boys came running out, their white shirts billowing in the breeze. They had plenty of room on that old stage, the lights were perfect and the orchestra followed the routine extremely well. The drum rolls properly dramatized the slow get-up tricks and the cymbals crashed in time with the *"saltos mortales."*

When the boys finished their act they came back for a bow and received enthusiastic applause. Then Chevalier, carrying the microphone and its chrome stand, came to center stage, where the boys were standing in the spotlight. He thanked

147

them for their performance. They were breathing hard, their chests visibly moving up and down. Chevalier, in a break with the usual one-act-after-the-other format, turned toward the audience, and in an "I have a surprise for you" tone of voice, began introducing the boys. *"Este es Edgar Mourino de Ponce, Puerrto Rrrico!"* ("This is Edgar Mourino from Ponce, Puerto Rico!")

As soon as Chevalier said *"Puerrto Rrrico!"* the audience exploded with one big, tumultuous cheer. Loud and intense, the sound roared out, filling the theater like a thundering waterfall, vibrating the whole building. It seemed more an emotional outburst than an ovation.

Chevalier, realizing the cheering wasn't going to subside, quickly interjected: *"Y este es Angel Rodriguez de Manatí, Puerrto Rrrico!"* which set off another cloudburst of cheering, clapping and yelling.

Chevalier raised his voice. *"Y este es Israel Gotay de Río Piedras, Puerrto Rrrico!"*

Another explosion of cheering, foot-stomping and hoorays surged forth from a thousand men and women. Some stood and waved their arms. Like some huge chorus they sang out their affection, their pride, their kinship. I could feel the sentiment welling up in their throats and in their hearts. Never have I seen anything like it. I shivered with the emotion of it all. Suddenly it was no longer a show, but a gigantic family celebration.

They were cheering Edgar, Angel and Israel from Ponce, Manatí and Río Piedras—from Puerto Rico—from home. Edgar, Angel and Israel, as the saying goes, had "brought down the house."

One has to understand the times to fully appreciate what was happening. It was 1960 and except for a few baseball players, Puerto Ricans in New York didn't have many heroes. Herman Badillo, who later became a United States Congressman and a strong contender for Mayor of New York, was relatively unknown. And only a short while before, Puerto Ricans had heaped their pent-up adulation on a professional wrestler, An-

148

tonino Rocca, who was really an Italian from Argentina. Add to that the negative images of Puerto Ricans projected by *El Diario,* the *Daily News* and other tabloids, which, almost daily, carried front-page photographs of uniformed cops escorting handcuffed Puerto Ricans into police stations.

And so here, today, in the San Juan Theater, they cheered. They cheered their fellow countrymen, not vague "Hispanics" or Latins of remote ancestry, but three of "their own." They cheered three Puerto Ricans who had, by their modest artistry, brought some measure of honor and joy to all Puerto Ricans.

The irony was that being Puerto Rican had never been an asset until this show. The *Ed Sullivan Show*'s trademark was discovering foreign acts. They weren't interested in local New Yorkers like the Antinos. In Canada and later in Mexico, producers and agents were glad to be able to call the Antinos "Americans from America—the entertainment capital of the world." In New York City, producers had always tried to pass off the Tumbleweeds and the Antinos as "Arabian Tumblers," and we refused several times to be called the "Mexican Jumping Beans." Even when negotiating for a show in Puerto Rico they wanted to identify the Antinos as Argentinians—exotic gauchos and all that. But here, today, the audience would have embraced the boys all the more if they called themselves the "Three Spics."

The review of the show in *El Diario* the next day was accompanied by a single photograph of three smiling young men in baggy-sleeved shirts, standing in the spotlight. The caption pointed out that Los Antinos were *"puertorriqueños."*

19

Mostly the Antinos were booked for what the contracts refer to as "club dates and casual engagements." This meant nightclubs, country fairs, conventions and one-show special events sponsored by fraternal lodges, organizations and such groups as the Letter Carriers of Yonkers. These bookings, paying from seventy-five to one hundred twenty-five dollars for each performance (divided three ways), weren't very lucrative, but with the advent of television and the demise of vaudeville, club dates, inadequate though they were, were the nearest thing to steady work for acrobats and novelty acts.

The Antinos played a weekend at Schwaben Hall, a hofbrau with waiters in Tyrolean hats carrying foamy steins of beer. The Antinos' mambo music accompaniment in that place had an unmistakable polka flavor.

At the Chateau Pelham in the North Bronx, they were accompanied by Anthony Armendolas and his "Funtabulous" orchestra, which played everything from the Charleston to Jewish tarantellas.

The Antinos did two shows on Friday and two on Saturday at the Sunrise Village, a nightclub on Long Island. At some noisy convention in the Waldorf-Astoria, they did a show in the Jade Room and then rushed over to do another in the Grand Ballroom. Israel pinched a bottle of champagne.

For two consecutive years they traveled to Washington, to

150

perform on Saturday and Sunday, amid the monuments of the nation's capital, at the annual Cherry Blossom Festival.

Between club dates, the Antinos continued to do benefits. These shows, besides being interesting, provided an opportunity to try out improvements in the routine, and most important, keep themselves in top shape.

In 1961 they toured the city with the Youth Board, which, in addition to its overall program to "Combat JD," was now sponsoring an extensive entertainment program to "divert youngsters from dangerous temptations." The American Guild of Variety Artists (AGVA), a union for entertainers, brought in big stars to perform at these shows and Local 802 provided the musicians for the orchestras. Thus Angel, Israel and Edgar performed on the same bill with such stars as Mahalia Jackson, Eddie Fisher, Sammy Davis, Jr., Brook Benton, and rock star Dion and the Belmonts ("The Wanderer," "Runaround Sue"), and were accompanied by the orchestras of Eddie Palmieri and Machito.

Backstage at one show they saw a famous rock-and-roll star sniffing cocaine. He graciously offered the boys a snort of the "dangerous temptation"—which they just as graciously declined.

They appeared at Loews Orpheum on East Eighty-sixth Street, with Clay Cole as the M.C. The "twist" was the rage then. The orchestra wove the twist rock music into everything: fanfares, entrances, exits and curtain calls. When Edgar got up on the roller-roller and started his swinging from side to side, preparatory to Angel's climbing up on his shoulders, where he would juggle the clubs, the orchestra injected a faint but catchy twist beat into the Antinos' mambo music. Edgar responded, not only by rolling back and forth to the music, but by twisting his body and rotating on the balls of his feet, coordinating both sets of movements—which was pretty good since he had never practiced it before. The orchestra leader, seeing Edgar pick up the twist theme, let the orchestra "take off." Edgar, inspired, was smiling broadly at the audience and twisting away like a shorter, paler Chubby Checker. By this time Angel was on the stage, in front of Edgar on the table, wildly twisting away also. Angel was quick to enter into the spirit of things. Israel, always more subdued, just faked it, so he wouldn't look out of place— or out of step.

The audience, realizing the genuine spontaneity of what was happening, stamped their feet and clapped their hands. The whole place was swinging. For the rest of their act the boys twisted instead of mamboed. They twisted while flying through the air and when standing on each other's shoulders. They twisted as soon as they landed out of their somersaults.

The *New York Mirror, El Diario,* the *Youth Board News* and many local newspapers carried pictures of the Antinos performing. They were personally thanked by Mayor Robert F. Wagner for their contributions to delinquency prevention. A big photo of that event appeared in *El Diario* the next day. Somehow the picture came out looking as if Israel were talking intimately with the mayor. In the album we added one of those balloon captions to the picture, attributing to Israel the words: "Listen, Bob, I want to tell you of the problems my people are having here in your city."

At the end of the Youth Board tour, after a dozen or more shows there was a big windup performance, with Machito's orchestra, in the ballroom of the Henry Hudson Hotel. The boys were sharp that day and the audience of teen-agers and adult leaders responded warmly. The comedian Joey Adams, who was president of AGVA and master of ceremonies for the evening's festivities, called the Antinos up to the microphone and publicly complimented their performance. Then he asked, "Are you guys members of AGVA?"

"No," Edgar answered, as Angel and Israel shook their heads in confirmation.

"Well, you are now!" said Adams with a flourish, as the audience applauded. "Come and see me in my office tomorrow."

And so the Antinos became card-carrying union members, which meant they were entitled to certain welfare benefits and assistance in contract negotiations, and naturally the union was trying to set minimum payments for various kinds of bookings. Union dues were almost four hundred dollars a year for the act, which the boys paid in installments—a percentage from each booking. When they occasionally fell behind in their dues, their attitude was: "Get us more bookings and we'll pay you more dues."

The Antinos got themselves booked into the famous Roseland Dance City near Broadway on Fifty-second Street, which opened in 1919 and holds 3,450 people. They performed on its ten-thousand-square-foot dance floor.

They performed in the center ring of the old Madison Square Garden on Fiftieth Street and Eighth Avenue (before it was torn down and rebuilt on Thirty-fourth Street) during a Channel 7 televised benefit circus for the New York City Fire Department.

"We felt like butterflies in that big place," said Angel. Israel was particularly impressed with performing there. Madison Square Garden was the most famous place he had ever heard of.

At the country fairs the boys never knew what to expect. They were held in armories, shopping centers, parks and the backs of trucks.

Once, in Jersey City, it was a high school football field that became the stage. Ordinarily a grassy area is ideal—a soft but firm surface with no height or space problems, and the boys were used to grass from their Central Park practices. But this show was at night—a black, moonless night with no stadium lights; just a single fixed spotlight. Everything went fine while the tumbling and stunts were clustered in the middle of the circle of light on the ground. When the Antinos got to their three-high ending, Israel climbed up on Angel, who was standing on Edgar, and prepared to stand to complete the human column. But as he stood up straight he went past the top edge of the area illuminated by the spotlight. He was in complete darkness. Only his legs from the knees down were visible. Is-

153

rael, enveloped in a black void, could see only Angel's head immediately below him, and the circle of light on the ground had shrunk to the size of a manhole cover.

Out there, where Israel had to fall slowly forward until that forty-five-degree angle before jumping clear, he could see only darkness. And he needed to see the ground to judge when to jump clear, not to mention the need to know where he was going to hit the ground.

"I can't see the ground," said Israel to Angel just below him.

Angel passed the message down to Edgar. "Edgar, Israel says he can't see the ground."

"He doesn't have to see to do the trick," said Edgar impatiently as he strained to hold Angel's legs firm against the back of his head.

Up the column via Angel the message went. "Edgar says you don't have to see the ground."

"How will I know where to land?" answered Israel with a touch of panic in his voice.

Down, via Angel, went Israel's reply.

"Tell him to just go!" said Edgar, exasperated and staggering slightly under the unwieldy two hundred sixty pounds of his two partners above him.

"Edgar says go anyway," said Angel to Israel. Israel's feet were beginning to pinch in on Angel's neck.

"I'm not goin'," said Israel stubbornly.

"He says he's not goin'."

"He has to!"

"I'm not goin'!"

"He's not goin'!"

"It's the only ending we have!"

And up. "Edgar says it's the only ending we have."

"I'm comin' down!"

"He's comin' down!"

"Tell 'im to stay!"

"Stay! . . ."

Too late. Israel had jumped for the small arc of illuminated

154

ground he could see in front of Edgar. Angel bent forward to ease him down and jumped after him. They all rolled, trying to fake it, but they weren't together. Israel sprained his ankle.

One rainy night, Angel's friend Wilfredo was taking them to Washington and the wheel came off his car on the Jersey Turnpike. With no help in sight, they set about trying to fix the wheel themselves. No good. They needed a new disk. Soaked, they sat in the car. It seemed like an hour before a police car pulled alongside. A tow truck was called. After another hour they were towed to a gas station—but the mechanic wouldn't be on duty until morning. They checked into the hotel across the street, which was described by the gas-pumping attendant as a place "where the fleas will steal your socks."

Wet, tired and hungry, they trudged up the front steps of the old wooden hotel building. As they walked into the lobby, Angel noticed the stares of several perplexed black tenants, who probably wondered why any nicely dressed young men would stay there. Angel, projecting the thoughts of the spectators, said, "There goes the neighborhood!" Everyone laughed, if only slightly.

Angel, Israel and Edgar were quickly disabused of the notion that show business was all glamour and big money. Although they rarely turned down bookings because the pay wasn't enough, some shows involved travel costs, meals on the road and hotel costs, and unpaid rehearsals and auditions. And then there was an average of two nights a week practice and more when they weren't getting bookings. Sometimes it hardly seemed worth the effort. And the thrill of performing was beginning to wear thin at times. But all three of them, even Israel, who complained the most about benefits and low-paying shows, got into the spirit of things when they heard the music and applause. They always gave their best, like the professionals they had become.

The three got along relatively well. Gone were the chronic disputes especially since Joe was no longer around as a thorn in

155

Edgar's side. Gone also was the whining and complaining about who was going to carry the equipment and costumes and about who was in charge. Angel and Israel were happy to let Edgar be business manager for the act. Leo Grund of International Attractions was their primary agent now and Edgar never had anything but praise for his consideration and straight dealing. Edgar was the contact person: he signed the contracts, negotiated the terms and handled the money. He painted the equipment, replaced parts, built a new, strong, high table for the roller tricks, and arranged for fittings when they purchased their tuxedo and jump-suit costumes (worn with silky, baggy-sleeve shirts). He arranged for photos, the making of composites, and their distribution to agents and producers. When necessary, he did everyone's makeup. And on those rare occasions when they did three shows a day, he massaged sore muscles, applied liniment and elastic bandages. He was like a trainer in a football locker room. On the road he did the cooking. He organized the practices and made adjustments in the routine.

Differences were minor and probably reflected their perspectives more than their incompatibilities. Edgar reveled in every aspect of show business. This was his milieu. He identified with show people. As soon as Edgar got to the dressing room, he would take off his coat and put on his red silk robe and walk around the dressing rooms talking to the other performers. Angel and Israel found Edgar's little pretensions an entertaining target.

"Edgar, I think you should wear your green robe today . . . and your stocking on your head . . . and your cowboy boots."

"You look sick, Edgar. Put on some suntan makeup."

Sometimes Angel and Israel would casually make decisions between themselves. "We're cutting out the pitch-backs tonight. Our feet hurt."

"Why wait until two minutes before we go on to tell me?" Edgar would say. "Those changes should be made during rehearsal." Exasperated, Edgar would continually scold them. "You guys are stupid. You got to be serious. You're in show

156

business now. You're professionals."

"No, Edgar," Israel would say, laughing. "We're amateurs."
Israel probably meant he and Angel were "outsiders."

In 1961 Israel's father died. Israel had stayed with him to the
end, even after his older sister and brother married and moved
out. For the last few months of his father's life Israel had to take
him a couple of times a week to the hospital for treatments.
Israel was holding his hand when he died.

Not wanting to go back to an empty house, Israel stayed for
a short while with his sister Noelia and her husband. Not many
months later Israel quietly got engaged to a nineteen-year-old
girlfriend and a month before his nineteenth birthday he was
married. Israel and his wife moved in with his wife's mother and
father, two younger sisters and a cousin, all of whom lived in a
five-and-a-half-room apartment on Eighty-third Street. By this
time Israel had left his Chicken Inn job and was earning a few
more dollars a week as a delivery boy at the Abbey Kent department store.

Almost immediately, strains were reflected in Israel's complaints about the difficulty of attending practices, rehearsals,
auditions, about doing benefits, and having to make excuses to
his boss when he took off from work to do shows. He also continually withdrew his share of the money in the Antinos' joint
bank account, which had been set up in order to have ready
cash for travel costs, costumes and equipment.

Every once in a while there were big paydays, like the time
the Antinos appeared on the Johnny Carson *Tonight Show*.
They were hired as stunt men, not to do their act. Acrobats
sometimes do stunt work because it pays well, and after all, they
are skilled at falling, jumping and taking risks.

This particular night Soupy Sales was filling in for Johnny
Carson. The comedian's trademark was hitting people in the
face with whipped-cream pies (he had revived that well-worn
comedy ploy for his kiddie show). To avoid having Soupy Sales

go through the almost obligatory pie in the face every night, someone decided that once and for all, someone would be thrown into a pie.

In the opening minutes of the first night of Soupy Sales's stint on the *Tonight Show,* Angel, Israel and Edgar came out on stage neatly dressed in dark suits, bow ties and regular street shoes—all provided by the show's wardrobe department. Before them was a huge tub about six or seven feet across the middle and about three feet deep, filled with instant-lather shaving cream. I guess it looked like the big whipped-cream pie it was intended to resemble.

After Soupy Sales explained to the audience what was going to happen, he asked the boys where they were from and without further ado said, "Who's it gonna be?" Edgar and Angel jockeyed a little for position before each of them grabbed Israel by an arm and a leg. Israel arched his back so he was like a sling. His head pointed toward the pie. Edgar and Angel swung him back and forth until they got him swinging a full one-hundred-eighty-degree arc, and then they swung him forward on "one," backswing on "two," forcefully forward on "three," and let him go. Israel sailed up and over the pie and *phhlopp,* he landed face down in the shaving cream, splattering some of the thick, creamy suds around the stage. Israel sank into the cream before he slowly crawled out, looking like the abominable snowman. He stood there letting the cameras get a close-up and allowing the audience to laugh, which they did, but only moderately.

Israel was disappointed that his suit was all messed up. He had liked that suit and had in mind to give it to himself for a bonus.

They shared $550 for doing that stunt.

20

As soon as Bernice Goodman, the program director at the God-dard-Riverside Community Center, heard that Joe and Ray were sort of retired from the Tumbleweeds and old enough to work in the center, she hired them.

Goddard-Riverside Community Center is really a settlement house with a variety of educational, recreational, social service, day care, camping, senior citizens' and community-improvement programs operating out of an assortment of buildings on the West Side.

In the fall of 1959, Joe, at seventeen, fresh out of high school, became a program aide, responsible for teaching tumbling and acrobatics to the younger children in the after-school program. He worked Monday through Friday, two and one-half hours a day, for which he was paid $1.60 an hour (sixty cents over the minimum wage, which had risen in 1955 to a dollar an hour).

Joe continued working part-time at Remy's Radio and TV Shop, and he worked half-time as a messenger for RCA. Later in the year he added a weekly paid session teaching tumbling at a Girls Clubs of America center. Joe liked to keep busy.

Because Ray was younger, he started as a supply closet attendant in the after-school program at $1.10 an hour. As soon as he got his first pay check, he opened a savings account and deposited the bulk of his earnings, as he was to do with every pay check, in preparation for paying his way in college.

Six months later, in the summer of 1960, Ray, seventeen and a year short of graduating from high school, became a full-time assistant group leader, responsible for teaching tumbling and acrobatics to the seven-to-eleven-year-olds in the Summer Vacation Play School. By fall, Ray was also earning $1.60 an hour, teaching acrobatics five afternoons a week in the after-school program.

Although Joe and Ray, on the basis of their fame as Tumbleweeds and their technical competence in acrobatics, quickly established themselves, they now had to learn new skills—skills which they had only begun to develop when they had helped me teach acrobatics in the past. They had to be teachers. They had to engage in that phenomenon of transferring knowledge and skill from themselves to other human beings. They had to learn to communicate, demonstrate, explain, encourage, motivate, organize progressions, analyze mistakes, systematize and conceptualize and use, instinctively or consciously, all those other techniques which make for effective teaching. It wasn't good enough to be skilled in the subject being taught, although that sure helped. Teaching required using one's head much more than one's triceps muscles.

Acrobatics and tumbling was an ideal activity for youth centers and settlement houses, which seldom had enough space or money to hire gymnastic coaches or purchase elaborate equipment like parallel bars or bulky, hazardous trampolines. Our kind of work required only mats. And the ability to teach tumbling and acrobatics was a skill specialty few people had. Joe and Ray had almost a personal monopoly, which soon brought them job offers from agencies all over the city. Ironically, as teachers they were in much greater demand than if they had been an acrobatic act in the show business market.

Bernice Goodman and others at Goddard-Riverside very wisely saw another dimension to Joe and Ray. Since most of the kids in the Goddard-Riverside program were Puerto Ricans, Joe and Ray were to be models for the younger kids, identifiable models—not a remote Ralph Bunche or Governor Muñoz

Marín, but Joe Ramos and Ray Sanchez, who, like the kids in the program, came from small towns in Puerto Rico, grew up in the neighborhood, attended P.S. 166, delivered groceries after school, played softball in Central Park—and who, in a modest way, had "made good."

By 1961, Joe was a full-time group worker at Goddard-Riverside. In addition to teaching acrobatics, he coached softball and basketball, supervised the game room, ran teen dances, recruited kids for the program, organized trips to parks, historical sites and the Goddard-Riverside camp, and took care of a host of other details generated by parents, kids and co-workers, all of which left a hum in his ears hours after he got home.

Not all the activities got equal treatment. Joe's trademark was still acrobatics and tumbling. Joe formed a special group of performers, who gave exhibitions that served to advertise the community center's program—and also advertised, to no small extent, Joe Ramos himself. The group consisted of seven Puerto Ricans and three blacks, of various sizes and shades of brown. They did many of the same tricks we had done as Tumbleweeds. They used the same music, they made the same red-dyed T-shirts and pants with the jagged-cut sleeves and cuffs. They began playing the same circuit of youth centers, schools and settlements that we had years before. They were a second generation of Tumbleweeds.

"On probation," they wrote on Ray's file when he was accepted into Bronx Community College in September 1961. Although Ray always got passing grades in high school, his average wasn't high enough for him to be accepted directly into the four-year City College, so he had to go to a two-year community college. But even here the admissions officer wasn't sure Ray was "college material." This was before the days of "open admissions" or the active recruitment of minority students. Ray was to be given a chance, but there were to be no special allowances. If he successfully completed his two years at Bronx

Community College, he could then go on to City College for the final two years and receive a regular B.S. degree.

Ray plunged into his schoolwork with single-minded determination. College had come to mean a lot to him. He hadn't grown up taking it for granted. Hardly anyone in the neighborhood had been to college. Most quit school as soon as they turned sixteen. Ray's mother thought college unrealistic and so did her friends. But Ray had always been receptive to new ideas and interested adults. I wasn't the only one to encourage him to go to college. There were teachers, social workers and community center workers who encouraged him and expressed confidence in his ability. The strongest influence professional people had on Ray was that they gave him a view of a life that appealed to him. Professionals had status and did dignified work. They lived well, dressed well, earned more and seemed to have more choices in their lives. They were, for the most part, decent people and Ray, quite understandably, wanted to be a part of all that. And the passport to that world was the college degree.

That's not to say Ray was one of those relentless upwardly mobile materialists. There was always a strong strain of idealism in him. When he was in his junior year in high school, he was one of the stars of Robert Cox's excellent teen theater productions (under the auspices of the Bureau of Community Education of the N.Y.C. Board of Education). Ray played the King in *The King and I* and displayed real talent. After a few performances in New York, the whole cast was invited to perform in the Tapia Theater in Puerto Rico. Ray subsequently appeared as Chino in another Robert Cox production, *West Side Story.* This led to a two-day job at one hundred dollars a day as an extra in the movie *West Side Story.* (If one watched closely, Ray could be seen in the background of a fleeting playground scene.) Years later I asked Ray why he never pursued a glamorous acting career. Without hesitation he answered, "I found working with kids more exciting." I knew exactly what he meant.

Ray concentrated on studying to the exclusion of other inter-

162

ests and much of his social life. He gave up acting and sports, limiting himself to short, efficient workouts with Joe and me. He drastically curtailed chasing around with Joe to clubs, dances and parties. Weekends were reserved for homework and study. Ray couldn't do schoolwork in his one furnished room with the chronic dripping faucet, the radio music and the frequent visits of his mother's friends. And he couldn't expect her to give up her radio and her social life. She was still in her thirties and after eight hours a day at the factory she deserved her moments of relaxation. So Ray camped out at the St. Agnes branch of the public library, on Amsterdam Avenue near Eighty-first Street. Whenever I wanted to get in touch with Ray I would go to the second floor of that library—poorly lighted, overheated in the winter, invaluable. Invariably I would find him, with his elbow in one book, several more stacked behind, writing painstaking notes. Seeing Ray in that drab room reminded me of those photos of immigrants I had seen in history books, bent over a flickering lamp, studying, persevering.

I thought it would be a good idea to involve as many people as possible in supporting Ray's efforts. I arranged for him to go to a reading clinic at New York University to improve his reading and comprehension skills. I arranged for testing and counseling at Columbia University Teachers College. When he finished the testing, Ray asked me to talk with the counselor because he felt his mother wouldn't understand or be able to make use of the findings. The counselor pointed out that Ray scored much higher on the nonverbal than the verbal tests. The counselor understood all about kids like Ray, who learned English as a second language, not performing as well on the tests when they had to use English. The counselor thought Ray could do college work and she told us so.

As Ray chipped away at his courses in history, English, sociology and math, I realized I was becoming more and more invested in his getting a college degree. That would be something, I thought, a kid from the "worst block in the city" earning a Bachelor of Science degree (Puerto Rican college graduates

163

were rare in those days). It would be equivalent, at least, to doing a Big Five pyramid.

Although Joe had talked about going to college, and I, Bernice Goodman and others encouraged him, I wasn't counting on him. Joe had the intelligence to do college work, but I wasn't sure he had the temperament for contemplative study or the discipline to allocate his energies judiciously. Joe was working full-time and overtime now and he was thriving. He wasn't ready to cut back and leave the "action" for the hallowed quiet of the library or the nit-picking of the classroom. Also, Joe's enthusiasm for college had been dampened by the fact that he would have to make up almost a year of academic courses that he didn't get in his vocational high school before he would be eligible to matriculate in college.

No, I wasn't counting on Joe, certainly not at this stage of his life. One college graduate out of five. I would settle for that. The difficulty was that my role in helping Ray in college was much more limited than the very strong influence I could exert in teaching him acrobatic stunts. With college study, Ray had to do it himself. And do it he did. By the end of his first year, his A-minus average got him taken off the "on probation" list and put on the Dean's List.

In the summer of 1962, Joe, Ray and I were all working for Goddard-Riverside. Joe was all over the neighborhood, whirling through playgrounds, gymnasiums, parks, streets and fire-hydrant sprinklers, with masses of white, tan, brown and black kids dressed in dungarees and shirts of summer yellow, white, red and green. There were softball leagues; punchball, paddleball, handball and dodgeball games; volleyball and jump rope tournaments; day camp trips to swimming pools, Orchard Beach, the museums and the Cloisters; dance pageants, block parties, parades, junior olympics, field days, sports days and dance festivals.

Joe's Tumbleweeds were performing all over town. He was elected chairman of the PAL Youth Council for the area. Youth

164

Squad cops and Youth Board gang workers referred kids to him and dropped in to track down rumors of "rumbles."

Joe was tireless and irrepressible. Just before the summer he had fractured his ankle, necessitating a cast and the use of crutches to hobble around. But Joe was up in the gym anyway, rolling around, demonstrating front rolls, headstands and cartwheels. Bernice Goodman had to fire him for a week to get him to follow the doctor's orders to stay off his leg.

Joe was coming into his own. His presence was felt and he was being noticed. Goddard-Riverside board members affectionately called him by his first name and were pleased when Joe used theirs. Teachers, principals, district superintendents, district leaders, precinct police captains, social welfare agency executives, made a point of periodically checking in with Joe—to keep channels open and the relationship warm.

Ray, again, was teaching his tumbling and acrobatics classes in the Summer Vacation Play School program. A couple of years ago most of the boys and girls in Ray's classes were Puerto Rican, but that had quickly changed when the middle-income white parents living on West End Avenue and Riverside Drive found out about the Ray Sanchez acrobatics classes. Instead of taking their daughters to ballet lessons or their sons to the YMCA, they took them to the Summer Play School, where they would ask, before enrolling their children, whether Ray would be teaching tumbling/acrobatics again this summer. Ray's work load swelled to five sessions a day with up to twenty kids in a class. Ray liked teaching kids and was buoyed by his success, but now he also complained. "I'm so tired of front rolls, back rolls, headstands, holding them, spotting them, helping them over."

I had just graduated from the Columbia University School of Social Work and accepted a summer job with Goddard-Riverside, coordinating and organizing community groups to use the neighborhood health and recreation facilities.

Every Tuesday, Thursday and Saturday evening after working hours, Joe, Ray and I practiced hand balancing, tumbling and pyramids in the corner of the huge Junior High School 44 gymnasium. We had in mind putting together a trio act, spending our three-week September vacation together in Puerto Rico, trying our luck at picking up weekend bookings in the San Juan nightclubs to defray the costs of traveling around the island.

Although Joe, Ray and I worked several blocks apart out of separate centers and didn't see each other very often during the day, I was occasionally reminded of their presence. Riding the Amsterdam Avenue bus or walking the streets, I would see some wiry eleven-year-old I had never noticed before break stride with a skip and, in the middle of the street, handspring or cartwheel gracefully from hands to feet. I liked seeing that, especially if the kid displayed certain unmistakable stylistic characteristics that stamped him or her as one of our products.

But Joe and Ray were not only acrobatic instructors, role models for the younger kids, and junior staff in the community center. Another role had evolved. In the surrounding Puerto Rican community Joe and Ray were now identified as *maestro* (teacher)—a title of considerable import in Puerto Rico. Spanish-speaking neighbors and parents accorded Joe and Ray the proper *respeto,* addressing them as "Mr. Ramos" and "Mr. Sanchez." Although Joe and Ray would ask to be called by their first names, it wasn't easy for old-country people to shake off their conditioning. The most common compromise I heard was "Mr. Joe" or "Mr. Ray."

Joe's and Ray's mothers proudly showed their co-workers at the factory snapshots of their sons in action, standing before attentive groups of children, hands posed in teaching gestures. Each took pleasure in telling relatives back home in Puerto Rico that her son was *un maestro sin título*—"a teacher without degree"—which some consider more prestigious than being one with a degree.

For the first time his mother treated Ray's college aspirations seriously. She became even more supportive and enthusiastic than I was about Ray's going to college. There was a look in her eye as if she was thinking maybe it would be possible for this son of a sugar-cane cutter, this child of a mother who never read a sentence in her whole life, to really become educated, and maybe, someday, be *un profesor*.

Naturally, Joe and Ray were like Pied Pipers in rounding up kids in the street to join the community center. And they did a considerable amount of personal counseling with the teenagers. When one of Joe's Tumbleweeds found out that his girlfriend, whom he intended to marry, was pregnant, he asked Joe to speak with his easily excitable father and explain to him this delicate, complicated situation.

Those Puerto Rican parents, who previously wouldn't let their children go on Goddard-Riverside–sponsored trips, willingly gave their permission if Joe or Ray was accompanying the group.

All this accrued personal influence and approbation by family, friends and associates profoundly boosted Joe's and Ray's self-images; it straightened their shoulders, lifted their heads, lightened their steps and gave them an engaging openness. They were quick to shake hands, touch one's arm or shoulder, or, depending upon size, stroke the head or pat the back. In public, they maintained a reasonably dignified demeanor. If Joe was sometimes pompous, it flowed from his insecurities and not from a main artery of his character.

Joe's image maintenance included dressing the part of a "professional." He wore Ivy League suits in soft browns, greens and conservative plaids, button-down oxford shirts, striped rep ties and mirror-shined cordovan shoes. Even in the summer he was fully outfitted with a short-sleeve button-down shirt, a summer-weight tie and a Dacron suit. He accumulated ten suits and eight pairs of shoes. Joe's mother had to give up her closet to his expanding wardrobe.

That summer Joe was one of several neighborhood people to become subjects for a series of short biographies published by the Board of Education, entitled "Heroes I Have Known." The "heroes" were local blacks and Puerto Ricans, and a few Italians, Irish and Japanese, who held jobs as teachers, firemen, clergy, civil servants, etc., whom the author expected would be realistic heroes for the minorities and ethnics in the city schools.

Although the biographies were too inspirational for my tastes —"these men and women have worked most of their lives to make freedom and personal fulfillment a reality"—I nevertheless thought Joe Ramos was a good choice.

According to the biography, Joe was influenced by me: "It was Fred who taught Joe gymnastics and tumbling. It was Fred to whom Joe went when he needed help or advice."

And since I had gone to college while working in youth centers, Joe is quoted as saying: "If he can do it, I can do it."

The story goes on to describe Joe's career: "Joe started at Goddard-Riverside as a part-time helper. Gradually, he was given more work, until in 1961, he became a full-time instructor. Here he supervises and teaches gymnastics, tumbling and basketball."

Then on to college: "With funds provided him by the center, Joe started in the evening session at Bronx Community College in 1962."

The story ends in 1962, with Joe reflecting on the future: "I want to be either a physical education teacher or a social worker. There's a great need for both. I wasted three good years by not going to college earlier. If you don't have a proper education you don't get a good job. I wish I could tell all the kids: Don't waste your time. You won't get anywhere, especially today."

Shortly after the book came out, Joe got a call from a junior high school teacher in a Queens "600" school (for students having difficulty adjusting to regular school). This teacher and the students had worked up a program using Joe's biography in "Heroes I Have Known." Could Joe come out and talk with the class?

When Joe returned from Queens, he spoke warmly of his experience. "You should have seen it, Freddy. Kids in the class acted out the story in the 'Heroes' book. One of the Puerto

Rican kids played me; a black kid played you. It was good. It was nice.

"And then they asked me questions and we just talked back and forth. I sat on the desk, natural and relaxed. Then they asked me a favor. Would I teach them tumbling? They had the mats all set up and ready in the gym and I gave them a lesson. It was good, Freddy. It was nice."

A week after Goddard-Riverside's summer program ended in September, Joe, Ray and I were in sunny San Juan, wading in the tepid blue ocean waters fronting on the Escambrón Beach Club. The next morning we made the rounds of the nightclubs and talked to managers and agents and showed our acrobatic pictures in hopes of getting a weekend booking. In the afternoons, after the steel band finished their rehearsing, we practiced our act in the Escambrón Ballroom.

Every club manager we talked with liked the idea of having an acrobatic act on the bill, especially one prepared to work as cheap as we would. But our timing was all wrong. We were too late for the summer season and too early for the winter season. One impresario wanted us to join his "Variety Extravaganza" opening at the Tapia in October. Reluctantly we turned it down. We had to get back to our jobs.

By the end of our first week, we abandoned our plan, rented a Volkswagen car and took off for the interior. We spent two pleasant days at Joe's grandparents' home in San Germán and an equally pleasant two days with Ray's grandparents in Rincón. We had a nice vacation, but our sharply honed acrobatic edge was wasted.

169

21

By 1962, the Antinos' third year, Angel and Edgar were contemplating a two-man act. Israel had begun drifting away. He missed practices, complained about how difficult it was to get off from work or away from obligations his wife had dumped on him. Angel and Edgar had to turn down a couple of shows because Israel said they were inconvenient or didn't pay enough. Once he missed a show because he was drunk.

Israel, now twenty years old, had been married a little over a year. Things weren't going well. His wife wasn't the person he thought she was. And living with his wife's family complicated and compounded simple everyday problems. Though the arrangement was economical because everyone worked except his wife's younger sister, Israel claimed his wife and her mother had overly ambitious living standards, which absorbed his earnings from the act and from his stockroom/delivery-boy job at the Abbey Kent department store.

Israel's drinking accelerated, as did the deterioration of his marriage. It wasn't long before he walked out. A three-month reconciliation failed and then he left for good, but not before he punched out the heavy pane of glass in the front door of the building, which tore a jagged gash in the pulse side of his wrist. The wound festered and two days later the emergency-room doctor at Roosevelt Hospital put in eight stitches and told Israel that if he had left the wound untreated for one more day he would have lost his hand.

Israel went from job to job and moved several times. He avoided his friends and stopped working with the act. Joe, who usually knew what was going on with everyone, didn't have anything on Israel except that he was living on the notorious Fox Street in the South Bronx. (The police refer to the area as "Fort Apache.")

Only once did the shreds of a story drift back. Israel, it seems, was working for a while in a bar on Fifteenth Street in Manhattan. Somehow he discovered that the cellar safe had been left open and he notified the owner, possibly saving him a couple of thousand dollars. The owner, through some kind of write-off manipulation, rewarded Israel with liquor from the storeroom. "Cases and cases of Scotch and beer," was the way someone described it. Israel used it for one big blowout, an open-house party for everyone on Fox Street.

I wondered about that party for a long time. Israel had once told me, "I never had a birthday party in my whole life." Maybe that was the first.

After that we heard nothing. Israel disappeared. Even Angel, his closest friend, didn't know where he was.

Angel had been living with his brother Chago and his mother and working steadily at a variety of no-skill, low-paying messenger-boy type jobs since he quit high school. His fifty-to-sixty-dollar-a-week pay checks went toward the seventeen-dollar weekly rent for their Eightieth Street furnished room, plus groceries, clothes, carfare and precious few miscellanies.

Chago's incarcerations were becoming more frequent and he was home less and less. Reynaldo was again in jail, where he had spent most of his life since coming of age. Angel's three older sisters had moved out and were living in traditional common-law marriage arrangements, with children of their own.

Angel's job situation was substantially improved when Joe Ramos helped him get a seventy-five-dollar-a-week office-machine-operator job in the Board of Higher Education office

171

on East Eighty-sixth Street. Two other young men were apply-
ing for the job, each with a high school diploma. One of them
didn't know how to operate the postage-stamping machine and
the other couldn't manage the mimeograph. Angel was able to
say he could operate both equally well—i.e., not at all. But
Angel was good with machines and Joe gave him a crash course
on the Goddard-Riverside mimeo machine. Angel was hired
with the condition that he get a high school diploma (required
by Civil Service) within the next two years. He was soon quite
expert with all the office machines and no one ever knew he
couldn't tell them apart when he started.

Angel was twenty-one when he moved in with Carmen
("Cookie") Arce, who was the same age and lived across the
street in a furnished room with her fifteen-year-old sister. Angel
had liked Cookie from the first moment he saw her two years
ago. She had long black hair, expressive dark eyes, a lightly
freckled fair complexion and a full, pretty mouth that alter-
nated between pouting and shaping words as if she were talking
to the hard-of-hearing. My first impression, seeing her on an
Eightieth Street stoop in tight pedal-pushers, talking and laughing with a cluster of guys and young women, was that she was
teen-age cute, kind of flirty, coquettish and . . . well, a Cookie.

Later I found out that Cookie was one of thirteen children,
two of whom had died in Puerto Rico at birth; another died
when very young, apparently from diseases related to malnutri-
tion. Her mother's first husband, and Cookie's father, died at
twenty-six, seemingly from a condition associated with alcohol-
ism. I also found out that Cookie stood all day behind a counter
at Gettleman's Five and Ten for forty dollars a week, out of
which she paid the rent, bought food and sent ten dollars a
week to her mother in Puerto Rico. She fended off the Eightieth
Street *machos,* cooked meals, made her own clothes, and despite her lack of education (two years of grade school in Puerto
Rico), had taught herself to speak, read and write English. She
was smart and tough. So much for first impressions.

A few months after Angel moved in with Cookie, he went to

172

his mother and told her he was planning to marry Cookie and live with her permanently. Angel's mother cried bitterly. She ranted and raged and tore Angel's shirt to shreds. She maligned Cookie, accusing her of some vague past infidelities that made her "unfit to marry." Angel, upset by his mother's reaction and stung by her words, cried also.

The next day Angel had a gray and worried look on his face. As we walked up Columbus Avenue, crowded with Saturday shoppers, Angel told me of his mother's accusing Cookie of unfaithfulness. I could hear the hurt and disappointment in his voice, and I could tell it had been eating away at him, for he talked about Cookie with increasing coldness.

After we had talked awhile, Angel agreed that maybe his mother's strong emotional reaction was due in part to her worrying about losing him, especially since he had never said anything to her about continuing to pay the bills. The thought of not doing so had never occurred to him.

Although my policy in personal matters with girlfriends and wives was generally to mind my own business, in this instance I did say a few words in Cookie's behalf—rather eloquent words, I thought.

I don't know how Angel worked it all out, but a week later, with his share from an Antinos pay check, he bought matching gold wedding bands.

Angel's mother came to like Cookie very much. Later that year, Jesse was born.

Before the year was out, Edgar had married Lydia, his old girlfriend. Lydia was as tall as Edgar, solidly built, light-complexioned, with long, dark straight hair and deep eyes accentuated by eye shadow. She seemed quiet, reserved and distant. I never got to know her, but it was easy to imagine her over a crystal ball, in the flickering candlelight, invoking spells to heal sickness, cast away evil, neutralize enemies or bring back a wandering husband. In every other way she seemed a traditional housewife. She spent much of the day with her mother,

173

who had trained her as a medium.

Soon after Angel and Edgar married, they moved into the same apartment building on Eastern Parkway in Brooklyn—Angel's family on the second floor, Edgar's on the third. Lydia gave birth to Eric in that building. Eric had his own room, as did Angel's and Cookie's Jesse.

Edgar hadn't found work as a keypunch operator when he graduated from the Monroe School of Business, so while carrying on the act, he held a variety of shipping clerk jobs in the garment center of Manhattan.

Angel's new household was just as hard pressed as before. Cookie had stopped working to take care of baby Jesse. Angel continued to support his mother and Cookie sent money to her mother in Puerto Rico.

Angel started getting asthma attacks—at least, that was the most frequent diagnosis. Respiratory infection, bronchitis and strep throat were also popular. Angel felt that his illnesses were due to having lived over the boiler in his Eightieth Street furnished room, where he inhaled the escaping fumes. He was often absent from work and took a lot of pills; his weight went down from a solid one hundred fifty pounds to a baggy one hundred thirty. Edgar and Angel stopped practicing the act.

When Angel began feeling better they started in again. Both Angel and Edgar were basically bottom men, yet Angel, who was almost a head taller, was trying to replace Israel as a top man. They worked "heavy." They weren't satisfied. They tried using some chrome equipment. Angel tried doing more juggling. They invented a swivel, which Edgar wore on his head like a knight's helmet. Angel was supposed to do a back swan on top of the swivel and spin around while Edgar was on the roller, but the first time they tried it Edgar's head was almost wrenched off his neck. They continued to practice, irregularly, without a clear-cut objective.

22

My stay at Goddard-Riverside stretched into a second summer and on into November 1963, when I was invited to return to a reorganized PAL as borough manager for the Bronx and Queens.

Although Joe, Ray and I still worked out together and even did our act in a few benefit shows, we didn't have as many after-work discussions in the corner bar as we used to. But it wasn't only my new job and the distance that separated us. My interests were expanding—pulling me out of the neighborhood, so to speak. Civil rights was an idea whose time had come and I, along with many others, joined the marches and demonstrations of the early sixties. Later we were in the "war on poverty" and the struggle for "welfare rights" and then the angry Vietnam war protests—and in the middle of all this my wife gave birth to twins, Guy and Erika.

Ray also had his hands full. He was going to school full-time and working at Goddard-Riverside from 3 to 10 P.M. He was given a difficult predelinquent group consisting of a dozen thirteen- and fourteen-year-old Puerto Rican boys. Ray's job was to try to channel their energies and aggressiveness into constructive or at least less destructive behavior.

"They're a wild bunch," said Ray. "Always getting into trouble, playing hooky, defying the teachers and disrupting the rest of the center."

Most of the kids in the group felt comfortable with Ray. All seemed to trust him. Part of the reason for this may have been his being Puerto Rican and not more than five years older than any of them. Unquestionably, the most important factor was Ray's personality. The kids felt they could talk to him, even about those confusing, awkward, personal, painful growing-up things.

The group became downright possessive about Ray and he was soon referring to them as "my group," or "my boys."

After several months Ray's group was proficient enough in acrobatics to give exhibition performances in other community centers, school talent shows and field days. Once they even performed on television.

"These guys," said Ray, "are *my* second generation of Tumbleweeds."

A mild debate began between Joe and Ray about how tumbling should be used with kids. Ray said, "I don't think working up a professional routine or doing shows is important. Tumbling should be a way of helping kids develop confidence. That was my experience. That's the way it affected me."

"But," Joe said, "doing shows is a way for the kids to get attention—which they want and need—in a positive way."

"It's a matter of emphasis," said Ray. "The primary goal is to develop the kids' confidence and not do a fancy routine."

"But you can't kid these guys," said Joe. "They're not gonna feel confident unless they can really do something. . . ."

I usually thought they were both right.

Joe and Ray had different styles of working. Ray was more open to incorporating new insights and quicker to learn from his mistakes. He accepted supervision and he watched and learned new techniques from many people. He was more comfortable than Joe was with letting a group decide what they wanted to do and how they wanted to do it. I like to think he got some of that from me.

Joe, on the other hand, was always the leader—controlling, demanding and sometimes intolerant. I felt this reflected his father's stern influence, but Joe would say, "I'm like you, Freddy. I don't take any bullshit. And these kids are shapin' up."

"But, Joe," I would say, squirming with discomfort, "if there is anything I learned in social work school it's that you have to be flexible . . . er . . . keep a balance . . . er . . . individualize. . . ." And then I would go dumb, trying to think of an example out of our common past of my doing any of those things.

As talented a mover and shaker as Joe was, he had to adjust his style—and learn some new tricks—when he was assigned to work with the Enchanted Angels, an active fighting gang of twenty Puerto Ricans, sixteen to nineteen years of age. These kids weren't predelinquents; many had already been involved in shootings, knifings, thefts and other assorted felonies.

Joe's task was to reach out, form a relationship with the gang, help them with individual problems, and whenever possible integrate them into the regular community center program. He, like the Youth Board gang workers, was to try and "cool the bopping" and help the group "go social."

The reaching out and getting to know the members of the gang were relatively easy, for Joe had grown up with some of their older brothers. Angel's brother Chago, for example, became a member of the Enchanted Angels.

But there were plenty of rough spots for Joe, especially in the beginning. Some of the guys in the gang already had problems relating to authority and bristled when hearing Joe's snappy commands. Some guys Joe didn't like and he couldn't bring himself to warm up to them. A few in the gang needed psychiatric or other kinds of specialized help.

Joe's approach basically was an individual one and it worked with the majority of the gang members. He referred them to jobs, got them back into school when they were suspended or expelled, and interceded in their behalf when they wound up in court. They called him when they got into trouble or asked him for help when they had specific needs, such as buying club jackets or planning a dance.

Joe's tumbling program was an asset. "It gives me a handle," he said. "I have something to offer. It's a basis to begin a relationship."

Ironically, Chago, during his sojourn with the Enchanted Angels, was one of the more constructive members of the group, and contributed to whatever success was obtained. Chago was the last elected president of the Angels, a position he held until they disbanded a year and a half later.

Ultimately, Joe's experience with the Enchanted Angels wasn't much different from the citywide "war on gangs." Gangs were broken up and the fighting and destruction of property were diminished, but the lives and needs of individual kids weren't changed very much. They still had problems with school, jobs, their families and neighborhoods. Maybe the cooling out of the gang fights kept teen-agers from making things worse for themselves. Or maybe, as Richard Cloward, one of my professors at the Columbia University School of Social Work, theorized, the rapid increase in drug use, which followed the suppression of fighting gangs, was "retreatist behavior." If teen-agers couldn't make it in the legitimate system of school and work and couldn't make it in the illegitimate system of organized crime (then controlled by whites), and if the fighting gangs—which conferred status, recognition (a "rep") and a sense of belonging on alienated teens—were extinguished, then there was nothing left but to retreat from a harsh reality by anesthetizing a worthless self with heroin.

In the 1960s the "heroin plague," as Claude Brown called it in his autobiography, *Manchild in the Promised Land,* was to become a leading cause of teen-age deaths. Heroin overdoses ran into the thousands.

On the wall in Joe's office in the Goddard-Riverside Community Center there is a photograph of Sexto Valenzuela, a good-looking sixteen-year-old, receiving a trophy for captaining the softball team to the league championship. Joe, who nominated him for the award, is standing proudly behind him. A year later Eddie Palenzuela was carried out of his apartment building in a green canvas bag, dead from an overdose.

178

Cliff Hyatt, one of Joe's husky Tumbleweeds, drifted away from the group and got sucked into the drug syndrome and then into dealing to support his habit and sometimes just because it paid better than anything else. Allegedly Cliff sold a bad dose (cut too much with milk sugar) and one night he was chased by three assailants, armed with club-length two-by-fours, into an alley near 106th Street and Central Park West, and beaten to death.

As soon as Chago outgrew the gang scene, he was getting into serious trouble again. I never could figure Chago. He was always so friendly, ebullient and smart. Once I put up my new Volvo as collateral for a bail bond to get him out of jail, never doubting he would keep his promise to appear for trial. He contributed very little to the family and borrowed whenever he could. He gradually left his mother's home, and like Reynaldo, his older brother, he was soon in trouble again.

Joe worried that his younger brother, Georgie, might get involved with drugs. He hovered over him, made sure he went to school, got him part-time jobs and warned the junkies to stay away.

Joe's other brother, Luis, who went with his father when his parents split up, had a difficult time with his father and aunt and uncle, who lived together far out on Long Island. Luis was a restless, adventurous kid, troublesome at times, and probably confused by his parents' separation. He got into more trouble, which provoked severe punishments and restrictions. At sixteen he ran away from home, and he never went back. He traveled the country from coast to coast, hitchhiking, bus-riding, working, and living by his wits. Eventually he ended up back in New York City. When last heard from, he seemed to be in good spirits and doing well. It wasn't clear what he did, but we knew he floated on the edges of that in-between world of hustlers, homosexuals, drug people and other outcasts.

With a regular salary, a well-stocked wardrobe and a visible public position in the community, Joe's natural social instincts flowered. He moved around the neighborhood like a politician running for office. When he wasn't attending the community happenings, he was creating them at the center. He charmed, impressed, and won friends among the neighbors, merchants, policemen and staff. The community center was his base. Here friends, neighbors and girlfriends knew they could find him. And Joe was still young enough to enjoy the social activities he planned for the older teens at the center.

Joe also liked to dance, and on weekends he liked "checkin' out the chicks" at the Caborrojeño, the Broadway Casino and the Club Casa Blanca.

As president of the Spanish Club at Bronx Community College, Joe organized ski trips, festivals and Latin dances. He was also president of the Alumni (later named the Rainbow Association), an organization of young Puerto Rican college students and graduates, whose ostensible goals were "to help their own," but who also considered social activities important.

Although Joe got the President's Award for his contributions to the life of Bronx Community College, his schoolwork suffered from all his flitting about. Joe dropped, failed and changed courses regularly. Progress was slow, but the tie was never severed, due in part to encouragement from the teachers and counselors and maybe to a nagging sense of competition with Ray Sanchez.

In 1964 Joe, at twenty-three, married Rudi Collazo, twenty, a bright, attractive, easygoing, full-figured, light-skinned long-time girlfriend. It had been an off-and-on romance, partly inhibited by Rudi's parents' objection to their daughter's marrying someone as dark as Joe.

That same year Ray, now twenty-one, married Ana Ortiz, a big, friendly, vivacious girl with seven older brothers. She was a high school graduate and worked as a clerk in a bank, but had the intelligence to do much more. She helped finance Ray's continuing education.

Joe and Ray now earned almost twice the $1.60 an hour they

had started with. Both couples moved into apartments on the West Side.

As each of the guys married, I made sure they knew where to go for birth control—which they did. And my wife offered to accompany any of their wives to the Planned Parenthood Clinic, which was necessary in only one instance. Religious considerations never came up in this matter, nor in any other. The boys' Catholicism was most nominal, being limited to identifying themselves as Catholics on application forms. Of course, their parents decorated their homes with plaster figurines of the Virgin Mary and Jesus, and bloody red hearts crowned with thorns and crossed with crucifixes. But these symbols were integrated with—if not subordinated to—their parents' stronger belief in spiritism.

As we became increasingly involved in our own careers and families—all except Israel would soon have a first-born—we saw less of each other. Ray and I continued to work out, but less frequently and then just to keep in shape. Joe came to my home to fix my television set or my Volvo (he had a Volvo of his own). Or he would invite me to see his Tumbleweeds perform in some show or another. They were very active and had become regulars at the half-time shows of the Harlem Wizards (a lesser Globetrotters) basketball games. Or Joe would ask me to come by the center because he wanted to discuss his latest job offer.

The years passed quickly.

23

At 5:27 P.M., on November 9, 1965, thirty million people in eight states and eastern Canada experience the largest electric power failure in history. The city is plunged into darkness. The Great Blackout.

Angel is at home. He looks out his front window and sees the headlights of cars—many headlights, and none are moving. Horns are honking like a squadron of geese. It's a traffic jam of dinosaur proportions.

Angel puts on his old night watchman's cap, the one with the shiny leather brim like a policeman's. He pins on his badge, tucks his night stick and handcuffs in his belt, and holding a flashlight in one hand and a whistle in the other, heads for the intersection of Schenectady Avenue and Eastern Parkway.

Angel blows his whistle. "All right, back in your cars!" People scramble into their cars, others stop honking. "Back up there! . . . Hold it up! . . . Move ahead!" he commands, gesturing with his hand and pointing the flashlight beam at those cars congesting the intersection. "Get those cars out of there! C'mon! Let's go!"

Angel alternates the "stop" and "go," giving each direction exactly two minutes to move through the intersection. After several minutes a police car pulls up behind a line of cars. Receiving Angel's signal to proceed, the police car drives slowly by. The officer in the driver's seat frowns at Angel, but as he glances around at the well-functioning intersection, he nods his approval.

For two hours the rush-hour traffic flowed smoothly at Eastern Parkway and Schenectady Avenue—more smoothly, in fact, than it did on normal days.

Angel had been working in the mail room of American Brands, Inc., since 1964. The Board of Higher Education had to let him go from his office-machine-operator job because he hadn't achieved his high school diploma. Angel had tried getting it by taking night courses, but he wasn't used to studying and his teacher wasn't sympathetic and Angel was working extra jobs to pay the bills, so he stopped going to night school.

For a while Angel had earned extra money as a night watchman. Then he drove a cab. He would wake up before 7 A.M. to get to American Brands by 8 A.M. He sorted, collected, stuffed and processed mail until 3:30 P.M., which gave him a half hour to pick up his cab. He drove until midnight, eating on the run, never getting home before 1:30 A.M. On Saturday he drove the cab a full day, beginning at 6 A.M. Angel remembered those days as a blur of mindless activity, chronic fatigue and constant coming and going.

For a time Angel earned extra money playing the big conga drum with Latin bands at clubs, dances and parties. He had learned to play when he was younger by drumming on the hoods of cars and by watching conga players. Initially he was invited to sit in with various combos or to substitute for a drummer who was sick, or sometimes a band would just get together for a special wedding party.

He played with several orchestras. He cut a 45-rpm record with Tommy Rosa and his Rhumba Bana Sextet. He did double conga solos with the Orchestra Impala. Once, on the way to a jam session in his car, one of the musicians asked Angel if he would mind picking up this blind kid named José Feliciano, who played the guitar and sang real good. The most famous group Angel played with was the merengue band Tipico Sibaeño.

According to Joe Ramos, who's a Latin music buff, Angel was highly regarded by other musicians. Angel knew nothing about written music. He was a natural.

But the weekend conga-playing strained his relationship with Cookie. Between sets there were drinks with the customers and the "groupies" of that circuit. Afterward there were more drinks, sometimes a little "fooling around," late, late hours, making up excuses, and often finding out he had spent the extra money he had made. Angel was also uncomfortable around hard drugs, which were so pervasive in the musicians' world he knew.

Both Angel and Cookie were relieved when he quit the conga-playing business. Cookie's new job as a dental assistant helped ease the financial strain.

With patience, persistence and plenty of practice, Edgar, pulling Angel along with him, bounced back into show business with a new act called Eddie (for Edgar) and Manny (Angel's middle name is Manuel). In 1965 they played the Puerto Rico Theater in the Bronx. They did two shows at the Premier Theater in Brooklyn, and in between auditions, did a couple of benefits.

But the act didn't click. Angel and Edgar could feel it themselves. Instead of the old smooth-flowing routine, with its carefully paced comedy, tumbling, balancing and get-ups, tested and refined before a hundred audiences, there was now only a patchwork of Angel juggling, too much of Edgar on the roller-roller, too much equipment, too much climbing. It lacked the exuberance and movement of the old Tumbleweeds and Antinos. Leo Grund, their agent, wasn't enthusiastic, but he encouraged them to keep working—which they did without much success.

Although the act was Edgar's obsession, he was always ready to try something new. He had an unquenchable enthusiasm for meeting people, learning hobbies, exploring, making friends, experimenting—and listening to the voices of salvation. Over the years Edgar was "saved" by the Espiritualistas, Pentecostals, Methodists and Jehovah's Witnesses. Even the Episcopalians had a crack at him.

Except for these religious searchings, I thought Edgar's capacity to enter into new endeavors, without preconceptions, prejudices or inhibitions, an admirable quality. Some interests I even encouraged. I thought he would have made an excellent physical therapist, but that required college, and with the family (Karen, his second child, had just been born) and everything else, he was only able to attend Manhattan Community College evenings for two semesters.

Edgar also had a short stint in drama school, which he soon gave up for karate and judo lessons, pursued until he had achieved a middle-level "purple belt." In addition, he played with his children, learned how to swim, lost some unwanted weight, became a good cook, built equipment for the act, had an awkward affair, and sold one of his oil paintings for fifty dollars.

But there was also a constant Edgar: the Edgar who always went to the gym to practice handsprings, roller-roller tricks and hand balancing. Even when Angel was sick, Edgar was there keeping in shape, sharpening his round-offs and nip-ups and thinking about new routines, looking over other gymnasts as prospects to join the act and dreaming about putting it all together, going out there in the footlights and "knockin' 'em dead."

Reynaldo, Angel's older brother, got out of jail in 1967. He was thirty-three years old. He began getting fainting spells. An exploratory operation found a cancerous tumor covering three quarters of his brain.

The surgeon confronted Angel with the options: "Cut it out, but if he lives . . . a vegetable. Close up his head . . . live a few more months. You decide!"

Reynaldo deteriorated rapidly. During the last weeks Angel rushed uptown after work to his mother's home, where Reynaldo was staying, to carry him to the bathroom, wash him, change the bed and bring him some favorite foods.

As the casket was being lowered into the ground, Angel very soberly suggested to his sister Rosa, who was standing next to him, the tears barely dry on her face, that maybe he should buy the adjoining plot for his mother. She had cancer also, and wasn't expected to live much longer.

As Angel was leaving the cemetery, his eye was drawn to Reynaldo's tombstone. The *y* had been left out of his name, "Renaldo," it said.

It was near midnight when Israel woke up in the intensive-care unit of Roosevelt Hospital with tubes in his nose and mouth, running down deep into his stomach, sucking up the blood from some hemorrhaging wound. Another tube, needled and taped to the vein in his arm, was connected to a suspended plasma bottle, which slowly dripped a solution into his depleted body.

Israel had passed out earlier in the evening at Edgar's father's small apartment on Fifty-sixth Street, off Amsterdam Avenue, where Israel had been living for the past couple of years. Eusebio had called the ambulance. It was May 11, 1967. Israel was twenty-four years old.

Israel had been sick, depressed and unemployed for several months. He had been drinking himself into a stupor almost every night.

It was three days before Israel was taken off the critical list and his head cleared enough for him to give up the terrifying conviction that he was going to die.

The young doctor who came to see Israel told him that if he had been older he wouldn't have survived. As the doctor moved the stethoscope around Israel's chest, he looked curiously at the old, bleached-looking scars scattered about his upper body: where an ice pick had punctured his chest and where a razor had slashed a four-inch wound in his shoulder and where several inch-long notches had been cut on his forearms, and there was that jagged scar he had got on his wrist when he punched and broke the pane of glass in the front door where he and his wife had lived. Israel attributed the scars to vague accidents that happened long ago.

The young doctor said he had learned from Israel's brother Juan that Israel had been an acrobat. Did he think he might go back to doing acrobatics again? Israel wasn't sure.

The tentative diagnosis was "bleeding ulcer." An operation was proposed. Out of instinct, fear or reasons unknown, Israel was convinced he didn't have an ulcer and refused to give his consent. Fifteen days later Israel was deemed well enough to be discharged. The young doctor referred Israel to Alcoholics Anonymous and warned him that if he started drinking again it could kill him.

Israel went back to living with Eusebio, who was in his late sixties and had been retired for the past few years. Eusebio had a small pension from the bakery and social security. He earned a few extra dollars by selling beer, milk and cigarettes from his apartment to the other tenants. The implicit arrangement was that if Israel worked, he contributed to the cost of running the household; when he was sick or not working, he wasn't expected to contribute. Eusebio cooked the meals, made no demands, and when Israel felt like talking, he always had a listener. Israel began referring to Eusebio as "my father" and Eusebio called Israel his "son." Israel later explained that this was done to avoid complications or delays if he should get sick again. And it may have been so.

Two weeks after his discharge from the hospital, Israel went to work at the Holiday Inn garage, parking cars. He had worked there for a while before getting sick. Every Friday evening he attended Alcoholics Anonymous meetings held in Roosevelt Hospital. Israel never spoke at the meetings, but he listened intently.

In three weeks Israel's hands had stopped shaking.

187

Bookings had fallen off, but Angel and Edgar continued to practice their act. It was pride in their skill and keeping in shape as much as being prepared for bookings that kept them working out every Monday and Wednesday at the McBurney YMCA on Twenty-third Street.

When Edgar heard Israel had just come out of the hospital, he began visiting him at his father's place, but Israel, whenever he could, avoided Edgar, other old friends, and even relatives, because he felt "ashamed." Edgar persisted and gradually cajoled Israel to come to the gym—"not to work out; just to visit."

On the first Monday in the corner of the Y's seventh-floor gym, with its overhead running track, its shiny varnished floor, its basketball players and judo enthusiasts, Israel stands and watches Angel and Edgar practicing. Sometimes he sits on the roller-roller table. He talks with Angel and Edgar between tricks.

The next night at the gym, Israel does the same, only this time he also touches his toes, stretches, does a few push-ups and a single front roll on the mat. Angel invites him to do a simple low hand-to-hand stand—as he used to do. Edgar offers to spot him. Israel begs off. "Haven't done anything in years . . . still outta shape . . . no strength in my arms. . . ." Edgar and Angel don't push him, but they say they expect to see him again on Monday night.

It's like a seduction. Angel and Edgar do tricks that leave something unfinished or need a third man to complete it, or they are done in such a way that an expert would be made uncomfortable and sorely tempted to show the performers "how it should be done." Angel does a handstand on Edgar's hands, but there is too much wiggling before they find the set position. Edgar holds Angel on his shoulders, walks a few steps and pirouettes, but nothing develops and Angel dismounts.

Israel begins testing himself. Unobtrusively, off on the side, he tries a cartwheel and a round-off and then a handstand on

188

the floor. It feels pretty good. Angel and Edgar praise and encourage him. Israel does a handstand on Angel's steady hands. It looks good. More praise—and more offers. Did Israel want to try a pitch? A stand on the shoulders? A back drop? A low one-hander? Could Israel still do a round-off back flip?

It isn't long before Israel is asking Angel and Edgar to try a high hand-to-hand with him . . . and a pitch-back . . . and a three-high. Israel's normally erect posture slowly returns, as does the strength in his arms and the bounce in his legs. Israel discovers he hasn't lost any of his old tricks. After years of abusing his body, he is delighted he can still do his whole repertoire. Edgar is amazed that Israel, in three months, is better than he ever was. Israel stops going to Alcoholics Anonymous meetings.

This time they called themselves the Galaxios—moon shoots, astronauts, satellites, *Star Trek* on TV, galaxies: it was the space age. Leo Grund, their agent, agreed "Galaxios" sounded topical and catchy.

Angel, Israel and Edgar bought new costumes—a black and a blue jump suit, and white, lavender and gold baggy-sleeved silky shirts which could be used interchangeably with the jump suits. They painted the equipment and covered the high roller-roller table with a black felt cover that had GALAXIOS printed on it in shiny starlike spangles. They got new music arrangements, a new set of composite pictures to be distributed to agents and producers. But the act—the routine—was the same one they had used as Antinos, when they were at their peak, before they broke up some six years before. Now it didn't seem so long ago.

The Galaxios looked good on *The Show of Shows*, a Spanish variety program on Channel 47. And they looked good at the Jazz Pavilion, which had stayed open after the World's Fair ended in 1966. And they looked sharp at the circus—all four shows—held on the State University's Stony Brook campus.

Cookie caught their act when they appeared at Manhattan Center. She thought they were better than she had ever seen them.

In a third-floor apartment of the same Fifty-sixth Street building where Israel lived with Eusebio, there lived one Josefa Padilla and her two children: Nilda, age nine, and Rafael, age five. She was as old and as tall as Israel, who never grew beyond his five feet, four inches. She had brown hair, soft brown eyes, a pleasant face, but with a gaunt sadness attributable only in part to the shape of her cheek and jaw.

Israel met her when he was helping the "super," which he occasionally did to earn a little extra money. Israel painted her apartment an unauthorized two coats in the unauthorized colors of her choice. Israel thought she was attractive and proper in her ways. She was responsible with the children, took care of her apartment, and she supported her family by working in a factory, where she made sew-on emblems, leather belts and novelty clothing. Israel had to make several visits to the apartment to finish the painting. Josefa Padilla was appreciative and sometimes she invited Israel for dinner or to watch television. A year later they had an official City Hall wedding.

Israel had money in the bank, a new car, a wife and family, and the Galaxios were working. "It was the beginning," Israel said, "of a whole new life."

24

It was a sunny June afternoon in 1968 when I set out for the ornate old Carnegie mansion at the corner of Ninety-first Street and Fifth Avenue, which housed the Columbia University School of Social Work. In the inside pocket of my suit jacket there was a ticket Ray had given me, inviting me to attend the commencement exercises for those Columbia students who, by successfully completing a rigorous two years of courses and field training, were to be awarded Master of Science in social work degrees. Ray Sanchez was to be one of them. Ray was going to graduate from the Columbia University School of Social Work —just as I had six years before.

When Ray had finished his two years at Bronx Community College, he had gone directly to City College. While attending school he had also worked for Ruth Frazier, district supervisor for the Bureau of Community Education—and good friend and supporter of both Joe and Ray. Ray had been assigned to the Junior High School 44 Community Center. He had risen to the position of teacher-in-charge and his earnings had increased to fifteen dollars per three-hour session. In 1966, after two years at City College, Ray had received his Bachelor of Science degree. With scholarship assistance from Goddard-Riverside and ASPIRA (an organization that encourages Puerto Ricans to continue their schooling), Ray had been able to enter the Columbia School of Social Work, where he tackled their Master's Program

191

with the same drive, discipline and perseverance he had applied to undergraduate school.

It was such a lovely summer day, I decided to walk across Central Park from my office on West Eighty-seventh Street—where I was now directing the Strycker's Bay Community Action Project—to the Carnegie mansion. I walked about a quarter of the way through Eighty-seventh Street, stopped, retraced my steps, and detoured downtown three blocks to Eighty-fourth Street. I thought it appropriate—even poetic—on this day to walk through Eighty-fourth Street, where Ray had lived when he came to New York City, and where I had first come to know him as a shapeless, seventy-pound ten-year-old. That was fifteen years earlier.

Huge chunks had been torn out of Eighty-fourth Street. The newly constructed Brandeis High School now occupied two thirds of one side of the street, and across from it the new Public School 9 occupied another third. There was still a row of grimy, deteriorated buildings, reminiscent of the old Eighty-fourth Street, at the Amsterdam Avenue end of the block. As I walked by, I could hear and feel the chips of wine-bottle glass grinding under the soles of my shoes. Mostly poor blacks lived here now. A chunky Puerto Rican woman holding a chunky baby leaned over the fire-hydrant spigot, out of which poured a slow stream of water, and rinsed the pacifier her baby had thrown on the soot-gray sidewalk. Several tired-looking blacks and dark-complexioned Puerto Rican men had relaxed their bodies into the angles of the stoop. Two black women, arguing loudly and patiently, competed with the shouts and yells of several teen-agers playing stickball. Smaller children were just getting out of school. They raced by me and got more numerous as I moved up the block. Few of them lived on the block.

Central Park was green and fresh with the scent of things blooming. I took my jacket off and carried it over my shoulder as I walked briskly under the trees on the grass, following the paved paths whenever they were going my way. Twenty minutes later I was standing in the shade in the tree-lined garden

192

of the Carnegie mansion, my shirt sticking to my sweating back.

Ana, Ray's wife, and his mother, Milagros, with her new husband, the placid and undemanding Carlos, were there, dressed and corsaged as if for Easter Sunday. They were glad to see me. They were nervous, but proud, and possibly a little uncomfortable in this unfamiliar setting, amid the extravagant old-wealth architecture.

We sat in the middle row on the wooden folding chairs that had been set up on the lawn. Hundreds of other parents and guests were seated around us.

The speeches were short, smiling and touched with decorous humor. The heat of the afternoon sun made me drowsy and dreamy. Sidney Berengarten, the acting dean, began calling the names of the graduating social workers in alphabetical order. They, each in their turn, walked, faces beaming, to the portable platform up front, where Dean Berengarten shook their hands and presented them with a large Columbia-blue folder containing their master's degree.

After calling about a hundred or so names, the dean came to the name of a woman from the Philippines. He interjected that this class had in it several students from faraway places like Australia, Greece and Argentina. "Some students," he said, "have come a long way to attend Columbia." When the dean got near the end of the roster of graduates and finally called "Raymond Sanchez," the thought struck me that Ray, too, had come a long way.

At twenty-five years of age, Ray became director of the East Harlem Children's Center—the youngest director in the history of the agency. This East Harlem Children's Center was the same one I had been director of exactly ten years earlier.

But Ray wasn't dogging my footsteps. Bernice Goodman, whom Ray respected, had left Goddard-Riverside and become program director of the Childrens Aid Society. She had recruited him. Probably the main reason Ray decided to take the East Harlem Center job was, as he said: "I wanted to start with something manageable, something I'm ready for. I want to work directly with people in the neighborhood, involving them in how the center is run. And naturally, I think I can be most effective with Puerto Ricans."

In 1969, Tom Wolfe, executive director of Goddard-Riverside, with the approval of the board of directors, appointed Joe Ramos director of their new Community Center on Columbus Avenue and Ninety-first Street. His annual salary was to be $10,500, which was pretty good in those days for a guy with only one year of college.

Joe's college career had been floundering along now for five years. His transcript was peppered with incompletes, withdrawals and failures. Nevertheless, he was still a registered student and he was still president of the Spanish Club, "the most successful club in Bronx Community College," according to Joe.

Joe's rise up through the ranks to the director's job hadn't depended upon his college credentials. There were other reasons. Being Puerto Rican helped.

Black Power! Puerto Rican Power! Power to the People! were demands born of the civil rights, student and poor people's movements of the sixties. Strong pressures (and sometimes intimidations) were put on social agencies to share their power by hiring blacks and Puerto Ricans, especially if those blacks and Puerto Ricans were from the immediate neighborhood, and especially if the agencies' clients were predominantly black and Puerto Rican. Goddard-Riverside had it easy. There was Joe— made to order.

Although Joe rode the wave of sentiment to hire minorities, he wasn't a "token Puerto Rican." He had a solid work record and strong personal qualities. He could handle responsibilities. He knew how to command. He had energy and drive. His exuberance and enthusiasm were infectious. He had a magnetism which attracted people. There were always people around Joe.

But Joe was a complex person. Things didn't always go smoothly. Those challenging his authority found him icily correct, barely civil, and were overruled. Those who knew him trod lightly during his dark moods. Supervisors with whom he differed found him to be alternately stubborn, surly, passive, depressed, forgetful or vindictive. Programs or policies that Joe opposed were sabotaged in such a way as to make them appear ill-conceived. The supervisors or bosses who got the most out of Joe were those who respected his very real talents and handled him with delicacy and diplomacy.

Because of Joe's popularity and many supporters, he was always able to boast, "I have the community behind me." Not only did Joe know just about everyone in the neighborhood; he had something going with them. He got local merchants to buy T-shirts and equipment for his softball teams. In return, Joe threw business their way or passed the word that their goods were okay. The merchants also felt they could ask Joe to keep the tough kids from hanging around their stores, scaring away business. Joe had influence with the street-corner kids because they occasionally used the center and sometimes Joe got them back into school after they were suspended or "pushed out"; or if they were picked up for minor delinquencies, the judge was always glad to accede to Joe's request that the case be resolved by a referral to his center. Joe sent kids to camp, occupied them after school and during the long summer months. He helped them have fun, meet friends and learn skills. Needless to say, the parents were grateful for the community center and were among Joe's most ardent supporters. A few mothers were constantly bringing him pots of rice and beans and special delicacies.

Joe always looked out for his close friends and went to great lengths to help them. One time a couple of his old Eightieth Street buddies were arrested for a robbery they swore they didn't commit. Joe arranged bail, got a lawyer from the Goddard-Riverside board of directors to be their counsel, and went scouring the bars looking for witnesses. Eventually his buddies were acquitted.

Some favors he did to enhance his image as a fixer, a wheeler-

dealer who could get things done. Joe was asked to join committees, boards, block associations and community corporations.
For a time he was vice-president of a neighborhood council.
Meetings weren't Joe's cup of tea—"Too much talkin'! Too
much bullshit!"—but he joined anyway to develop contacts,
hear the neighborhood news, find out where the foundation
money was going, and get his "piece of the action."

Ironically, Joe often joined organizations and committees
with the implicit understanding that he would be balancing the
ticket, integrating the group, acting as *the* Puerto Rican representative. But Joe was a very assimilated Puerto Rican. His
behavior, attitudes and life style were mainland American.
After all, he had spent only the first four years of his life in
Puerto Rico. Over twenty years had been spent in New York,
much of that time, in recent years, outside the Puerto Rican
ghetto. Ordinarily there wouldn't have been a problem, but
times were changing. There was a reaction in the schools, generated by Puerto Rican intellectuals, activists and sympathetic
educators, against Puerto Rican children's mindlessly absorbing
the television world of American culture. Puerto Rican studies,
and programs fostering a pride in one's Puerto Rican heritage
and language, were initiated in all levels of education.

As a community leader involved in the education and sociali-
zation of Puerto Rican children, Joe was invited to conferences,
caucuses, forums and meetings to discuss Culture Conflict and
the Puerto Rican Migrant, or variations on that theme. Joe was
careful to speak Spanish, at least part of the time, at these
meetings, putting himself on record as knowing the language
—a minimum requirement for being a bona-fide Puerto Rican.
(The Young Lords, a Puerto Rican gang which turned to political action, were greatly handicapped when they tried organizing Puerto Ricans without being able to speak Spanish.)

When the young Puerto Rican militants on the West Side
began challenging the "welfare colonialism" and "cultural im-
perialism" of the schools and social agencies, Joe effectively
kept them off his back by pointing out that he, an indigenous

196

Puerto Rican, was the *jefe* directing this community center. Increasingly Joe could be heard introducing himself as José Rrramos.

Joe got on especially well with policemen. To the police, Puerto Ricans were sometimes hostile, strange and difficult to handle. Joe wasn't like that. Joe was a Puerto Rican they understood. Joe was reasonable, cooperative—an all-right guy.

Joe, for his part, wasn't so different from the cops he knew. Many were about his age. They could relate to Joe's rough, tough, no-nonsense approach with kids. They usually had a common interest in sports and in hoisting a few at the bar. In many ways Joe was as "American" as they were. He shared the same values about work and getting ahead and even about "law and order." He sought the same comforts, cars and gadgets. He had the same chauvinistic attitudes toward women and prejudices toward "bullshit politicians" and "higher-ups" who don't understand how it is "out on the streets."

Uniformed cops on the beat regularly dropped in at the community center to say hello, use the bathroom, have a smoke, tell Joe their troubles, pass on a little station house scuttlebutt, and listen to Joe's complaints about the high price of steak and *aguacates*.

The Youth Patrolmen who ran delinquency-prevention sports programs were made to look good when Joe entered dozens of Puerto Rican kids in their softball and basketball leagues. Joe became a member of their precinct youth councils and was elected to the executive committee of the 20th and 24th Precinct youth councils.

The first stop for Community Relations cops on the West Side was always Joe Ramos. And if these cops reported to their superiors that they had made contact with the "Puerto Rican community"—by meeting with Joe—their claim wasn't totally unjustified.

Word of Joe's reputation reached the Deputy Commissioner of Community Relations. Soon he was calling Joe to ask his opinion on some matter or another or to request that Joe meet with a group recruiting minorities for the Police Department. Or, in one instance, to recruit Joe as an occasional consultant (at sixty dollars a day) to the Police Community Relations program.

One of Joe's tasks as a consultant was conducting small-group discussions aimed at "sensitizing" policemen to the feelings and culture of Puerto Ricans. I don't know how much the cops learned of Puerto Rican culture, but the human relations material Joe injected was common-sense stuff about how you treat people decently ("Don't curse at the kids!").

Understandably, Joe acquired considerable leverage. He could get extra cops assigned to his special events, parades and play streets. Even the Spanish radio station WBNX recognized Joe's role with the police. They gave him their Community Service Award—a plaque with the inscription: "For your outstanding contribution to the better understanding between the New York City Police Department and our Spanish-speaking community."

But the ultimate accolade Joe received from his police friends was a "testimonial" held in a private upstairs room of the Playboy Club on Fifty-fourth Street. The Precinct Youth patrolman invited me. "We want all of Joe's friends to be there." Rudi, Joe's wife, came, as did several of the high-ranking brass from "headquarters." There were eats, drinks served by Bunnies—and another plaque for Joe's wall.

It was a sedate and dignified affair, unexpectedly so, expressing warm feeling for Joe. Joe appreciated it.

25

Big things were in the wind for the Galaxios. In June of 1970 they had just played Mexico City. There was now an offer for a nine-week tour of Japan at $750 a week. And maybe Las Vegas after that.

Edgar saw this as the ideal time to take the risk and go into show business full-time, something he had always wanted to do. Angel and Israel weren't so sure. They had their jobs, family responsibilities, their apartments, bills had to be paid regularly. It was complicated. They had to consider. They had to discuss it with their wives.

Edgar stalled for time by stretching out the negotiations for the Japan tour. He asked for round-trip plane fare to be included in the contract. The producer accepted. But before the final contract could be settled and signed, the Galaxios were again booked for the *Siempre en Domingo* TV show in Mexico. Apparently, "they loved them in Mexico City."

It was the same deal as before, $450 for two consecutive Sundays, plus plane fare and hotel costs.

A final decision on the Japan tour was to be delayed until they returned from Mexico—to give Angel and Cookie and Israel and Josefa more time to consider. But they didn't have to wait that long. Angel knew, down deep, this Mexico show was going to be their last. The Japan tour only crystallized the issue. The realization had come to Angel at Kennedy Airport. They had just cleared the checking in and ticketing of their luggage and they all turned for a final wave goodbye to their wives, standing dourly on the overhanging balcony. All of them were pregnant, Cookie due any day. Josefa, Israel's relatively new wife, was big of belly also, carrying the only child Israel ever fathered. Lydia was expecting her fourth.

Israel had told Edgar and Angel of his wife's ultimatum: "Japan or me!" and they knew if it came to that, Israel would stay with his family. They also knew their wives had picked up some stories about "geisha girls" and "massage parlors" in Japan, and that didn't sit well with them at all. Besides, the wives had never liked their husbands being out most evenings doing shows or practicing the act. Angel and Israel were also beginning to feel the evenings away from home were getting to be a bit of a drag, especially after a tiring day's work. Israel cherished quiet evenings at home and he hated making excuses to his boss to get off from work to do shows.

The Galaxios gave a good performance on Sunday. Leo Grund, who was mixing business with a Mexican vacation, caught their act on his hotel television set. Except for the usual suggestion that Israel smile more, the agent thought the boys were "great!" He looked forward to big things.

And then one bright, cloudless morning, Angel, Israel and Edgar rent a car and drive some thirty miles outside Mexico City to Teotihuacán, a vast ancient city of shrines, temples, priestly palaces and pyramids spread over seven square miles.

They walk past the Temple of Quetzalcoatl and down the Street of the Dead, dividing the City of the Gods, which they learn was built some two thousand years ago. They take some snapshots. They stand looking up at the towering four-sided Pyramid of the Moon and the Pyramid of the Sun. They learn the Pyramid of the Sun is the highest of all—as high as a nine-teen-story skyscraper—and that it probably kept ten thousand laborers toiling twenty years to build.

For some reason, or no reason, they decide to ascend to the

top of the Pyramid of the Sun. They start climbing the rough rust-brown blocks of stone. It's strenuous going, for the steps are almost two feet high, as if for a giant. Sometimes they lean on their hands as they put one foot after the other up on the shelves of stone. They climb slowly and steadily, feeling the fatigue creep into their legs. Looking around, they see a few clambering tourists, some of them taking pictures. It takes forty-five minutes of climbing to reach the top of the pyramid. It's flat and as big as the infield of a baseball diamond.

Between their breathing and puffing, Angel, Israel and Edgar squeeze out exclamations of wonder at the spectacular view. A sea of green surrounds them and fades into a lighter green as their eyes sweep out to the distant snow-capped mountains silhouetted against an endless sky. Israel says the people on the ground look like ants. Even the other pyramids look small. The sun is hot, very hot, but billowing winds are soothing-warm and blow stronger here than down below.

For several minutes they stand, catching their breath, looking out, kind of hypnotized by the expanses of green and blue and the horizon of majestic mountains. It's serene and contemplative. Quiet, too.

Angel, Israel and Edgar have many thoughts, but nothing special. Just a feeling of well-being.

Then Angel and Edgar lift the leather camera straps over their heads and put their cameras down on the stone. Angel grips both Edgar's hands. Edgar spreads his legs, bracing himself as Angel climbs to a stand on his shoulders. Angel wiggles his feet to adjust his position. When he feels set, he reaches down and pulls Israel up to the usual standing position on top of his own feet.

From there, Israel climbs, grabbing and holding Angel's hands and arms, and he eases his way up to a standing position on the shoulders of Angel, who is standing on the shoulders of Edgar.

Israel raises his arms high over his head, as he always does to

201

complete the three-high. Israel leans into the wind, ever so slightly, for counterbalance. It feels good: steady and solid. They hold the three-high for a long time—longer than ever before. There isn't a sound. Israel feels the warm wind rushing between his fingers.

26

All of a sudden, it was summer 1974. And 1974 was special. It marked the twentieth year since the Tumbleweeds had formed. Twenty years was half my lifetime and more than half the lifetimes of Ray, Joe, Angel, Israel and Edgar, who were now all in their early thirties.

Our association over the years had had its ebbs and flows. And there were times when it was dormant. But we were most intensely together at an impressionable period in our lives. For better or worse, we were irrevocably changed by the experience. Some more than others, myself as much as they.

I decided to talk to Ray about a twentieth-year reunion of the Tumbleweeds. Maybe I would also write a story about them.

The Broadway IRT express screeched loudly into the Chambers Street station. I fell in with the disembarking passengers. Coming out on the sidewalk, I saw looming in the not-too-far distance the giant rectangular twin towers of the World Trade Center. The tops of the buildings were obscured by mist and clouds, giving the appearance that the buildings emanated from the heavens and had touched down about a half mile south, near Wall Street. I strode east on Chambers Street, amid briskly walking people, until the squat "Tweed" courthouse building came into view. Then I turned left and walked one block to the modern, glass-paneled Federal Building, where

Ray had been working during the past year for the Department of Health, Education and Welfare.

The express elevator went rapidly and quietly to the thirty-seventh floor, the top floor in the building, a fact that reminded me—allegorically—that I had always urged the boys to "go higher." I had always felt sure of what that meant, but in recent years, many of my notions and attitudes had changed. I wasn't so sure anymore what "success," the "big time" or "going higher" meant—not even if it took one up to this thirty-seventh floor.

"Hey, Freddy! *Cómo está?*" said Ray as I walked into his functionally equipped office with file cabinet, bookcase, swivel chair, and a telephone on the corner of the desk. Several children's crayon drawings were Scotch-taped to the wall along with a couple of large posters promoting youth programs. Ray closed the thick manila file he was reading and tossed it on top of a pile of other folders as if he welcomed the interruption. Ray's modest mustache was as black as his hair, which was long, but styled, and held in place carefully with hair spray. His cheeks had always been full, but now they looked a bit puffy, though that was more first impression than fat. He looked tan and healthy. His jacket and pants were the latest youth style, good quality double-knits in deep blue and brown. He seemed almost as tall as my six feet, but I knew he was three or four inches shorter.

"Let's go sit in the conference room," said Ray. "It's more comfortable."

Although Ray's position as assistant director of the Office of Youth Development (for which he was paid $23,500 a year) required visits to program sites as far away as the Virgin Islands and Puerto Rico, it was mainly a desk job. He reviewed proposals for grants, read and wrote reports, and went to meetings: unit meetings, division meetings, department meetings.

"How's Gretch and the kids?" he asked.

"Fine!" I said. "Gretch is working on her doctorate. Conrad's a junior in college now. He wants to teach. He's been working

204

at camp. He likes working with kids."

Ray shook his head as if he couldn't believe the passage of time and was remembering his junior-high-school days when he used to pick Conrad up at the day care center.

"Little Gretch," I continued, "is fifteen now and the twins are ten. How's Ana and your kids?"

"Fine, so far," he answered. Ray had been separated for almost a year, after being married for ten years. "We're careful not to use the kids in any destructive way. I take them on weekends. Ana's mother takes them when she's working. We had explained the situation to them. They seem to be taking it okay."

"How old are they now?"

"Melissa's eight and Ramon's four."

"They sure are handsome kids," I said, remembering how impressed I was when I last saw them.

"How's Ana doing?" I asked, and immediately felt that was an awkward question.

"Ana and I are still friends. We talk. We try to be sensitive to the kids. . . ." Ray's answer was smooth, reassuring, and disconcertingly interspersed with such irritating words as "feeling tones."

Ray and I drifted over to the chairs and sat across the conference table from each other, stretching our legs out, slouching with our elbows on the armrests of the chairs. I told Ray about the proposed reunion and about writing the story of the Tumbleweeds.

"Fine!" he said. "Do you want me to tell Joe?"

"Okay, good!" I said. "I'll contact Angel, Israel and Edgar. I haven't seen them for a while."

Ray went on to tell me how he and Joe, both bachelors now, occasionally get together in the Under the Stairs restaurant— one of the "in" places for the young, integrated middle class that came to the West Side with urban renewal. Here he and Joe meet friends and talk about their kids, the burdens of paying for two households, jobs, and women.

"You know my mother's going back to Puerto Rico?"

"No! Really! I know you said she was going someday, but those 'somedays' seldom arrive."

"Yeah, she and Carlos bought a house in Caguas. It's small and it's in a development, but it's all they need. She has her retirement pension. She worked twenty years at that factory. And she gets a small disability check from Social Security for the time she hurt her shoulder. So she's secure. Anything Carlos makes, if he finds work—it's hard to get a job now in Puerto Rico—will be gravy. She feels fine and she's only forty-nine."

After a short lunch in the sixth-floor employees' cafeteria, Ray had to leave for a meeting. He waited with me for the elevator.

"Come over to the apartment for a drink tomorrow," Ray suggested, "and we can talk some more."

Early evening the next day found us sitting on kitchen chairs out on the small fifth-floor balcony of Ray's three-room apartment in Park West Village, a middle-income development, at the corner of 100th Street and Columbus Avenue. We put our feet up on the balcony railing as we drank beer from Pilsner glasses and looked out at the stars, the streetlights and the lit-up windows of the surrounding buildings. A faint breeze chased the day's sweltering heat.

With an edge of weariness, Ray talked about his job. The federal appropriation establishing the Office of Youth Development was to end in another year. "It's just as well," he said. "I'm ready to move on. I had a chance to travel and that was good, but most of my time is with paper, behind a desk. And we can't start any new programs. We're just monitoring the ones we have going. . . . I think I'd like to get back to working directly with people and communities, planning programs with them. I don't know about running a community center. At least not for a while. I was at East Harlem for five years and that was draining."

"Do you have any prospects?" I asked.

"Lucky I didn't take that assistant commissioner's job with

the Youth Services Agency," said Ray, laughing.

"That's right!" I said, remembering the major scandal which hit that agency soon after Ray was offered the job.

Ray had also been offered a high-ranking position in the Dominican Republic, setting up social service programs for the entire country. He could have worked for the Puerto Rican government, but the arrangement hadn't been quite right. But he had met Governor Rafael Hernández Colón and had helped prepare some material which the governor used in a major speech about federal programs in Puerto Rico.

Ray had turned down the directorship of the Puerto Rican Studies Department at Rutgers. He had taught one course in group work at the Columbia University School of Social Work. "I like teaching," said Ray. "I think I'd like to get into it full-time, sometime in the future. Right now, it doesn't pay enough."

Ray mentioned that the Childrens Aid Society wanted him to come back—in their main office as a program director for all their community centers. A Puerto Rican classmate of Ray's at the Columbia School of Social Work, who was now on the selection committee for Ford fellowships, told Ray he could probably get a grant to work on a Ph.D. degree. The most lucrative offers would have involved him in politics. "And I don't want any part of the infighting and hassling that goes with politics," said Ray emphatically.

"Someday," added Ray with a sigh of fatigue, as he looked out at the sky, "I'd like to live in Puerto Rico . . . in the country. Have a garden, raise some animals . . . earn just enough to live on."

After another beer, Ray's mood lightened. We reminisced and laughed about job experiences we had in common. Ray began speaking with much more confidence about himself. "I think I've put the pieces together and am now ready to move on. The past year especially has forced me to be introspective, because of my broken marriage. I was super sensitive about the breakup because of my own mother and father. But then I accepted that marriages do break up—and kids don't have to be screwed up because of it.

"And my father and I recently came to terms. He's sick, you know, and not expected to live. The kids have gotten to know him. He likes them. They're going to miss him. Of course, I feel guilty about not having come to an understanding sooner, but I'm glad we settled things before it's too late.

"I also have a better idea of what I want to do now. I turned down being politically used as a Puerto Rican. I'm not out to make it politically—to be a commissioner or something like that. And I don't feel I have to prove I'm a Puerto Rican. Down deep I know I'm a *jíbaro*, so I don't have to show it off, or be or do something just because I'm a Puerto Rican. Like when they changed the spelling of my name from Ramon to Raymond. I got used to 'Raymond.' All my documents are 'Raymond.' Later, when I became more aware of who I was, it wasn't worth the trouble to change it back. I knew who I was and the spelling of my name wouldn't change that.

"I'm also aware of my limitations. I'm quiet and soft-spoken and not the politician type. My idea of making it is not making more money or having a big position." Ray chuckled and added, "Of course, I want to get out of debt.

"No, I want to do something that is gratifying to me and makes a contribution in some small way. I need to feel I did what I could to make an impact."

"On what," I asked, "do you want to make an impact?"

"Well," he answered, "I want to help, in some way, other Puerto Ricans, but I feel a commitment to poor people in general. I'm conscious of the needy everywhere, the rights of people. And I think I'm more conscious because of my own experiences."

It was late in the afternoon, several days later, when I stopped by the Goddard-Riverside Community Center to see Joe, as is my practice when in the neighborhood. School had just let out and chattering, jostling children were beginning to pile up around the desk at the center's entrance.

Joe sees me through the window of his sidewalk-level office. Smiling broadly, he waves me in. I pick my way through the swarm of kids, wincing slightly in the hall as the magnified din of high-pitched voices hits my ears. I step into Joe's office.

"Freddy, I want you to come to my graduation. I'm finally graduating from Bronx Community."

"I'm honored!" I say, opening my eyes wide with surprise. "How long has it been?"

"Ten years," says Joe, still smiling.

"Ten years!" I say, shaking Joe's hand. "Congratulations! That's great! You really hung in there. . . . Are you sure you have enough tickets?"

"Sure! I know the guy who gives them out. Ray's comin', too. And my mother, my kids and some friends."

"Good!" I say. "Now we have a double reason to celebrate. Did Ray tell you about the reunion?"

"Yeah, he did, and I think the best place to have it is at your house."

"Poppi!" says Lysette, Joe's daughter, a big, soft, rosy-cheeked nine-year-old, as she breezes into the office followed by her seven-year-old sister, Adrian, who is much smaller, but has her father's coloring and solid build. "Poppi!"

"Whooah!" says Joe with feigned severity. "Say hello to Mr. Johnson first." They dutifully say hello. "Now what is it?" says Joe, smiling again.

Joe spends a great deal of time with his daughters even though he has been living in his own apartment, far uptown, since his second and seemingly final separation from Rudi over a year ago. Lysette comes to the center after school and Adrian after the day care center. They join in the regular program until their mother gets home from work. I remembered that Joe once told my wife he was glad he had daughters because the whole area of father-son relationships was conflicted for him and he wasn't sure of himself. That was a good insight for Joe to have, I thought.

Lysette and Adrian ask their father about going on a trip. Joe

209

gives them the rough-gruff treatment, asking them questions about how, where, whom they were going with and when they would return. I can see in Lysette and Adrian's eyes that they aren't taking their father's grilling too seriously. They seem relaxed and happy. And Joe is obviously proud and concerned about them.

The separation from Rudi had been hard on Joe, especially in the beginning when he had to live alone.

But Joe was bouncing back. "You have to meet Judy, my new girlfriend, Freddy. *Muy saludable* [very healthy] and very athletic."

"I'd like to meet her."

Joe, sitting in his swivel chair near the corner of his desk, alternately waves to people passing on the sidewalk and says hello to those in the hall who poke their heads in the door as they pass. A secretary calls him out of the office. I stand and occupy myself by looking at a couple of the larger gold-plated trophies fastened to marble bases with inscribed nameplates indicating they had been awarded to Goddard-Riverside teams for winning softball or basketball tournaments. Among the plaques and photos I notice a plaque I hadn't seen before: a "Citation of Merit" awarded to Joe by the United Fund of Greater New York. Joe sweeps back into the office.

He begins to describe how several minor Puerto Rican politicians have been warming up to him, soliciting his support, inviting him to political dinners and testimonials and asking him to put in an appearance at this or that affair. (Joe's friend and vice-president in his Rainbow Association, Pete Rivera, was soon to become assistant district attorney of the Bronx.)

"But I don't give them any bullshit," says Joe, sounding apologetic. "I give it to 'em straight, Freddy. I don't give 'em any bullshit. No bullshit, Freddy!"

"Keep all the doors open," I say, trying to reassure Joe that I didn't think he would be corrupted on contact.

We talk briefly about Joe's most recent job offer. Though after he has had a bad day Joe sometimes talks convincingly about making a move, he usually decides to stay. He feels secure at Goddard-Riverside. He's been here full-time for thirteen years. He earns $16,537 a year. And he, along with several others from settlements around the city, will be honored at the 75th Annual Celebration of the United Neighborhood Houses, as one of the "Leaders of Tomorrow."

"What happens," I ask, "now that you are finished at Bronx Community?"

"I think I'm gonna go to Adelphi School of Social Work. You remember George Lockhart, the camp director at Goddard-Riverside, and Bill Stafford from the Youth Board?"

"Yeah."

"Well, they teach out at Adelphi and they want me to come there. In one year I could get a bachelor's degree in Social Welfare because they would give me a year's credit for 'life experience' and Goddard would give me time off to take a full load of classes. After that I could go for my master's degree."

"Sounds like a good deal to me," I say. For several minutes we discuss the pros and cons of the latest job offer and going to social work school. Then I get up to leave. "See you at graduation," I say.

"*Cójelo suave!*" says Joe.

"*Cójelo suave!*" say I.

27

On the phone, Edgar nearly bubbled over with enthusiasm at the mention of a reunion. Briefly we updated each other— whom we had seen and what they were doing and what we were doing. Edgar said he worked at The Gym, a health salon, where he taught exercises and simple tumbling. He expected to be working there full-time soon, but he also worked part-time in the diamond-cutting business.

I told him I had quit my last job training social workers and was considering writing about the Tumbleweeds.

"That would be real good," said Edgar. "I have all the contracts for the shows we did. And pictures of the act, too, if you need them."

"That's great!" I said. "Can you bring them when we meet tomorrow?"

I waited for Edgar in the lobby of the Lerner Building, at the corner of Thirty-third Street and Tenth Avenue. It was a tall, bustling, functional building, with a rough cement-finished exterior, which housed offices, light manufacturing and diamond-cutting shops.

Edgar stepped out of an elevator a few minutes after twelve noon, our agreed-upon meeting time. He was the same five feet, six inches as Joe, but now, with an extra inch of heel on his highly polished shoes, he looked a little taller. He was as broad-

212

shouldered as ever, but thinner than I had seen him in recent years. His hair was fashionably long and hung down to his collar in the back. His red print shirt had a long, wide mod collar and his blue polyester trousers were tight around his barrel thighs and flared at the cuff. His sunny, smiling, dimpled face was as always.

"You look trim and fit," I said, shaking hands. Edgar attributed his slim figure to his special diet and to his being "into health foods."

"Is it possible for me to see where you work before we eat lunch?" I asked.

"Sure!" he said.

We took the elevator to the fourteenth floor. Edgar peeked through an eye-level slit in a heavy metal door. A buzzer rang and he pushed open the door. We went in and passed through a large room, vibrating and whirring with the sound of many small electric motors rotating thin, sharp grinding disks which were cutting into tiny objects clamped into mounted vises.

"Those are cutting the diamonds," said Edgar. "They are fixed and left to cut them. Sometimes it takes half a day to cut through a diamond. Diamonds are hard. After they're cut we get them in here." We walked into a room with three long workbenches. About fifteen men, sitting on stools at intervals along the benches, were seemingly engaged in a process of holding a diamond up to the light while looking at it through a jeweler's eyepiece, then fixing the diamond to the end of an instrument similar to the arm of a record player. Next the arm, with the diamond where the record-playing needle would ordinarily be, was placed on what looked like a spinning LP record, which of course was really a grinding stone. The process was repeated over and over again.

"This is what I do," said Edgar. "I'm called a 'bunker.' I grind down the facets on diamonds. You know, like the grain in wood, diamonds have a grain, too, which we call facets. It is what makes diamonds sparkle." Edgar took a small diamond, which

213

he called a "pansy," out of his workbench drawer to illustrate. He handled the "pansy" with his three-fingered right hand, using his thumb and third finger with dexterity. He gave me the eyepiece and the diamond, instructing me to look for the facets. "The experienced guys," Edgar continued, "get the big stones, the emeralds and rubys. I still get the 'pansys.' "

Looking around, I saw that half the "bunkers" were Orthodox Jews in dark clothes, with yarmulkes on their heads. The other half were Puerto Ricans, who had radios on their benches, *Playboy* centerfolds taped up on the wall next to them. Edgar introduced me to his cousin, a dark, handsome Latin about forty years old, with gold in his front teeth, who got Edgar into the diamond business a couple of years ago. Edgar described his cousin as one of the most experienced "bunkers" in the shop. He had trained Edgar over a period of several months, an apprenticeship that ordinarily would have cost several hundred dollars. Edgar said his cousin had learned the trade in a diamond-cutting shop in Puerto Rico, where many skilled New York Puerto Rican diamond cutters came from.

"I rent work space," said Edgar, "and buy my own tools. I also have to replace the grinding wheels." He handed me a gray, fine-grit grinding wheel to examine. "Like all these guys, I'm in business for myself. It's piecework. You get paid by the diamond."

"Are there fringe benefits?" I asked.

"No; no benefits, vacation or pension. We pay for that ourselves if we want it. . . . I only work mornings here. I work at The Gym in the afternoon. Between the two places, in a good week, I average three hundred to three hundred twenty-five dollars a week. But there were times when the diamond business was slow and I didn't make anything here. Business has been picking up lately."

During lunch we continued our discussion. "Last I remem-

214

ber," I said, "you were working for the National League of Nursing."

"That's right; I was there for almost six years. I started as a shipping clerk at seventy dollars a week. Then I became a keypunch operator and worked my way up to one hundred thirty dollars a week."

"Why did you leave?"

"It was so boring," said Edgar with a pained expression. "It was so boring, I don't know how I stayed that long, sitting at the keypunch all day long, punching letters and numbers on cards. It was mostly research statistics. Boring! . . . Now it's better. With the diamonds I make my own hours. Pretty soon I might be able to work at The Gym full-time, but it depends on business and somebody leaving. . . . And I'm also working on a new act," said Edgar, laughing. "With a girl. I never give up. I still want to be in show business."

Walking to the subway, Edgar talked warmly about his kids, but awkwardly about his wife, Lydia. It was fairly clear it was only a matter of time before he and Lydia broke up. I tried to ease his discomfort by telling him Ray and Joe had been in the same boat.

The Gym, where Edgar and I had arranged to meet two days later at six in the evening, was on Fifty-fourth Street, near Third Avenue, where the rent for their advertised "7000 square feet of exercise area, dressing rooms, saunas, showers, waiting room with video tapes of gymnastic events" was three thousand dollars a month. It's run by Gary Novickij, a young Russian ex-soccer player and disciple of Kounovsky, a well-known figure in physical culture circles. Men and women using The Gym pay seven dollars for an hour-long class (limited to six students), in which "increased muscle tone, suppleness, and stamina are developed through the use of the basic techniques in tumbling and apparatus."

215

"C'mon in and watch for a while," said Edgar. "I have to teach a class."

"Okay," I said, glad for an opportunity to see Edgar in action. The exercise rooms on the sixth floor were bright, clean and uncluttered. Gray and blue vinyl-covered mats lined the floors. One large room contained basic gymnastic apparatus—rings, parallel bars, side horse and climbing ropes.

Edgar went into one of the small exercise rooms. He exchanged greetings with five clean-shaven, well-groomed men in their late thirties, wearing shorts, T-shirts, sweat socks and sneakers. They looked like the $40,000-a-year advertising executives Edgar had said some of them were.

Edgar led them in light warm-up exercises. Then he had them do some interesting stretching movements, which were probably specials of the house. Then Edgar began what was obviously *his* special.

"Squat down, put your hands on the mat.... Duck your head. Keep bending forward until you can look up between your legs and see the ceiling...."

Edgar was teaching them a front roll—the same front roll we had done when we started tumbling so very long ago.

"Roll on the back of your shoulders—not your head or neck. ... Grab your knees as you roll forward. ... Stand up!"

The step-by-step instructions were exactly the same, including our distinctive grabbing of the knees at the end.

The men seemed to enjoy the exercise. They jumped up with enthusiasm after completing the roll, which they did very well. They looked to Edgar for a nod and a few words of approval, which he gave. Their faces expressed a sense of satisfaction.

All the way home I was smiling.

I wasn't startled by Angel's conservative blue, stylish, wide-lapeled business suit or his close-cropped beard or his serious demeanor or his modern air-conditioned office with the beige floors and walls on the third floor of the new American Brands

Building on Park Avenue. After all, I had seen Angel in business suits before and I had seen him at work running office machines. But in the back of my mind I still carried this picture of Angel Rodriguez as the young, reckless, chaotic, *mañana* street vagabond. So I was startled by the incongruity of seeing Angel sitting behind a big, tidy desk surrounded by the artifacts of organization: an "in" and an "out" box, a telephone with a row of extension buttons, alphabetized files, a rotary address file, an adding machine, a desk file, a typewriter, pens, pencils, rulers, "From the desk of Angel Rodriguez" note pads at the ready, an "American Brands Directory" and two volumes of the *Manual of Procedures.*

He smiled as I came in, that same big smile, and he had the same alert, mischievous gleam in his eye. Yet there was also something subdued, quiet and somber about him that I hadn't noticed before. He and Ray had turned out to be the tallest of the five boys, but Angel was huskier than Ray. He had an extra layer of muscle and flesh all over his still symmetrical body. He weighed one hundred seventy pounds; five pounds less than I. He looked powerful.

"How's Cookie?" I asked.

"Fine!" he said. "She looks forward to seeing you again."

"How long have you been married now?" I asked.

"Twelve years," he said, and without a trace of self-consciousness, he added, "and we still love each other."

"I'm glad," I said. "And how long," I went on, "have you been on this job?"

"Ten years."

"Boy, are you the steady one!"

We talked about our families. Angel's son Jesse was now twelve and their second son, Oggy, was two. He and Cookie were thinking of maybe having a third child, but they weren't sure. Angel asked about my kids and my wife and he told me what little recent information he had about Edgar and Israel, and I told him about Joe and Ray. He mentioned that he had seen Ray being interviewed on TV.

217

After ten years in the mail room, Angel had just been appointed office manager of the Mail Department at an annual salary of $12,500.

"Two heart attacks," he said, "retired the previous office managers. I wasn't looking for the promotion because I was waiting to get into the Police Department. But now, with a couple more increments, this job will look even better. Besides, it's beginning to look like the city's in all kinds of money trouble. They might not be hiring anymore."

"How did you come to be interested in the police?" I asked.

"First I wanted to be a fireman. They were hiring at the time and it's a civil service job with security, good pay and a good pension. It was just a good job. But you had to have a high school diploma, so I started studying for the high school equivalency exam at the same time I studied for the fireman's exam. I took the equivalency twice and failed it twice. On the third try I passed it. By then I had so much practice I passed the police exam the first time. Then I wanted to be a policeman."

"Were you interested in any specific aspect of police work?" I asked.

"From what I understand," he said, "they need Spanish-speaking cops. And they need cops who understand the people —and who understand some of the problems I lived through. That's what I think I could do well—work with people. I'd like to help others profit from my experiences. I'd like to pay back for the help I got. I think I'd even like to have a Tumbleweeds group like you did."

"Seems to me," I said, "you work with people here."

Angel agreed and proudly pointed out that he supervised fifty-three people, who included twenty "co-ops" (high school students who alternately worked and attended school). "C'mon. Let me show you around." Angel began introducing me to the employees in his Mail Department. Some of his introductions were worthy of the M.C.'s out of our past.

"This is the most important person in the mail room," he said of the teletype operator, a middle-aged woman with an Italian surname, who denied the assessment, but obviously appreciated the remark.

"This guy is the work horse," said Angel of a leathery older man tying bundles of mail. "I don't know what I would do without him. And Frank here is my right hand. He's in charge when I'm gone." He introduced me to an articulate, unassuming Puerto Rican in his early twenties, who went to college in the evening. Angel obviously liked the young man, but out of earshot, he said, "That guy is planning to go back to Puerto Rico. He says he feels his place is there, with his people, working for his own country." Angel's face frowned, as if he had thought a lot about this. "And I have nothing against that. That's okay for him. I respect that. But I feel my place is here. I've been here a long time. My kids are growing up here. There's a lot of work to be done here. There's a lot of my people here and they're going to be here in the future."

A red-faced man with white curly hair, wearing a blue-gray suit that matched the color of his eyes, walked past and in a gruff, flippant voice said to Angel, "Hi there, Geraldo!" Angel offhandedly returned his greeting.

"Some guys call me Geraldo," explained Angel, "because they say I look like Geraldo Rivera of Channel Seven News."

I was a little suspicious of Angel's being called "Geraldo," because I remembered the times when, having a beer in the West Side bars and hearing the old timers—who were immigrants themselves—all Puerto Ricans were called "Pedro."

"How did he feel," I asked, "about you becoming the boss?"

Angel smiled and said the man had jestingly said, "The Puerto Ricans are pushing me out of my neighborhood, and now I have to work for one."

We returned to Angel's office. I leaned back in one of the upholstered chairs, and Angel began to talk about his son Jesse.

"I tell Jesse, 'You better appreciate me. You're lucky. I never had a father to play with me when I was a kid.' I do try to take time to play with Jesse, even if I'm tired. I'd like for him to have a stable home, not like mine, with fathers comin' and goin'. Like, Edgar says to me, 'Let's do an act,' but I can't go runnin' around like that anymore. I got other things to do. With a family, it's not worth it."

An opened letter on Angel's desk caught his eye. He picked it up, smiled and handed it to me. "Fred, I thought you'd get a kick out of seeing this." It was a formal congratulatory letter from the president of the American Brands Company, informing Angel Rodriguez that he, having recently joined the "management team," was now entitled to use the "Executive Dining Room." Visions of an anemic twelve-year-old Angel Rodriguez scrounging in the park for uneatable berries flashed in my head. "That's great!" I said, giving him a knowing look, indicating that I, too, saw the irony.

The red-faced man who had passed in the hall earlier, the one who had called Angel "Geraldo," breezed into the office and with an air of casual irritation began asking Angel questions about procedures and assignments. Angel introduced him to me as Mr. Shanahan, and then quickly answered the questions. He then thanked the man for getting him the king-size thermos bottle, left over from one of the company's promotions, which Angel had wanted for his upcoming Florida vacation. Angel picked up a square package, neatly wrapped in brown paper and tied with string, with a package handle attached to the top.

"Don't mention it!" said Shanahan. "Don't mention it! I didn't pay for it!"

"But you wrapped it up for me," said Angel.

"It's nuttin!" he said. "It's nuttin!"

"And you didn't have to give me a going-away-on-vacation card," said Angel, holding up the white envelope, confronting Shanahan with this evidence of sentiment.

"Awwrr! I stole it off the rack," said Shanahan, with a denigrating wave of his arm, as he walked out of the office.

Angel's soft brown eyes were shining. He smiled as he put the card back in the envelope. In a warm, private voice, he read the bold letters on the envelope: "Geraldo."

Angel was an active member of the company's bowling team. He brought Cookie to the social events. Occasionally he had a "night out" with his buddies from the company. He coached the women's softball team. "Why don't you come," he said, "and watch them play tomorrow in Central Park?"

"Okay," I said.

Angel and I got together once more before the reunion. I had told him that my wife and I were going up to the State University at New Paltz to visit our son Conrad. Angel suggested that he take us in his car. He wanted to see the college and he wanted to give his family a day in the country.

So Angel, Cookie, Jesse, Oggy, my wife and I drove up the New York State Thruway toward the university. On the way Angel talked of his determination to send Jesse to college. "No one in the Rodriguez family has ever gone to college. Jesse will be the first. And if I have to work two jobs to send him, I will."

I suggested that when we got to the university we ask Conrad to take Jesse on a tour of the college campus to see the classrooms, labs, dorms, library and gymnasium, "as a way of getting him used to the idea of going to college." Angel was interested in that. So was Jesse. Cookie wanted to go, too.

Several days later Angel called me on the phone. "We had a good time at Conrad's school," he said. "I asked Jesse how he felt about the visit and he said this is what he wants to do, go to college. And I felt good about that. But you know, Fred," Angel added plaintively, "I also felt, as I was walkin' around the campus, I would have liked to be one of those students myself, going to college. And I've been thinkin', I'd like to try it. I have free time. I'm gettin' bored watching television all the time. And what do I do on weekends? We visit Cookie's mother or her sister or my sisters, I go fishin' once in a while and fool around with the bike—you know, the motorcycle. I'm lookin' for something else to do. Of course, I'd have to go nights in the city. And my job encourages going to college. In fact, they pay for courses related to your work. Cookie wants me to try. A little at a time, I thought. Only a few credits to see if I can do the work."

And then, in a much more determined voice, he said, "So what can you tell me about getting started?"

28

Joe and I had a difficult time finding Israel. We hadn't seen him in over a year. He wasn't at his old address or his old job. The telephone company wouldn't give us his number because it was "unlisted." Joe ran one of his informal checks and found out that Israel lived somewhere in the Frederick Douglass Houses, a low-income public housing project of several hundred apartments beginning at 104th Street and Columbus Avenue. Although Ray lived in an adjacent development, he hadn't seen Israel. I checked back with Angel and he told me Israel still worked for the Holiday Inn parking garage. I called there, but Israel wasn't on duty yet. His was the four-to-midnight shift. I left my number. That old feeling of frustration began to come over me just as it used to whenever I chased around the streets looking for Israel or Angel, trying to find them in time for a show or a practice.

But this time Israel called me back a few minutes after he had got my message. He was glad to hear from me and apologized for not keeping in touch, but he added, "Even though I still got problems, everything else is pretty good." We started telling each other of recent events, but had to cut ourselves short because Israel had to get back to work. We made arrangements to talk further at my apartment at ten o'clock Tuesday morning, Israel's day off. Israel said he liked the idea of my writing about them and the reunion. He looked forward to seeing everyone again, especially Angel.

Tuesday morning, Israel appeared at my door at ten o'clock sharp. He was clean-shaven; his curly hair was now wavy and reached his collar. He wore a casual print shirt and an expensive-looking leather jacket—"from Mexico," he said, fingering the lapels. Except for a broadening of the shoulders, he looked the same, trim and firm. His one-hundred-thirty-pound top-mounter body was all muscle and bone.

"You look good!" I said, genuinely impressed.

"And you look exactly the same," he said.

"I'm in good shape," I answered. "Mostly from tennis, but I still do a little hand balancing with Erika." Israel remembered Erika, one of the twins, because I had taken her with me several times to the Twenty-third Street YMCA to work out with the Galaxios.

"You should see my daughter, Teresa," said Israel with enthusiasm and pride. "She's two—my only child with my wife. She stands in my hand. She's not afraid. She can do a front roll on the bed. She likes it. But my wife doesn't want me to teach her. She's afraid she will want to go out of the house to go on the stage." Israel smiled as if his wife's fears were not to be taken seriously.

We sat in the dining room and leaned back in the imitation-leather office chairs, our elbows on the armrests. Israel swiveled slightly from side to side as he looked out the side windows at the Hudson River just beyond the trees of Riverside Park. He refused every offer of food and drink. Sanka was the strongest thing he drank—and that "only once in a while." Recently he had taken to drinking hot Ovaltine, which he fixed for his daughter in the mornings. "According to the news reports I've been reading," I said, "you have to be careful what you eat today."

"I eat whole-wheat bread," said Israel. "You taught us to eat whole-wheat bread instead of white bread."

I had forgotten. "If I did that," I said, "I'm glad." I went on

224

to explain that scientists have come up with new findings about the harmful effects of some foods. "Either the food has too many chemicals or it's too high in cholesterol. Meat, for example, especially beef, isn't the best source of protein."

Israel listened attentively, nodding his head sympathetically in understanding. But after I had finished explaining my point about meat, Israel, with absolute aplomb, without any indication of disagreement, and in a voice pitched to equanimity, said, "I eat meat twice a day—every day." By the way he said it, I knew my cautions were but mere logic. Obviously, eating meat twice a day had a significance for Israel going beyond considerations of health. It was as if he ate meat twice a day to celebrate his having achieved—in at least one area of living—the good life. And eating meat, not cheese or protein substitutes, was the symbol which, twice a day, reaffirmed that he no longer had to feel hungry; that he was "eating high off the hog."

Angel and Edgar had told me that after Israel stopped drinking he had gradually become a habitual user of cough medicine. I suspected Israel had become addicted to the codeine found in some nonprescriptive cough medicines. I asked him about it. He said he used to take cough medicine for his asthma and whenever he felt "lousy." The cough medicine, he said "makes me sick now. I can't use it anymore."

"That's just as well," I said.

Israel smoked continuously. "But I keep in shape," he said, "running up and down the five flights of stairs at the garage, getting and parking the cars. And sometimes when things are slow I do a few handstands in the back. The guys at work ask why I don't go back to being an acrobat. I tell 'em I'm too old for that kind of pounding. They're amazed when I tell them I'm thirty-one; they thought I was in my twenties. But you know, Fred, I think I could still do all the old tricks."

"I'll bet you could," I said.

I asked Israel about his previous job, driving a laundry truck.

"My wife," he said, "told me to take this parking job because they have a union, Blue Cross and Blue Shield, and the money is pretty good. With tips I make more than two hundred dollars a week."

Throughout the morning Israel continually prefaced his explanations with, "My wife said . . ." or "Josie said . . ." or "my wife wants . . ." and "I have to see if Josie has any plans. . . ." There was no indication he felt nagged, nor was he complaining. He was very positive about his wife.

"Why do you have an unlisted number?" I asked.

"So people don't bother me."

"What do you mean?"

Without hesitation, Israel said, "When I'm not workin' I like to be home. My wife wants me to be home. I eat and watch TV. Sometimes I take the kids to the park." Israel's face brightened. "You know, I took my daughter to the Bronx Zoo last week. That's some place! I've never been there before." Israel picked up answering my question by describing how each day after his wife goes to work and Rafael, now twelve, and Nilda, now fifteen, go to school, he fixes breakfast for himself and his daughter. Then he dresses her, combs her hair and plays with her until he has to go to work. Then he turns her over to his wife's mother, who lives near the Holiday Inn garage.

"Sometimes I clean the house or cook," he said. "Mostly I just stay home. My wife says I'm a 'house person,' and I guess she's right."

Israel said he watched TV every day. He looked forward to it. Although he watched daytime interviews and quiz shows, he also watched news programs and *60 Minutes*. He was fascinated by science and animal programs. "And I watch sports. The Mets and the Knicks. And gymnastics whenever it's on. But lately I have been watching those crooks. Nixon's friends. Boy, that's something!"

"You mean the Watergate business?"

"Yeah! That's why I never liked politics. They're all crooks!"

Israel went on to say he never voted and never intended to. For a moment I tried to think of some political figure who might give a little balance to Israel's cynicism, but every day there

226

were new revelations of corruption everywhere in the country and it seemed you couldn't be sure of anyone.

Israel mentioned that he hadn't seen his married brothers and sisters for years and I assumed he was back to elaborating on his answer to my original question about the unlisted number. He had got pulled into some of their domestic squabbles and he didn't want any more of it. "Even Noelia I haven't seen for six months," he added.

He talked about the dangers of just hanging around the street, the bars or the poolroom. Once he even got arrested walking to the store. The cops had raided a sidewalk crap game and grabbed everyone in the vicinity. He was released only when the crap shooters swore Israel had nothing to do with the game. He recounted a series of other incidents he knew of where someone was shot or stabbed. Then he laughed and said, "You gotta watch out for these Puerto Ricans—they'll mess you up."

Israel looked out the side window, up toward Grant's Tomb and the George Washington Bridge. Absent-mindedly he took a black-handled switchblade knife out of his pocket and flipped it in his hand. I couldn't tell how long the blade would be when opened, but it would be a lethal size. When Israel caught my disapproving glance, he smiled and said, "This is only in case I'm getting beat up bad. If you get mugged today, it's bad. More vicious than it used to be."

"Take care," I said, "you don't create even bigger problems for yourself."

Two hours had passed. It was noon. Israel had to go. We arranged to meet again a week from Friday.

"By the way, Israel," I asked as I cleared the coffee cups, "where did you go when you first disappeared—after your first marriage and all your troubles?"

"Oh," he said, smoothing his hair with his hand, "you mean before I went to the old man's house, Edgar's father's house. I stayed for about a year with Orlando. Remember him from Eightieth Street?"

227

"Oh, yeah," I said, nodding my head. I remembered him. Orlando was one of the older homosexuals whom Israel, Angel and the others visited and exploited when they were younger. The boys had always spoken well of him. Israel didn't bat an eye when he said he stayed with Orlando. For a second I didn't know what to make of it, but then I thought that was about the time Israel was probably looking for a little mothering.

Friday morning slipped by and Israel hadn't come. I called his home. No answer. In the afternoon, when Israel would ordinarily be working, I called the garage. They said Israel wasn't working there anymore. That evening I went to his apartment in the Frederick Douglass housing project. Josefa let me in. She was almost in tears. In a desperate whisper she said, "Israel started drinking again. The first time since he stopped. . . ."

I went to the bedroom. Israel was watching television out of half-closed eyes. He was in his underclothes, partially covered by a blanket. He seemed dulled and drugged. He had a large black-and-blue mark on his shoulder and stomach. His eyes were bloodshot. His answers to my inquiries about his condition were vague. He felt sick.

I told him I was worried because I had called the garage and they had told me he wasn't working there any longer. Israel admitted he had got into a fight with the foreman. "But he's not the big boss. I'm gonna see the boss on Monday about my job."

I suggested we talk again tomorrow if he felt better. "We could talk about your problem with the job if you want." Israel nodded his head tiredly in agreement.

Josefa walked with me down the three short flights of urine-smelling stairs past heavily graffitied walls. She told me that after an argument a few days ago with one of the foremen, Israel "started drinking, only a little, but soon he was drinking so much he couldn't drive the cars. They sent him home. He fell down and the door hit his shoulder. That's how he got those marks on his body. I took him to Roosevelt. They gave him tranquilizers and I took him home. They said bring him back tomorrow if he is still drinking."

228

Before I left Josefa, she said, "He doesn't want me to tell you about the drinking, so . . . please, don't say anything I told you."
I felt terrible. Some social worker I was! Some friend I was! I resolved to work it out so Israel could feel comfortable talking to me when he felt things closing in on him. I had to change whatever it was I was doing so Israel could get past feeling ashamed and hiding all his big troubles. I had never been much help to Israel, I thought, especially when he most needed help.

Saturday morning Josefa called and said Israel was still sick and couldn't meet me. The next day, Sunday, I called Israel. No answer. I called again in the afternoon. Still no answer. All day long I envisioned Israel's inexorable deterioration, the classic pattern of the alcoholic: he drinks and loses his job, causing more drinking. He fails to be a father to his kids, and a husband to his wife. He fails his beloved Teresa. More guilt and more drinking. He drinks up the food money, the rent money, and the money for the bills. He gets sicker (the doctor told Israel drinking again could kill him). The alcoholic hits bottom.

Monday morning I went to Israel's home. No one was there. I left a note, knowing that if Israel was drunk, at least Josefa would see it and know I'd been there. I went to the corner bar, half looking for Israel even though my primary intention was to use the telephone to call Roosevelt Hospital. Israel wasn't in the bar, and according to the admitting officer at Roosevelt, he wasn't there either.

I was gone all day Monday. When I returned home about eight o'clock in the evening, my older daughter had a message for me. "Israel called," she said. "He's at work, at the garage. Call him there anytime. He says you know the number."

A week later, looking clear-eyed, rested and none the worse for his ordeal, Israel walked into my apartment holding little smiling, dimpled Teresa by the hand. We sat down; I poured the coffee. Teresa went off to my daughter Erika's room to play.

Israel's only mention of his relapse was to describe that Monday-morning scene with the boss, who Israel said liked him.

229

According to Israel, the boss said to the foreman, "He stays!"

Although I had in mind to ask Israel questions about our old acrobatic routines, I remembered my resolve to try and open up communications, so I lay back and let Israel take the conversation wherever he wanted it to go. Teresa came into the room again, seemingly to reassure herself her father was still there. She took off her wrist watch, which looked fancy and silvery, and gave it to Israel, telling him in Spanish to hold it. Then she left once more.

Israel, with an air of resignation, drifted into telling me of his financial woes. He had debts, bills, expenses, loans, and interest payments on the loans. Since he earned a reasonable salary and his wife earned a little over the minimum wage and they had a reasonable rent, I asked him why he was so strapped.

"My wife and I really throw money away." He gave as examples their buying furniture on credit, charging his wife's trip to Puerto Rico to visit relatives and taking out a loan to pay off another loan. Taxis were another extravagance. He and his wife often took taxis to and from work. "And it's two dollars here, three dollars there." Israel rationalized some of his own taxi riding, saying he got out of work after midnight and there usually was a long wait for the bus. Beyond that, Israel couldn't convincingly justify his taxi riding to me—or himself.

I jokingly said something about his being out of debt in no time if they would give up taxis. "In fact, you'd soon be rich," I added with a laugh. Israel agreed, but the tone of his voice lacked conviction. He said he expected he would jump in a taxi when he left me today, despite the easy access to subway and bus. Taxi riding for Israel, I concluded, was like his eating meat twice a day. It wasn't a simple matter of dollars and cents or doing what was best.

Israel launched into a complicated story about the problems he had with his color TV. He had bought one of the most expensive models and it hadn't worked very well; several visits from the repairman failed to improve the reception. So Israel had gone back to the store and insisted they change the set. "I got tough with them," he said. "You gotta talk to them like the colored people today. If you don't, they don't listen. I told them, 'You think we don't know nothing and you can get away with givin' us a color TV that doesn't work.' I said, 'I'm gonna report you to the Department of Consumer Affairs . . .' like you told me about. I said, 'You people sold me a banana!' Hey, Fred, is that right—if somethin' don't work you call it a banana?"

"You meant a lemon, I think."

"That's right, a lemon." Israel shook his head disgustedly, mumbling to himself, "Stupid! A banana . . . Stupid!"

Then we both laughed.

"Hey, Fred," he said, "I don't mean to just talk about my problems."

"I'm interested," I said. Having drunk up a pot of coffee, and not wanting to interrupt our conversation by making another pot, I quickly boiled water and poured it over the grains of instant coffee in our cups. We passed each other the cream and sugar.

Israel said he probably would take his vacation in Puerto Rico because he could stay for free in the Holiday Inn in San Juan. "I've never been back. But I want to go and see places in Puerto Rico. I've never seen anything. My brother says don't stay with the relatives because if you are from New York they think you are rich, and if you are staying with them, in their home, and you eat with them, they expect you to buy the meat. They expect you to buy steak for everybody. And down there they think I'm a big shot. My sister sent them pictures of the act and pictures from the newspapers. . . . My wife's mother, Josefa's mother, is going back to Puerto Rico, to stay."

"Ray's mother is going back, too," I said.

"Oh, yeah," said Israel. "I had a dream about her, that I was eating at her house. . . . I haven't seen Ray in a long time. He's a little stuck-up, I think. He lives near me."

"He's real busy," I said.

"Josie wants to go back, too. But I tell her, What jobs could we get down there? And if we get jobs, how much would they

231

pay? There was a guy up here, a Puerto Rican, from the Holiday Inn in San Juan. Down there he does the same job I do. He makes twenty-five dollars a week. I tell him a quarter tip is nothing up here. He thinks it's a lot. And the prices in Puerto Rico, especially San Juan, they say are higher than in New York for some things."

Looking more comfortable and obviously feeling more voluble, Israel leaned back, put his feet on another chair, as I was doing, and said in a confident, philosophical tone, "Things are changing too fast. The ideas of the kids today. They take pills, stay out late, and the way they dance! And the clothes—raggedy old dungarees, and they go to school that way. Skirts up to here. And they wonder why the boys are after them.

"But me and my wife feel school is the most important. That's the future for the kids. That's what we will leave behind. My wife and I are . . . I don't mean washed up, but we are finished with school. We know what we have to do—the work we have to do. And if the kids want to go to college, we have to be ready for that.

"I tell Rafael. I talk frank to him. I tell him I don't have much education, but I know about drugs and how that can mess you up. And I tell him to stay away from gangs. And he listens. . . . And I tell him, When they ask you what your father does, it's nothin'—this job, that job, the laundry, the garage. You can say I was an acrobat. I traveled to Mexico and other far places. I met people. People applauded me. You can show them the pictures. At least I did something. I was somebody. I was an acrobat."

29

The first hour of the reunion seemed like a blur, with everyone chattering away at once. Joe, Ray, Edgar, Angel, Israel, Gretchen and the kids and I were crowded around the large dining room table. Ice cubes clinked in glasses as we sipped beer, Scotch, sangria or ginger ale. We all tried to talk to individuals across the table at the same time we tried listening to the conversations around us. There was a lot of catching up to do. It had been a long time since we were all together—and it seemed good.

Joe and Angel were the only ones who could occasionally command everyone's attention, but then only for a short burst of a sentence. And funny or not, someone made a crack and everyone laughed.

Edgar and Joe went out of their way to be gracious to each other, as if they felt guilty about having had so many arguments in the past.

There was a barely perceptible pattern to the festivities. First there were comments on physical appearance. Someone noticed Joe's few gray hairs and the slight thinning on top. Ray was joshed a little for his chubbiness. Most of the comments were expressions of surprise at how well everyone looked.

"Cookie and I," said Angel to my wife, "hope to look as good as you and Fred when we get your age." Embarrassed, Gretchen stuttered her thanks.

The conversation shifted to checking up on each other's parents. Joe announced that almost all his many relatives, including his father, had gone back to Puerto Rico. Only his mother and his brothers Luis and Georgie remained. Ray said his mother had returned to Puerto Rico only a couple of weeks ago. Edgar said his father had been sick recently, "but considering he's near seventy, he's holding up pretty well."

No one's family or relatives lived in the Eightieth Street neighborhood anymore. Like Angel's sisters and Israel's brothers and sisters, they had moved to the Bronx or the East Side. One of Cookie's sisters had moved with her family to New Jersey and Edgar's brother and his family had moved to Long Island.

Everyone was disappointed to hear that Angel's favorite sister, whom we all knew, had gained weight. "My brother Chago," he said, half laughing, "went to Boston. Then Angel, seemingly wanting to be less public, turned to Joe and me, who were standing closest to him, and said, "That Chago . . . drives around in a Cadillac that's paid for! He's always got a wad of bills. He's been involved in some heavy stuff. He'd better watch it.' "

Then, it seemed, it was time for the "Whatever happened to . . . ?" questions. Most of the people they asked about from the early community center days I had lost touch with or they had died. I was surprised they remembered so many.

Joe announced that Abe Rodriguez, who had often been like a sixth Tumbleweed, was now going to Hunter College. "And you know Sorraida," added Joe, "Sorraida Molina, who used to hang around with us? She's a legislative assistant to Al Blumenthal (New York State assemblyman and majority leader.) I helped her get the job . . . I see Carmen Martell all the time. She's active in El Comité. She's an Independentista."

"You know Mr. Douglass?" asked Israel. Everyone murmured praise or approval of the science teacher at Junior High School 44, a black man. He had been Israel's teacher; the others knew him from the community center. Israel was happy to report, "Rafael, my son, now has Mr. Douglass for a teacher."

"Anyone heard from Titi [Angel Cruz]?" asked Angel. No one had.

Joe and Ray said they had visited Bernice Goodman (who had first hired Joe and Ray at Goddard-Riverside) at her part-time home on the Puerto Rican island of Vieques. They reported that she was writing a book on the prospects and problems of lesbians as adoptive parents.

"I read about her work in the *Times*," I said. "Apparently she's the pioneer in that subject."

"Right," said Ray.

"You all know Alba," I asked, "from the East Harlem Center. She worked her way up to being a family worker—doing social work with families at Union Settlement in East Harlem."

"Freddy," said Joe, "remember Josephine from Eightieth Street—the dark, pretty girl with the high voice; the one you liked?"

"Yeah," I said. "Whatever happened to her?"

Joe shrugged. "This guy she was married to shot a guy on the corner of Seventy-seventh Street."

"I heard about that," I said. Not wanting to hear any more about that part of the story, I changed the subject. "Hey, Ray, remember Jo Ann Borda, the girl who got the PAL Boy and Girl of the Year Award with you, when you were about twelve or so? The one in the picture we have with Mayor Wagner congratulating both of you."

"Yeah," said Ray.

"Well, I met her in Teachers College library, over here at Columbia. She's finishing up her Ph.D. thesis on Hostos, the famous Puerto Rican writer and leader.... By the way, who was Hostos; what did he do?" No one knew.

Angel was downright sentimental. He remembered ancient kindnesses: a single Christmas at the home of a Youth Board

235

worker; a Salvation Army "civilian" who for a few short months before he died encouraged Angel to play the cornet. He remembered co-workers of mine who surely had forgotten him. He talked of his dead brother as if he was never a burden to the family and told us that every Easter he puts flowers on his mother's grave. It was as if he used these meager memories, over the years, to warm himself against the chilly winds of neglect, swelling them in his mind to whatever dimensions he needed to soothe the hurts and feed the hunger.

Then Joe told a story. Everyone listened. Only a few weeks ago, Joe had received a phone call from an official of Operation Springboard, a federally funded rehabilitation program which paid ex-offenders and senior citizens for working in community agencies. The official had said there was an Antonio Lopez there in the office who was saying he knew Joe and wanted to be placed with him in the community center. Joe had told the official, "I never heard of Antonio Lopez!" And that ended that. "Later," Joe said, "Antonio Lopez came around personally to see me. And who do you think it was?" Blank, attentive stares. A couple of heads shook side to side, indicating they didn't know.

"Sonia Fish!" said Joe happily. *"La alcaldesa*—the mayoress of Eightieth Street. He's old now. And he has rheumatism, and couldn't get a job."

Everyone was surprised—and interested. Angel and Israel urged Joe to continue.

Joe said, "I picked up the phone and told those Operation Springboard people I wanted Antonio Lopez assigned to me. Right away! He's workin' with me now, helping with the senior citizens' lunch program. He's doin' very well. He's very domestic, you know." Joe smiled with an air of self-satisfaction.

"That's good," said Israel.

"I'm glad to hear that," said Angel.

Then a sadness came into Joe's face. "Do you know the last thing Sonia Fish said to me that day he came by the center?"

236

Joe paused. Everyone was quiet. "He said, 'But, Joe, you didn't even know my name.' "

I could tell by the way Joe said it that he had felt bad when it happened. The others, hearing the story, felt bad, too. They hadn't known his name either.

Israel, I guess, started the talk about children when he passed around a snapshot of Teresa, which he had taken from his wallet. He bragged about how smart she was and how she could stand in his hand and do a front roll on the bed. The German shepherd next to Teresa in the snapshot, Israel pointed out, was for "protection."

Angel told how active and demanding his son Oggy was at home as contrasted with his orderly behavior in nursery school.

Joe and Ray mentioned that their kids went to Public School 84, a highly regarded, integrated school on West Ninety-first Street. Their kids liked the school and read above grade level. It turned out that all their school-age children read above grade level. Rafael recently got a certificate acknowledging his accomplishments in reading and other subjects. Ray's Melissa read above grade level in Spanish and English. Edgar's son Eric recently got a scholarship to take special art courses at the Metropolitan Museum of Art.

"You should see Adrian, Freddy!" said Joe. "She can do a dive and roll over six kids laying down—like Israel used to do." Adrian was the star of his junior Tumbleweeds group. I had seen her perform recently. At seven, she had that unmistakable Ramos muscle and explosive power.

I was going to remind them not to force their kids to learn acrobatics, but I changed my mind. They knew that as well as I did. And as they talked, it became clear their kids had all kinds of talents and interests, which they encouraged.

While bringing Joe another scotch and water, I heard him say to my wife, "Women's lip, I call it!"

"What do you mean?" Gretchen asked in her subdued, Socratic way.

"Some of them women's libbers talk nonsense," he said. "I'm

237

for equal rights, sharing in marriage, equal pay and opportunity, and that kind of stuff. . . ." Joe's jaw muscles flexed.

"Fair enough," said my wife, with an amused, perplexed look on her face, as if she was still trying to figure out where Joe stood.

Joe firmly summed up. "Now, if anyone were to push Adrian aside from participating in tumbling because she was a girl, they would have to see me."

Joe's discussion—or diatribe—on women's liberation set me to thinking. What was their political perspective? What did they think of other liberation movements? I knew most of them were disdainful of electoral politics and they had a TV-news awareness of what was going on in the world, but they didn't get worked up over civil rights, Vietnam, military versus social spending, or American's support of foreign dictatorships. Even the controversy over the status of Puerto Rico didn't stir their passions. They were neither Independentistas, pro-statehooders or Commonwealthers. Joe and Ray, who were politically the most sophisticated, were still playing it cool. Ray had said, "I'm going to pay more attention to the issue." And Joe had said, "There are some good points on all sides . . . and some negatives on all sides."

Looking back, I realized we all grew up together during the fifties—the Eisenhower years, when political activism wasn't very popular and even I didn't have any compelling political interests.

But the major reason for the boys' "apolitical" orientation was obvious. They had bought the American Dream—and I had mixed feelings about that. Like most Americans, they had a reasonably comfortable standard of living. (Two incomes and birth control had been crucial.) Like most Americans, they pretty much spent what they earned. Although there were differences, they all used credit cards or installment buying to pay for TVs or stereos, or furniture or loans or automobiles. Some had private school and nursery school fees to pay. Edgar even had a mortgage on a plot in the Poconos. They wore the latest fashions. Nothing was secondhand. They believed in hard work, in getting ahead, and like most Americans who get a small piece of the pie, they were wary of changes that might threaten what they had.

A question popped into my head. "Do all your kids," I asked, looking around the table, "speak Spanish?" Everyone nodded. "Oh, yeah," said Ray. "We believe it's important for the kids to identify as Puerto Ricans and be proud of their heritage—and speaking the language is an important way to achieve that."

There was a period of milling around, changing seats, stretching legs, side conversations, refilling of drinks and clearing of dishes. Then Ray and I told everyone that Joe, just last week, had graduated from Bronx Community College. I passed around the graduation program so everyone could see Joe's name on the list of those receiving the Associate in Arts diploma.

"After going for ten years," said Joe, "everyone thought I was a professor." We all laughed.

Joe smiled broadly; the gold in his teeth sparkled, his burnt-brown face glowed radiant and expansive. He announced he was going to become ". . . a sos'cial woika, en ees abowt tine! I bean een dis cuntree fi jears en all I lairn ees de forrking baad worrds!"

"Joe, show them the poster," I suggested.

Joe went over to the cabinet where he had set down his rolled poster. He unfurled it for everyone to see. "This is my latest edition of Tumbleweeds," he said. The one-by-two-foot poster, made from a photograph, showed five teens in long, tight-sleeved shirts and long pants doing a Big Five pyramid. "They just won first place in a talent contest sponsored by the New York City Housing Authority."

Everyone was impressed, for the Big Five was the best of the pyramids we had done as Tumbleweeds. But no one dwelt on comparisons. The handstand topping the pyramid just didn't have the classy lines and elegant toe-point of the Israel handstand.

239

Edgar passed around three color snapshots and explained, "These are pictures of me backstage at the Metropolitan Opera. Last month I had a small part as an acrobat in the opera *Les Troyens.*"

Joe said something about the costume looking like an oversize jockstrap and everyone laughed.

"How long," I asked, "were you in the show?"

"Eleven performances," said Edgar, "at one hundred fifty dollars a performance and five dollars an hour during rehearsals. It was fun!"

Angel then jumped in with his story about "the first and last night" he worked at Polyclinic Hospital as an elevator operator. He had had difficulty lining up the elevator with the floors. Once he was about ten inches too high, and one man stumbled out of the elevator onto his knees. Angel mimicked himself as the elevator operator, looking down at an imaginary man hobbling on his knees. "Watch your step!" he giggled, making the story sound funnier than it really was.

Edgar went back to their teen-age years with a story about the time Angel and Israel had come to his house trying to get something to eat. Edgar described how he had opened the door a crack and whispered that he had a girl inside with him and could Angel and Israel come back in an hour. Edgar laughed and pointed to Israel and Angel and said, "And these bums came back in fifteen minutes and started pounding on my door."

"We messed up Edgar's thing," said Angel. "We didn't mean to, but I remember we were really hungry." Angel put his fists over his head and described how he had pounded on the door, all the while yelling, "Criminal! Let us in! Criminal!" "And this guy," added Angel, pointing to Israel, "was yelling, *'Satanás! Tengo hambre!'* "—"Satan! I'm hungry!"

Drinks were refilled, legs stretched, and trips made to the bathroom. Everyone wandered around, drifting from one small cluster of chatting people to another.

Angel, carrying a can of beer, bumped into me coming out

of the kitchen. "How's your mother and father?" he asked.

"They're fine," I said. "Both are in their seventies. Later Joe is going to show the movie we made out at their house seventeen or eighteen years ago."

"We should go out and say hello sometime," he said.

"They would like that," I said.

Angel remembered our visits to my parents' home, exploring the swamps and marshes nearby.

"All new houses have been built there on that land," I said. "Black families have moved in. The neighborhood is mostly black now—and it's all spruced up. I go out there to fix up my parents' place because I don't want it said the whites are 'bringing down the neighborhood.' "

Angel laughed and told me about his own building, which was "all black" when his family and Edgar's family moved in. "The blacks complained the building was getting run down and they gradually moved out." He laughed. "Now it's all Puerto Rican." he said. "There goes the neighborhood!" We both laughed.

Israel, holding a glass of ginger ale, ambled over and put his arm around Angel's shoulder. Angel put his arm around Israel's shoulder. They stood and looked at each other.

"Boy!" said Angel. "Are you hard to get ahold of, old buddy."

"I went to see you a bunch of times," said Israel, "but you were never home."

"Tell me you're comin' and I'll stay home," said Angel.

"You know," Israel said to me, "I never see this guy anymore."

"That's nothin'." Angel chuckled. "Edgar lives upstairs in my building, and I never see him."

"This guy," said Israel again, addressing me, "was my good friend. He's my daughter's *compadre* [godfather]. We did everything together. I used to copy him."

Angel, a little embarrassed, said, "Yeah, we were through a lot together."

Israel, with a laugh, quickly added, "He used to get me in trouble."

241

Joe, sitting on a chair next to the projector, signaled that the film was ready to be shown. Everyone shuffled into the living room. Some sat on the floor, others on the sofa. I dragged in a couple of chairs from the dining room.

"Hit the lights!" said Joe.

The movie is in color and the opening sweep of the camera over the small green patch of lawn on the side of my parents' house picks up a shiny new black car parked on the street in the background. It's a 1955 or 1956 Oldsmobile. Everyone laughed because the car looked so ancient.

The boys, looking tan and brown, except for light-skinned Edgar, come running out from behind the house in their pinkish-red, jagged-edged costumes. They look young, puny and amateurish as they jerkily go through an early Tumbleweeds routine.

Pride was mixed with the laughter of the viewers.

"That's a good move!" someone said.

"I forgot we could do that trick."

"That's neat!"

The more difficult tricks, shakily performed in those days, evoked shouts of encouragement. As Angel climbs up on Edgar, whipping the roller back and forth under his feet, someone said, "Hold it, Edgar! Hold it!"

"Up, Joe! Up!" said Angel, as Joe in the film struggles to his feet, holding Ray aloft on his one arm.

Everyone laughed at the scene of my then chubby two-year-old son Conrad scrambling up to a three-high standing on Ray's shoulders. Joe reminded the viewers that Conrad was now almost six feet tall.

A shaky four-man pyramid ends with Israel jumping off and landing heavily on the ground. Israel, sitting next to me, groaned as if he were feeling that landing all over again.

There's a scene of Angel, in a shapeless hat, juggling the clubs. Ray comes into the picture and with one hand he takes off Angel's hat, places it on his own head as he begins moving in front of Angel, taking one, two, three spinning clubs from him

242

without interruption. Ray juggles as Angel goes around him and repeats the process, taking the hat and intercepting the clubs. They speed up the exchange and begin laughing and we, in the audience, knew they would soon become too giggly and someone would drop the juggling clubs. But the film ends before that happens.

The lights went on. Everyone was squinting. Angel stood and said, "Let's do this again—soon!"

"We can take turns using each other's house," said Joe.

"I want to work out in the park," said Israel.

A picnic was tentatively planned, so wives and children could also come.

Edgar and Ray turned pages in the Tumbleweeds photograph album on the coffee table. There was one old faded snapshot of the boys in T-shirts and shorts, with sunny, smiling, hairless faces. There were photographs of us tumbling and balancing in Central Park and copies of professional composites of the Antinos and Galaxios. There were yellowing clippings and photographs from *El Diario,* old programs, a photocopy of the seven-hundred-dollar check the Antinos received for the Canada show, a thank-you letter from Joey Adams for performing at an AGVA benefit. There was a photograph of a delicate balance with Angel and Israel doing handstands side by side and me doing a handstand on their necks, and another picture of lovely Alba standing on my shoulders, with Ray doing a handstand on her back. And several photos of Joe, Ray and me doing our trio pyramids. The latter section of the album had an assortment of photos of Joe's second and third generations of Tumbleweeds.

It was late. The twins had unobtrusively slipped off to bed. The rest of us settled ourselves in the living room. Angel and Israel sat on the sofa and put their feet on the coffee table. Edgar stretched out on the rug. Joe draped himself into the butterfly chair. My daughter hovered about, listening. My wife sat next to Ray. I went to check on the coffee.

As I came back into the living room, Angel was saying, "Re-

243

member the times we used to baby-sit for Conrad?"

"And take showers," interjected Israel, laughing, "and eat all the food in the refrigerator."

In a voice heavy with nostalgia, Israel recalled the time he did something "wrong" and I had booted him in the behind. Although Israel insisted he deserved the boot and Ray defended me to my daughter—"Sometimes he had thirty kids. It was hard"—I insisted my action had been wrong. Joe told about the time they had all stolen warm-up jackets but never wore them around me for fear I would discover they were stolen. Angel and Israel told similar stories of doing "wrong" and being worried I would find them out.

"Remember the time we almost got into that fight," said Joe, smiling at me, "and you said, 'Nobody swings until I do!' "

Edgar, laughing to himself, managed to squeeze out, "Remember the audition for *Gypsy*"—he slapped his three-fingered hand against his thigh and laughed again—"when we dropped the juggling clubs so we could look under the curtain at the girls dressing? . . ."

"And remember," said Ray, "the first time you took us to a cafeteria? . . . And the time on Columbus Avenue when we were carrying the equipment and the cop stopped us? . . ."

"Remember! Hey, remember bouncing off the ropes at St. Nicholas Arena? . . ."

One story triggered another and soon there was a torrent.

"Remember Joe's front-flip landing on top of us doin' handstands? . . ."

"Remember the Ted Mack show—all of us in makeup? . . ."

"Hey, remember the long subway rides out to Miccio Center? . . . Remember!"

"Remember the workouts in Central Park? . . . Whatever happened to what's-his-name—the guy who does the one-arm planche? . . ."

"Remember the split pants? . . . Israel comin' down from a Big Five and crashin' through the platform? . . . Remember!"

"And remember those girls in the Youth House . . . and remember those retarded people upstate in that institution? . . ."

"Remember, hey, remember Mount Sinai Hospital . . . all the shows . . . each floor . . . the kids liked our act. . . ."

"And remember . . ."

I remembered. And as I sat there in my living room, warm with memories of the old days, I remembered what a wide-eyed gaggle of grimy, ragtag street nomads these five guys appeared to be when I first saw them. And now, whenever I walk through a city street, crowded with scruffy, noisy, insistent kids of every shade of black, brown and white, looking to try the world out for size, I am reminded of Joe, Ray, Edgar, Israel and Angel, when they were just like that.

I thought of all those kids out there—so many of them. What of their futures? I didn't know. The world today is confusing and unpredictable.

And I thought of the children of my good friends in my living room: Adrian and Lysette Ramos; Melissa and Ramon (Jr.) Sanchez; Rafael, Teresa and Nilda Gotay; Jesse and Oggy Rodriguez; Eric, Karen, Renier and Kevin Mourino. What of their futures? Their world will be different from their fathers'.

At least they have a good start. They're healthy, well fed, maybe a little overfed. They go to reasonably good schools. Their parents take them to beaches, parks, zoos, rides in the country, and sometimes they even go to Puerto Rico or Disneyland for vacations. They have toys, books, bikes, spending money, sports equipment and the latest-style sneakers. They probably watch too much television, but they are rigidly supervised in doing their homework—and no one, but no one, roams around the streets. All of them will probably be able to go to college. Most will be expected to go. Some of them may finish their growing up in the suburbs of Long Island or New Jersey. Undoubtedly they, too, will become more "American" and suffer to some degree the identity problems of second-generation children wanting to be assimilated and accepted. I hope they will retain those qualities of their Puerto Rican heritage which Ray describes as ". . . a feeling for people and the use of

245

language; a sensitivity—a serenity."

And when they become adults they will also have to face, among other things, the dilemma of "keeping up with the Joneses" and deciding what to do with their lives. . . . But who can say? The world is a different place today. New ideas are more accessible. Old ways are being challenged. I'm heartened by the fact that their parents have done such a good job so far, their mothers especially, because they have been with them most of the time. But their fathers have also contributed their love and influence. On good days, the "old man" was a tough act to follow.

Yes, the Ramos, Sanchez, Rodriguez, Gotay and Mourino kids have a good start. Who knows how high they will go?

And who, for that matter, knows how high the five original Tumbleweeds will go?